The Will to Learn

THE WILL TO LEARN
A Guide for Motivating Young People

Martin V. Covington

University of California, Berkeley

CAMBRIDGE
UNIVERSITY PRESS

PUBLISHED BY THE PRESS SYNDICATE OF THE UNIVERSITY OF CAMBRIDGE
The Pitt Building, Trumpington Street, Cambridge CB2 1RP, United Kingdom

CAMBRIDGE UNIVERSITY PRESS
The Edinburgh Building, Cambridge CB2 2RU, United Kingdom
40 West 20th Street, New York, NY 10011-4211, USA
10 Stamford Road, Oakleigh, Melbourne 3166, Australia

First published 1998

Printed in the United States of America

Typeset in Palatino

Library of Congress Cataloging-in-Publication Data
Covington, Martin V., 1938–
The will to learn : a guide for motivating young people / Martin
V. Covington.
p.   cm.
Includes bibliographical references (p.) and index.
ISBN 0-521-55353-9 (hard). – ISBN 0-521-55679-1 (pbk.)
1. Motivation in education – United States. 2. Self-esteem in
children. 3. Learning. I. Title.
LB1065.C658   1998
370. 15′4—dc21   97-21296
                                              CIP

*A catalog record for this book is available from
the British Library.*

ISBN 0 521 55353 9 hardback
ISBN 0 521 55679 1 paperback

CONTENTS

1

THE FUTURE AND ITS DISCONTENTS

We know nothing about motivation. All we can do is write
books about it.
> Peter Drucker

INTRODUCTION

CERTAINLY MUCH HAS BEEN WRITTEN ABOUT MOTIVATION. TO
this extent Drucker's observation is correct. But what is less
clear – and this is Drucker's concern – is the *nature* of our understanding. Although we actually do know a good deal about motivation, our knowledge on closer inspection is quite uneven. We
know *how* to arouse people to greater effort, especially for short periods of time – how, for example, to arrange incentives for factory
workers so that production improves and absenteeism falls, and
even how to rearrange the social organization of schools so that
students are more willing to learn for its own sake. But knowing
how to motivate people is not the same as knowing *what* motivation
is. Here Drucker makes his point. Whatever is being aroused by the
clever use of rewards and incentives – namely, motivation itself –
remains mysterious and elusive. Motivation, like the concept of
gravity, is easier to describe (in terms of its outward, observable effects) than it is to define. Of course, this has not stopped people
from trying.

The first goal of this book, then, is to introduce the basic principles of human motivation and consider various attempts to define
its essential nature. The second goal is to explore how the lessons
to be learned from research on motivation can be applied to the
task of educational change and reform. In essence, we will ask, If
encouraging the will to learn is a major objective of all schooling,

1

then how can we best restructure the learning experiences of young people to achieve this objective? Put differently, we will arrange the research on achievement motivation in ways that lead to various recommendations for improving the educational experience of millions of schoolchildren today and many millions more tomorrow.

In effect, then, this book is intended, first, as an introduction to the principles of human motivation and, second, as a guide for responsible educational change. But there is more.

We will also deal with the future. Clearly, these two topics – motivation and the future – are closely linked. As Harry Lauder once remarked, "The future is not a gift, it is an achievement," and, it might be added, an achievement built in equal measure on discipline, realism, and joyful dreaming.

In this first chapter, we begin with a brief exposition of the future and of the desperate need for schools to face constructively the challenges that a changing future will certainly bring. We will then unveil the broad outlines of what it means to undertake a motivational analysis of classroom life.

BUILDING THE FUTURE

> My interest is in the future because I am going to spend the rest of my life there.
> Charles Kettering

If the future is an achievement, as Harry Lauder argues, then teachers are futurists along with politicians, filmmakers, and journalists – those individuals who, according to J. McClellan (1978), "make other people's futures more real to them." Indeed, at its best, education should provide young people with a sense of empowerment that makes their futures "real" by moving beyond merely offering them a few plausible but limited alternatives to indicating how their preferred dreams can actually be attained.

But of what should this future-building legacy consist, especially since no one can know the future, at least in any detail? First, we

2

can suggest that, in preparing for the future, students develop viable occupational skills. Learning a discipline – whether it means becoming a plumber, a rodeo performer, or a writer – and doing it well provides the foundation for a sense of purpose, security, and confidence in adulthood. It is confidence that propels the future and, conversely, feelings of incompetency that cause us to fall short of what is best in us.

Second, students should prepare for change. Change, to recall a cliché, is the future's only constant. There is a need to accept with grace the inevitability of change – to be part of the process of change, whether this means facing up to ever shifting personal relationships, accepting change in the prevailing social order, or understanding fluctuating global economics. As we shall see, change is best handled, and even welcomed, when individuals possess a well-developed arsenal of mental skills associated with original, creative, and independent thinking. This suggests that schoolchildren should cultivate the capacity to deal thoughtfully with future circumstances that they and even we, their mentors, cannot fully imagine.

Naturally, of course, change should not be accepted uncritically. It must first be evaluated in the light of both its potential benefits and inevitable costs, an observation that calls to mind the "cliffhanger" theorem: "Each problem solved introduces a new unsolved problem" (O'Brien in Dickson, 1978). Avoiding the pitfalls of change requires careful problem analysis, critical thinking, and the ability to anticipate the results of change.

Third, and above all, the greatest legacy of education is to encourage in our students a will to learn and to continue learning as personal circumstances change – in short, to promote a capacity for resiliency and self-renewal. This point was anticipated over a half century ago when John Dewey (1938/1963) remarked that "the most important attitude that can be formed is that of the desire to go on learning" (p. 48).

These are brave sentiments and some would say hopelessly romantic and unattainable: a sense of commitment, self-confidence, and resiliency in the face of change. No one can be against these values, yet who among us is immodest enough to say precisely how to

3

achieve them? As a result, these values are often honored more in their absence than by their observance. Today too many students graduate or drop out of school without a single achievement for which they can feel uniquely responsible or justly proud. Moreover, the majority of our students understand neither the history of change nor the forces that shape their individual lives; and their loyalties often run to self-indulgence and near-term gratification.

Little is new about these values (Cuban, 1990). Repeated calls for encouraging them have been matched by a long history of failure to do so, dating back at least as far as Greco-Roman times, when an anonymous observer lamented that "our students have grown lazy and are disrespectful of authority. They slight their tutors, mislead their teachers, and fail to attend to their lessons" (Covington & Beery, 1976, p. 1). These same troubling themes have echoed down through the ages and find their most recent embodiment in American ghetto youngsters who, according to Shelby Steele (1989a), "see studying as a sucker's game and school itself as a waste of time. One sees in many of these children almost a determination not to learn, a suppression of the natural impulse to understand, that cannot be entirely explained by the determinism of poverty" (p. 506).

But now there is something *new*, not the values themselves but a fuller understanding of how to shape the educational experience of youngsters in order to encourage self-renewal, self-discipline, and resiliency. But before meddling with the future, we must be convinced that new, alternative visions of education are likely to fare better than "business as usual" or, stated differently, that future prospects are so horrifying that virtually any reasonable change in the current ways of schooling will be welcome. Enough is now known for us to develop plausible scenarios of future events if trends continue unchanged. These trends project a dismal, downward course. If things are going to get worse, how bad are they now?

The Class of 2010

The high school graduating class of the year 2010 just recently entered kindergarten. Like so many other students before them, they,

4

too, have approached the future with enthusiasm. Yet unless things change, their enthusiasm, like that of previous generations, will also dwindle and soon evaporate. Kati Haycock and M. Susan Navarro (1988) describe the "process of deterioration" in this way:

> For many, this process will begin very early in their school careers. Even in first grade, some youngsters will get the sense that something is wrong with them; that somehow they're just not doing things right. . . . By the sixth or seventh grade, many will not be proficient in the basic skills. . . . Though still in school, they will have dropped out mentally. Before high school graduation, they, and many of their peers, will drop out altogether. (p. 1)

Indeed, three out of ten students entering the ninth grade today will not graduate from high school, a rate that has doubled since 1970 (Haycock & Navarro, 1988). Moreover, these figures are conservative when we consider Hispanics and blacks, whose comparable dropout rates in California are now close to 50 percent.

For many of those who remain in school, the prospects for learning are equally shocking. For instance, the nationwide reading achievement scores for recent graduating high school seniors reflect a ninth-grade level of proficiency, which likely explains a U.S. Navy report that one-quarter of its recruits could not read well enough to understand basic safety instructions (reported in Wurman, 1989, p. 54). Writing skills fare no better. For example, according to Albert Shanker (1988), former president of the American Federation of Teachers, only 20 percent of those youngsters still in high school can write a minimally acceptable letter applying for a job in a local supermarket. Moreover, a majority of junior high school students can name more brands of whiskey than they can past presidents of the United States. And in a recent survey conducted by the ABC television network, two-thirds of the teenagers interviewed could not identify Chernobyl (one youngster guessed it was Cher's real name).

Current events may not be their strong suit, yet American schoolchildren show even less aptitude for problem solving, if that seems possible. For example, one group of first-grade and second-grade children blithely solved the following word problem, mostly by manipulating the integers 10 and 26: "There are 26 sheep and 10 goats on a ship. How old is the captain?" (Reusser, 1987). None of these students saw anything odd about this question. This is an example of students calculating but not thinking, trapped by the mindless rote application of rules that unfold automatically, irrespective of their relevance to the problem.

Overall, this dismal scene can be put in stark relief by a single statistic: thirteen million students – nearly one-half of all school-age youngsters – are at serious risk for failing academically (Bringing Children Out, 1988). Also, more often than not, school failure clusters with delinquency, substance abuse, and teenage pregnancy. One study sponsored by the Carnegie Corporation (Dryfoos, 1990) estimates that at least three million adolescents between the ages of ten and seventeen have fallen prey to all or most of these high-risk behaviors, and that another four million are at substantial risk of destroying their life chances. These seven million youngsters represent one out of every four adolescents in the United States.

These statistics make grim reading. For example, consider the dislocation and waste of talent created by such underachievement. In the technologically sophisticated society of the late twentieth century, the need for unskilled labor has plummeted, and is likely to continue downward at least in the near term. Over the next two decades, the majority of new job openings will require some form of education beyond high school. At present, however, less than 40 percent of our youth enter any form of postsecondary education, including technical trade schools, and far fewer than half of these individuals complete their course of study.

Change is the watchword. For instance, it is estimated that after students in the graduating class of 2010 enter the permanent work force, they will change careers – not just jobs, but careers – an average of five times before they retire. Yet given what can be deduced from all of the statistics just cited, a near majority of our youth will face an unknown world utterly unprepared. Without the capacity to participate in and learn from change, and to weather the occasional upheaval, these youngsters will become crippled, confused, and overwhelmed by a vastly altered society, one in which they will no longer know how to participate. Such observations take on a special imperative in light of America's shrinking role as the economic engine and prime mover of the world economy. Clearly, we cannot hope to compete in a technologically advanced world game when many of our players are illiterate or underprepared.

Clearly much is amiss. For many children, growing up in America today has become a perilous, dispiriting business. And unless things change, the overwhelming likelihood is that the situation will worsen. Before we begin rethinking the mission of education, however, several other observations are in order.

Who Is Responsible?

The first of these observations concerns the matter of assigning blame. Who is responsible for the mess? The present crisis in schooling cannot be attributed solely, or even largely, to the failure of any particular educational policy. Many other factors outside the influence of schools are also involved in this decline – poverty, the loosening of public morals, broken homes, and the drug epidemic, to name only a few. In fact, it can be argued that without the steadying presence of schools, for all their limitations, things would be even worse.

Be that as it may, finger pointing is of little value because in this maelstrom of abuse, abandonment, and personal failure, what is *cause* and what is *effect* become blurred. Take just one example. There can be no doubt that the failure of schools to teach contributes directly to youngsters dropping out of school (Finn, 1989), but then so does becoming pregnant. Teenage pregnancy is a leading cause of leaving school in America. Nationwide, more than one million girls in the class of 1986 became pregnant before high school graduation (Riessman, 1988). Yet even this number underestimates the problem. The babies born to these mere children, often raised in unrelenting poverty and frequently abused, neglected, and drug exposed themselves, may in turn become handicapped in *their* social,

7

cognitive, and emotional development, so that yet another generation becomes failure prone (Landrigan & Carlson, 1995; Patterson,
1987; Schorr, 1988). And the deprivation can be elemental. Some
children enter kindergarten never having used a pencil, others never having held a fork or spoon.

Not only are the causes of school failure many, but the burden
imposed on schools grows daily. Increasingly, schools are expected
to act as custodians for a growing assortment of youthful misfits
and incorrigibles. Schools also are expected to stem the rising tide
of teenage promiscuity through instruction in a secular version of
morality training, and to act as the first line of defense against public health dangers of truly catastrophic proportions, including the
AIDS epidemic.

It would be foolish to argue that issues of drugs, sex, and violence
are not part of growing up educated in America today. Nor can
schools easily abandon their responsibilities in these areas. But their
resources are limited. To these burdens we can add other responsibilities that in part represent failures of wider social policy or stem
from public indifference. These additional demands involve the legitimate need for everyone to succeed – ethnic minorities, the economically disadvantaged, learning-handicapped pupils, and the
burgeoning populations of immigrants from non-English-speaking
homes (Rumbaut, 1995). The enormity of this challenge is reflected
by the fact that at last count some ninety-one non-English languages and dialects are spoken in the Los Angeles County schools.
And the experiences in this one county remind us in turn of the
pressing need to teach children throughout the United States how
to cooperate with peoples of diverse political, cultural, and reli-
gious backgrounds, especially in the face of a potentially hostile
world whose boundaries shrink daily.

In the waning years of the twentieth century, there is altogether
too much evidence that American schools have become a dumping
ground for the unwanted and unacceptable and for seemingly unsolvable problems: a place of failed individuals and of failed social
policies. It is an enterprise for which too much has been demanded,
with too few resources made available. As a consequence, schools

do too few things well; and when they do achieve excellence, too few students benefit. This situation has occurred despite the Herculean efforts of many dedicated, hardworking teachers, administrators, and staff. If energy and devotion alone could solve our educational problems, then solutions would be far more advanced than is now the case.

I will argue that teachers can do little to shorten the terrible odds arrayed against them and their students unless there is a fundamental reconsideration of the motivational dynamics of learning, and of *what* should be taught as well as *how*. Actually, I will argue that teachers are victims, too, ensnared by the same outmoded views of motivation and learning that hold their students hostage.

What Answers Do We Seek?

Now, a few words about the kinds of remedies to be offered in this book. First, the recommendations will focus on those that follow uniquely from a motivational perspective. In effect, I will ask if there is any special contribution that research on achievement motivation can make to our understanding of the exceedingly complex phenomena of school learning and school failure.

Second, these recommendations are intended to be compatible, insofar as possible, with other analyses of the school crisis that come from quite different starting points: from the business community, from minority neighborhoods, and from Main Street.

Third, recommendations will be restricted to those considered eminently practical and capable of implementation by schools and by individual teachers within a relatively short period of time, say, within five years. This condition implies that the recommendations are not particularly new, but are largely untried and in need of more emphasis. Moreover, they are familiar enough to be implemented without a massive overhaul of the educational system. Indeed, all these ingredients for change are well known to educators, but they are often overlooked and underappreciated.

Fourth, there must be a reasonable prospect that these changes, if initiated even in modest ways, can influence youngsters here and now – those who will graduate in the year 2010 – and not be delayed in their impact until some distant, future time. This caveat is not meant to imply that a total reformation can occur within such a brief span, but only that hints of positive payback should emerge soon, portending greater dividends to come. Actually, any changes in schools of the magnitude ultimately needed must be worked out in terms of generations, not just decades, time enough to reshape public beliefs about the mission of schooling and to revitalize teacher training.

Finally, we must remain mindful of the classic predicament of all reform efforts captured in the picturesque lament, "Who can think about draining the swamp when we are up to our asses in alligators?" The answer, it appears, involves a little swimming, then a little draining, and an occasional hop up on the bank to gain the perspective (and safety) of distance. Hopefully, modern views of motivation can provide this perspective.

But does a motivational perspective admit to such possibilities, even in theory? And, seriously, what is the hope for any practical successes, especially given the fact that student indifference, truancy, and poor achievement often go hand in hand with classroom violence, drug dealing in the school yard, and other deplorable forms of abuse and exploitation? Obviously, academic failure is as much, if not more, the result of the inevitable pressures and risks of growing up in a dangerous, unforgiving world as it is the fault of any misguided educational policy (Mushak, 1992; Schaffer, 1994). Perhaps in the end there is little that schools can do to reverse the horrific statistics of failure and despair cited earlier. We must be prepared for the possibility that in the final analysis the massive failure to learn is merely the end result, and not the cause, of a steady accumulation of various social ills. But to abandon the search for school-related solutions now is to admit defeat prematurely. Basically, I will argue that even if schools were drug free, uncompromised by hatred and fear, and not a dumping ground for the rebellious and the unwanted, certain aspects of schooling would still be a threat to the future of our children. It is these dangers – no matter how modest they may be, compared with the larger circle of threat – that will drive our recommendations for educational change.

10

It is important that we now introduce the topic of achievement motivation and reconnoiter the psychological landscape over which we will soon travel.

THE FAILURE TO LEARN: A MOTIVATIONAL ANALYSIS

People compose for many reasons: To become immortal; because the pianoforte happens to be open; because they want to become a millionaire; because of the praise of friends; because they have looked into a pair of beautiful eyes; or for no reason whatsoever.
> Robert Schumann

Just what is a motivational analysis of classroom life? Simply put, motivation deals with the *why* of behavior. Why, for example, do individuals choose to work on one task and not on another? Why do they exhibit more or less energy in the pursuit of the task? Why do some people persist until the task is completed, whereas others give up before they really start, or occasionally pursue more elegant solutions long after perfectly sensible answers have presented themselves?

In essence, the answer to all these questions is that, like Schumann's composers, different people have different reasons to achieve. In school, some students learn in order to earn gold stars and may stop when these rewards are no longer forthcoming. Other students strive to develop new skills for the sake of self-mastery and will not stop until they are acquired. Still others seek to demonstrate superior ability either by outperforming others or by achieving notable successes with little or no effort. From these few examples, it is not difficult to appreciate that what students learn, how much they remember, and how engaged they become in the process depends largely on which reasons for learning dominate. In effect, for our purposes motives are equivalent to reasons for learning.

Over the past several decades, two broadly different conceptions of achievement motivation have emerged (Covington, 1992). One

11

perspective views motivation as a drive, that is, an internal state or need that impels individuals toward action (Heyman & Dweck, 1992). This motives-as-drive approach typically views motivation as an enabling factor – a means to an end, with the end being improved status or better test performance. A drive perspective dominates popular thinking whenever schools are admonished by politicians or newspaper editorials to motivate (drive) students to do better as the answer to those horrifying achievement statistics cited earlier. A particularly crude but unmistakable expression of this reasoning was directed at education professor Michael Kirst (1990): "One legislator told me, 'I just want the little buggers to work harder.'" The underlying assumption is that if we can provide the right rewards and enough of them, or threaten sufficient punishments, we can arouse (drive) otherwise dispirited, lazy students to higher levels of achievement. Then there is the corollary: that arousal is greatest when these rewards are distributed on a competitive basis, that is, with the greater number of rewards (e.g., high grades) going to those who perform best.

We will find that a motives-as-drive mentality encourages largely negative reasons for learning, including the threat that if one does not perform well he or she will be punished.

A second perspective considers motivation in terms of *goals* or *incentives* that draw, not drive, individuals toward action (Heyman & Dweck, 1992). This tradition assumes that all actions are given meaning and purpose by the goals that individuals seek out, and that the quality and intensity of their actions will change as their goals change (Dweck, Chiu, & Hong, 1995). Considered from this perspective, motivation is a unique human resource to be encouraged for its own sake, not simply a means to increase school performance. Indeed, by this analysis, fostering meaningful, goal-directed behavior and positive reasons for learning becomes the ultimate purpose of schooling. These positive reasons are noncompetitive and intrinsic in nature, that is, they beguile and entice individuals into action for its own sake and generally for ennobling purposes – for the sake of "a pair of beautiful eyes," to recall Schumann, or "for no reason whatsoever," save perhaps curiosity. And, finally, because goals are always the creatures of the future, the motives-as-goals tradition is heavily future oriented.

The research that draws its inspiration from the drive-theory tradition helps clarify the basic causes of school failure today and their motivational roots. For example, whenever students are savaged by competition as a means to drive them to learn, they react in ways that characterize the current educational crisis: students become defensive, resistant, and angry and may even doubt themselves despite doing well. This drive-theory analysis of the *causes* of school failure will occupy us for the first half of this book. By contrast, the second half deals primarily with *solutions* to the educational crisis, which are the province of the motives-as-goals approach. Whenever students are drawn to learning out of curiosity, to understand the world in which they live, or for the sake of some valued personal goal, they act in ways we all admire and wish our students would emulate: they become absorbed in learning, committed, and oblivious to the passage of time.

We will now consider each of these two traditions in somewhat more detail, but still only briefly, in order to introduce the basic line of arguments to be presented later.

Motives as Drives

Need Achievement Theory. The most sophisticated view of achievement motivation as a learned drive was developed initially in the 1950s and early 1960s by John Atkinson (1957, 1987) and by David McClelland (1965). This theory holds that human achievement is the result of a conflict between striving for success and avoiding failure. These two motives are couched largely in emotional terms. For example, *hope* for success and the anticipation of *pride* at winning are said to encourage success-oriented individuals to strive for excellence. On the other hand, a capacity for experiencing *shame* and *humiliation* is thought to drive failure-oriented persons to avoid situations where they believe themselves likely to fail. It is this difference in emotional anticipation (pride vs. shame) that was thought to answer the questions of *why*. Why do some individuals approach learning with enthusiasm and others only with reluctance? Why do some choose easy tasks for which success is assured, whereas others tackle problems for which the chances of success are exquisitely balanced against the chances for failure?

Attribution Theory. Beginning in the early 1970s researchers led primarily by Bernard Weiner and his colleagues (Weiner et al., 1971) posed a radical reinterpretation of Atkinson's theory. Weiner reasoned that cognitive (thought) processes rather than emotional anticipation were the agents primarily responsible for the quality of achievement. In effect, what people *think* was given priority over how people *feel* as the prime mover of achievement.

More specifically, Weiner proposed that *how* individuals perceive the causes of their prior successes and failures is the deciding factor in choosing whether to work on a particular task and in deciding how long to persist once work begins and with what amount of enthusiasm. For instance, persons who attribute their past successes to their ability are more likely to undertake similar challenges in the future because they anticipate doing well again. By the same token, people are less likely to be optimistic about the future if they attribute their prior successes to good luck.

From a theoretical perspective, a subtle change occurred as the result of this cognitive reinterpretation. The classic question of *why* individuals achieve or not, which was answered originally in terms of feelings (pride vs. shame), was now treated more as a question of *how* – how people interpret events and attribute meaning to them. Although this shift is admittedly subtle, it is immensely important, especially for its educational implications. For example, if the rational, cognitive side of our nature truly controls motivation, then educators would be well advised to put a premium on teaching students how to analyze the causes of their successes and failures in the most constructive, yet realistic ways possible.

One feature of attribution theory is its focus on the role of effort in achievement. This emphasis is justified if for no other reason than the widespread belief that student effort can be controlled by teachers through the application of rewards for trying and, when necessary, punishments for not trying. Whether this premise is true or not (and we will come to have our doubts), at least teachers act on it: students whom teachers see as having studied hard are rewarded more in success and reprimanded less in failure than students who do not try. From this pattern of rewards and punishments, attribution theorists have concluded that students should come to value effort and trying hard as a major source of their personal worth.

But if this is true, then why is it that so many students do not try in school? Recall Shelby Steele's depressing observation that "One sees in many of these children almost a determination not to learn, a suppression of the natural impulse to understand." And why do other children hide their efforts or refuse to admit that they study hard? The answer to these questions lies in the domain of self-worth theory.

Self-Worth Theory. In our society human value is measured largely in terms of one's ability to achieve competitively. For example, researchers have found that nothing contributes more to a student's sense of self-esteem than good grades, nor shatters it so completely as do poor grades (Rosenberg, 1965). Thus, it is achievement – and its handmaiden, ability – that dominates as the ultimate value in the minds of many schoolchildren. Given this reality, it is not surprising that the student's sense of self-esteem often becomes equated with ability – to be able in school is to be valued as a human being, but to do poorly is evidence of inability, and reason to despair of one's worth (Beery, 1975).

Here we have the makings of a profound conflict in values. On the one hand, attribution theory emphasizes as most important those sources of worth that come from complying with a work ethic – being dedicated and trying hard – whereas, on the other hand, self-worth theory emphasizes those sources of worth and pride that follow from feeling smart. But why should there be any conflict at all? Cannot students become competent by working hard and feel smart in the process? Yes, in theory, and sometimes even in practice – but all too often schools are arranged so that learning becomes an ability game. In this special game, the amount of effort students

15

must expend to learn provides clear information about their ability. For instance, if students succeed without studying much, especially if the assignment is difficult, then estimates of their ability increase; but should students try hard and fail to do well anyway, especially at an easy task, attributions to low ability are sure to follow.

Thus effort becomes what Carol Omelich and I (Covington & Omelich, 1979) have called a "double-edged sword," that is, trying hard is valued by students because teachers reward it, yet trying hard is also feared by students given its potential threat to their worth should they fail.

Self-worth theory contends that the protection of a sense of ability is the student's highest priority – higher sometimes even than good grades – so that students may actually handicap themselves by *not* studying in order to have an excuse for failing that does not reflect poorly on their ability. A number of strategies for avoiding failure, or at least avoiding the implications of failure – namely, that one lacks ability – have been identified by researchers (e.g., Birney, Burdick, & Teevan, 1969). Some of these failure-avoiding strategies are favored by middle-class white students and others by impoverished youngsters and ethnic minorities, but all of these strategies – no matter who employs them or what form they take – undercut the will to learn and compromise school achievement.

This self-worth analysis is useful because it helps us understand what are *not* the causes of the massive default of the will to learn in schools today. Two noncauses can be mentioned in advance.

First, we must be wary of blaming the failure of students to learn simply on a *lack* of motivation. The absence of behavior – docility, passivity, and listlessness – is surely just as motivated as is a lively abundance of behavior. According to a self-worth analysis, the reluctant learner who may refuse to study is already motivated, driven by circumstances to protect his or her self-esteem. Thus, the failure to achieve is just as likely the result of being *overmotivated* but for the wrong reasons, as it is of not being motivated at all! This suggests that educators must alter the reasons that make for truancy, poor achievement, and belligerency rather than simply raise the stakes in what is already a losing game by increasing rewards for effort and punishing not trying more severely.

16

Second, self-worth theory makes clear that the present educational crisis is not merely a matter of poor performance. Slumping achievement scores are only symptoms. Rather, schools face a crisis in motivation. Once teachers transform the reasons that students learn, from negative to positive, the symptoms should coincidentally disappear, like the breaking of a fever.

This is not to say that current proposals for school reform inspired by drive theory are irrelevant. But they are surely incomplete and certainly lacking in imagination – "*More* academic courses, *more* hours in school, *more* homework, *more* tests, *more* hurdles for prospective teachers, *more* units for graduation . . ." (emphasis added) (Russell, 1988, p. 4). Basically, these recommendations follow a strategy of *intensification,* or what we might call "tinkering" – simply continuing to do what has been done for years, but more of it. This strategy assumes that the present mode of schooling is fundamentally sound, and that no basic changes are needed. However, taken by themselves these approaches are at best insufficient, if not too tame, and at worst counterproductive (Covington, 1996).

The potential dangers inherent in following a policy of intensification are particularly great for the failure-prone child, the underprepared, and the disenfranchised youngster from an underclass ghetto or barrio. As things stand, simply adding days to the school calendar will condemn many of these youngsters to waste more time, often in depressing, dilapidated, and abrasive environments. Nor is the solution as easy as adding new course requirements or raising academic standards, as has been done recently by many states and local school districts. If students cannot now measure up to old, presumably less demanding requirements, or pass the courses already on the books, then these increased demands would seem rather pointless. Effective solutions lie elsewhere – elsewhere being a paradigm shift in our thinking about schools (Wiggins, 1991).

In summary, those who would champion a drive interpretation of motivation typically assume that the best way to arouse students to action is to put them in competition with one another, where too many students scramble after too few rewards in what we have referred to as an ability game. In this circumstance, negative reasons for learning are encouraged – achieving for fear of losing, for fear of being left out, or out of anxiety over being unmasked as incompetent – with disastrous consequences for the quality of learning. And what is doubly bad is the fact that the kinds of rewards typically associated with drive theory – praise, applause, gold stars, and grades – are largely *extrinsic* in nature, that is, basically irrelevant (or external) to the act of learning. This means that once the need for recognition is satisfied or the threat of failure removed, there is no longer any particular reason to continue learning. Moreover, the pursuit of such rewards creates a highly noxious situation because the dominant reinforcers are negative – success is counted largely in terms of avoiding something that is bad, not necessarily achieving something that is good. These circumstances detract from true learning and focus students' attention on performance per se, without regard for what is learned or its meaning to one's life. Self-worth theory is useful because it alerts us to these and other dangers of applying drive-theory notions to schooling.

Motives as Goals

The answer to school reform lies not so much in increasing motivation – that is, arousing existing drive levels – as it does in encouraging different kinds of motivation altogether. The key to this transformation is to view motivation not in terms of drives, but in terms of goals, and goals that are largely intrinsic in nature (Deci, 1975; Harackiewicz & Eliot, 1993). Intrinsic motivation refers to the goal of becoming more effective as a person. For instance, when a student willingly completes a reading assignment on nutrition because he believes a proper diet will help him remain fit, we say he is intrinsically motivated. So, too, is the student who pays close attention to the lecture on how to write persuasively so she can convince others, through her writing, not to do drugs. In these cases learning becomes valued for what it can do to enhance one's effectiveness or to help others. Additionally, individuals may seek out answers or information simply to satisfy their curiosity – to find out why, for instance, some shoes squeak and others do not.

The key to understanding the concept of intrinsic motivation is that the payoff resides in the actions themselves – that is, the act of learning is its own reward. Put differently, the repetition of an action such as satisfying one's curiosity does not depend as much on external inducements such as praise or a good grade as it does on satisfying a personal interest.

Intrinsic reasons for learning have several special characteristics. Because intrinsic rewards arise from within the individual, they are open to all persons, inexhaustible in number, and largely under control of the individual. Unlimited and equal access to the rewards of learning is the essential condition needed for what we will call an "equity game," as contrasted to an "ability game." In an equity game all students can approach success, and for positive reasons available to everyone. But how can everyone win? And what is the basis for equity when students are so unequal in so many different ways? The answers lie in the concept of "motivational equity."

Motivational Equity

Obviously, not everyone is equally bright, nor can all children compete on an equal footing intellectually. But at least schools can provide all students with a common heritage in the reasons for learning. Everyone can experience feelings of resolve and a commitment to think more and to dare more, of being caught up in the drama of problem solving, and of being poised to learn and ready to take the next step. Low ability is no barrier to this kind of excellence. In this sense, everyone can be equal – equal in terms of motivation. In the second half of the book we will argue that the challenge for schools is to create a motivational parity for all students, with everyone striving for positive reasons by arranging payoffs that promote curiosity, that establish meaningful rewards for self-improvement, and that encourage increased knowledge.

Encouraging motivational equity is not easy. Several questions arise whenever the notion of fostering intrinsic involvement is proposed. The first issue we will consider concerns the sheer frequency of rewards. If learning becomes its own reward with the happy prospect that, as Alice put it during her Wonderland adventures, "everyone has won and all must have prizes," will not the value of these freely available rewards be cheapened? In short, who wants to play games in which everyone wins?

Second, sometimes it becomes necessary to reward students extrinsically (with praise or grades) in order to involve them long enough so that what they learn will eventually become valued for its own sake. This most often occurs in the early stages of learning, especially for tasks that are seen as chores (e.g., learning the multiplication tables). But how can students become truly involved if they were originally paid to learn? Will not students conform just long enough to win the prize, as many observers fear, and then disengage once these rewards are removed? These questions, too, will be considered later.

Thinking about One's Future

Establishing motivational equity is only one ingredient for encouraging the proper reasons for learning. In the second half of this book we also will consider another critical factor. This involves learning how to think about one's future and addressing the question of *what* to teach – in effect, asking what is worth knowing as students begin to create their own futures. Two kinds of knowledge stand out: (1) knowing *how to learn*, that is, how to acquire specific facts and information – what can be called the raw material of thought; and (2) knowing *how to think*, that is, how to arrange this information in ways that permit solutions to significant problems. We will see that an emphasis on teaching students *how* to think is important for at least three reasons.

Discipline and Freedom. First, encouraging intrinsic learning goals requires that students have considerable freedom – freedom to set their own learning objectives within reasonable limits and then to decide how best to achieve them. Such freedom requires the monitoring of one's own progress toward these goals, and the ability to plan. These qualities are rare enough, and they are particularly in short supply among children who see learning as a threat to their sense of worth. For these youngsters, something more is needed than simply providing an opportunity for unlimited rewards.

They must also be trained in the skills of intellectual self-discipline that form the essential complement to freedom.

Ability as a Learnable Resource. Second, improving one's ability to think encourages the will to learn. Learning how to think fosters the view that ability is expandable through experience and practice – the "incremental" view of intelligence (Dweck, 1986, 1990; Dweck & Bempechat, 1983). Students who hold this view tend to tackle more difficult problems, for longer periods of time, and with greater resolve and confidence than do students who hold an "entity" view of ability. An entity belief presumes that intelligence is a fixed, immutable factor likely of genetic origin that does not yield to effort or improve through the accumulation of knowledge.

Future Survival. Third, instruction in the skills of thinking is also critical to future survival. We can no longer safely assume that what is presently taught in schools will satisfy future job and civic responsibilities or help children adapt to radically different life-styles and to a myriad of other changes that can only be dimly perceived today. The future is overtaking our children at a rapidly accelerating pace. At the center of these changes is the knowledge explosion with its growing glut of facts. Robert Hilliard of the Federal Communications Commission estimates that "at the rate at which knowledge is growing, by the time a child born today graduates from college, the amount of knowledge in the world will be four times as great. By the time that child is 50 years old, it will be 32 times as great and 97% of everything known in the world will have been learned since the time he was born."

Hilliard is serving notice that more information than ever before is needed to remain functional, literate, and adaptive, and that the range and breadth of such knowledge will continue to expand at a staggering pace. Worse yet, information itself is subject to increasing obsolescence at an astonishing rate. As Alvin Toffler (1970) explains it, "We are creating and using up ideas and images at a faster and faster pace. Knowledge, like people, places, things and organizational forms, is becoming disposable." Indeed, the half-life of facts today can be measured in terms of months or weeks, even days.

21

Today schools largely grapple with only the first aspect of the "knowledge explosion" – that of mastering the sheer volume of ever increasing information – by trying to make learning more efficient (sometimes through computer-based instruction) or by requiring students to spend more time at their studies. These solutions are easily recognized as part of the intensification mentality. Merely spending more time will not solve the problem; there will never be enough time.

By far the more important challenge is the rapid turnover of information, an issue that has gone largely unaddressed by schools. Clearly, schools must do more than merely dispense facts to be memorized and reproduced later, so-called reproductive thinking (Covington, 1986). Schools must also instruct in broader, future-oriented skills that include strategic forms of thinking and problem solving. Among other things, being strategic in one's thinking in the twenty-first century – or in any age, for that matter – means having a keen sense for which information is relevant. As Krates the Elder remarked some twenty centuries ago, "One part of knowledge consists in being ignorant of such things as are not worthy of being known." Today as the computer age hits its stride, individuals will be confronted more and more with virtually infinite amounts of information, only a fraction of which will be relevant to any given problem. Students must learn to cope with this information glut so that they, and not the machine, will be the master.

A MORAL TALE

> Only a tiny minority of us ever are involved in inventing our present, let alone our future.
> Harvey Rubin

The children of Fidel Castro's Cuban revolution of the 1960s provide a provocative view of the problems facing American education today. When asked to describe the study of history, these young

Cubans hotly proclaimed that *they* were history in the making, the wave of the future. When American schoolchildren were also asked, it seems that history is something that happened in the past. Cubans: 1, Americans: 0.

Prolonged social upheaval was the price paid by these young Cubans for their forward-reaching, charismatic view of change. We must find other less tumultuous means to instill the belief in our children that it is *they* who are the architects of the future, and not for just a short, frenzied time, but for years to come. Fortunately, according to Lawrence Cremin, former president of the Spencer Foundation, a uniquely American solution is available. "Education," Cremin noted, "is the characteristic mode of American reform. In other countries they stage revolutions. In the United States we devise new curricula." It is to this task that we now turn.

But before proceeding, it is important that we first lay a foundation in modern motivation theory. This will allow us to explain, among other things, how two learners can see the same achievement differently, one perceiving it as a success and the other as a failure, as well as why success does not always increase a learner's self-confidence. The answers to these and other puzzles related to motivation and learning are revealed in Chapter 2.

SUMMING UP

1. The greatest legacy of education is to encourage in young people the will to learn and to continue learning over a lifetime.

2. The will to learn is threatened not only by the risks of growing up in a dangerous world, but also by misguided theories of human motivation.

3. The drive-theory view of motivation gives rise to wrongheaded proposals for school reform that follow a policy of *intensification* – *more* hours in school, *more* homework, *more* tests, *more* hurdles for prospective teachers, and *more* units for graduation.

4. Actually, many students are often already motivated, but for the

wrong reasons – motivated to avoid failure or at least to avoid the implications of failure, that they lack ability.

5. True educational reform lies not so much in arousing or intensifying existing drive levels, as it does in encouraging different reasons for learning altogether. We must view motivation not as drives, but as goal seeking – goals that draw and entice students toward learning.

X 6. Viewing motivation as goal seeking depends on establishing motivational equity. Everyone can experience a commitment to think more and be poised to learn more. Differences in ability among students are no barrier to this kind of excellence. It is in this sense that everyone can be equal – equal in terms of their reasons (motives) for learning.

ACTIVITIES

Activity 1: Theorizing about Theories

Chapter 1 introduces several theories of achievement motivation. What are theories anyway, and what is their purpose? These questions are best answered by example. Following is the description of an everyday event. Read the first part, then make a guess about what is being described. This guess is your theory. Next, read the second half of the description. Does your theory account for these additional facts? If not, start over with a new theory. When you are satisfied, check Appendix A for at least one possibility that seems to cover all the facts.

First Part. The procedure is very simple. First, place things into different piles. One pile may be enough, depending on how much there is. It is important not to do too much at once. If you are not careful problems can arise. A mistake can be expensive.

Second Part. After the procedure is finished, you can arrange these items into different piles again. Then they can be put in their proper places. Eventually they will be used again and the whole procedure will be repeated.

Activity 2: Asking the Right Questions

Theories are clearly important. But of equal importance, theories must address the right questions. In the realm of education it is teachers, students, and parents who most often ask the right questions, not necessarily researchers. For this reason, you may find it useful to study the following quotations from four different individuals. Think about each statement in terms of questions you believe researchers should be addressing about schools. Then, as you read this book, periodically review your questions. Ask yourself if what you are learning is helping to answer your questions. In other words, how useful is our motivational analysis of classroom life for solving the problems implied by these statements?

High School English Teacher. "What are teachers to do? When you've given your all and there's no hope for students . . . that's too much."

Educational Researcher. "American ghetto youngsters see studying as a sucker's game and school itself as a waste of time. One sees in many of these children almost a determination not to learn, and a suppression of the natural impulse to understand, that cannot be entirely explained by the determinism of poverty."

High School Dropout. "I was invisible, man. I knew it. I sat in those schools for two years. I sat in the back of the room and did nothing. I didn't speak to anyone and no one spoke to me. Nobody said, 'Do your work,' or nothing. Then one day I said it, 'Man, I'm invisible here.' I got up and walked out of the door and never went back."

Ninth Grader. "Somebody is in charge of everything at the regular high school – attendance, schedules, lunch. But nobody is in charge of caring."

Activity 3: Prioritizing the Future

In the opening pages of Chapter 1, we considered a short list of the qualities of mind needed to build a successful personal future, qualities that schools should encourage: a capacity for self-renewal, self-confidence, and self-discipline. What additional human characteristics would you add to complete your "mission statement" for what schools should be all about?

Be sure to return to your list from time to time as you read this book to test how well these goals are being served by our motivational perspective.

2

MOTIVES AS EMOTIONS

Emotions are feelings with thoughts incidentally attached.
David Hume

THE BEGINNING

THERE ARE MANY INDIVIDUALS AND EVENTS IN THIS CENTURY THAT can lay claim to the beginnings of the scientific investigation of achievement motivation. We begin with a little known drama of great importance.

THE PLAYERS: Professor Kurt Lewin and his laboratory assistant, Ferdinand Hoppe.

THE TIME: 1931–1932.

THE PLACE: A small laboratory at the University of Berlin.

Professor Lewin's laboratory was crowded with the research paraphernalia of his time, including an odd conveyor-belt device. This contraption allowed a series of pegs to move on circular rollers at a uniform rate of speed, much like a row of ducks in a shooting gallery. This unlikely apparatus would provide the key to the question of how, psychologically, humans define success and failure. There are few consistent yardsticks when it comes to judging whether a particular achievement is successful – certainly not in the same sense that we can objectively measure height, weight, or temperature. Success and failure mean different things to different people. The same accomplishment can elicit pride in one person and self-rebuke in another, giving rise to the truism that "one person's success is another person's failure." For all the subjectivity involved, however, these judgments do proceed in lawful ways as Professor Lewin and Ferdinand Hoppe were to discover.

27

Hoppe (1930) invited an assortment of local tradespeople and university students to practice tossing rings on the moving pegs at various distances from the target. He found that some subjects felt satisfied after placing, say, eight rings, while others expressed extreme frustration at only twelve correct tosses. Additionally, Hoppe found that the performance level needed to arouse feelings of success changed over time for each individual. A score that was initially judged a success might well be considered unacceptable on a later practice trial.

Levels of Aspiration

These curious behaviors make sense only in light of the individual's personal goals, or as they eventually came to be known, "levels of aspiration" (Diggory, 1966). Hoppe found that judgments of success or failure depended less on the actual levels of performance of his subjects than on the relationship between their performances and their aspirations. Thus when Hoppe's subjects achieved their personal goals, say, tossing ten rings correctly, they felt successful. By the same token, when their performances fell below their self-imposed minimums, they experienced feelings of failure. As we shall see, these same mechanisms operate in schools where success and failure are real – not artificial creations of the laboratory.

Self-Confidence

Hoppe's revelation prompted a cascade of crucial insights. For instance, it was now possible to give meaning to the concept of self-confidence, another psychological state of mind like success and failure. There is no accounting for self-confidence in objective terms. Some individuals may discern a gleam of hope in a situation that seems hopeless to everyone but themselves. At the same time, others may express a vote of no confidence despite the fact that they have everything going for them. Basically, self-confidence reflects the extent to which individuals believe themselves able enough mentally to win the prize, strong enough to turn back the foe, or possessing sufficient hand–eye coordination to toss enough rings correctly in Hoppe's experiment.

Expectancy

The notion of expectancy also comes into play here. In its current usage, the term expectancy generally refers to perceived estimates of eventual success – how sure individuals are of doing well in the end, but not necessarily that they themselves are the cause of their success. Thus "expectations" and "confidence" are not merely interchangeable concepts. For instance, students may remain optimistic about an outcome, say, achieving a passing grade on a geography test, not necessarily because they judge themselves equal to the test, but because the assignment may be quite easy – something anyone could do – or because they may be counting on help from others. From this example we can deduce that depending on its perceived causes, success may or may not act to increase self-confidence.

Hoppe was amazed at the cleverness with which individuals maintained a balance between their success and failure experiences. By raising or lowering their aspirations, his subjects created a check-and-balance mechanism involving what researchers have subsequently called a "typical shift" (e.g., Atkinson & Raynor, 1974). After a success Hoppe's subjects typically shifted their aspirations upward and, conversely, after failure they usually shifted them lower. In the latter case, they protected themselves against the possibility of repeated failure, and by raising aspirations after succeeding they avoided getting bored. So pervasive were these self-correcting maneuvers that subjects would often unconsciously lean in closer toward the pegs after a failure or two, or after committing themselves to a particularly high performance goal, thereby making the task easier without necessarily having to change their aspirations. In fact, the distance that individual subjects stood from the target, when given a choice, became recognized by later researchers as an important measure of the person's willingness to take risks.

Realistic Challenges

Hoppe's subjects also understood intuitively what researchers would later confirm empirically. The key to sustained involvement in learning requires that a realistic match be established between the individual's present capabilities and the demands of the achievement task. This point is well illustrated in an experiment conducted years later by Charles Woodson (1975) who created varying degrees of match and mismatch between student ability levels and the difficulty of an upcoming school test. Those students who experienced a close match (i.e., high ability, difficult test; or low ability, easy test) learned the most, and this was true for both bright and less bright students. On the other hand, a mismatch interfered with learning at all ability levels, but for different reasons. Those more able students who competed against easy standards became bored, while those less able students from whom too much was required simply gave up when they failed to deliver.

Absolute and Merit-Based Standards

Hoppe's experiments also illustrated the importance of setting achievement goals for oneself. When Hoppe's subjects set their own goals, they usually challenge the upper limits of their present ring-tossing capabilities and not beyond, thereby assuring that success was always within reach and never in short supply. Moreover, these self-generated goals remained a more or less constant target until the individual achieved them. For this reason we can refer to self-defined goals as constant or "absolute" in nature. They can be distinguished from achievement goals that are defined in relative terms, that is, by comparing one's achievements relative to those of one's peers. In this latter case, the measure of success is constantly changing, and as a result always depends not only on how well the individual does, but also on how well others do, something over which the individual learner has little control.

Another yardstick for measuring success involves teachers, not students, in setting the standards. Here success is merit-based, that is, anyone who attains a goal set by the teacher merits a reward. For example, Hoppe might have told his subjects that "Anyone who tosses eight out of ten rings correctly on two consecutive trials has succeeded." There are many real-life examples of merit-based achievement goals outside the laboratory. Consider, for example, the boy scout who is working for a merit badge in photography. Any number of merit badges can be awarded because success does not depend on doing better than others, but on completing a specific set of requirements satisfactorily. The struggle to achieve success in this case focuses on the obstacles imposed by the requirements of the task itself, and on the varying levels of excellence required, not on individuals competing against one another for diminishing rewards.

Absolute standards, whether self-generated or set by others, will form an important part of our recommendations for educational change. Motivationally speaking, absolute standards are invaluable because they foster a positive interpretation of failure, should it occur (Kennedy & Willcutt, 1964). When students expect to be held to a well-defined standard of performance, and not simply expected to outperform others, the failure to attain the prevailing standards tends to motivate students to try harder next time. In this case failure implies falling short of a goal, whereas competing with others and failing implies falling short as a person!

Absolute goals also provide built-in criteria for gauging one's progress, or lack of it, and for judging when one's work is finished or still incomplete. Unfortunately, in competition one's work is never done, unless of course one drops out. The structure that absolute standards provided is especially important for anxiety-prone students who, in the absence of clear, unambiguous guidelines for success often think the worst of themselves, no matter how well they perform (Wiggins, 1989).

Finally, setting one's own achievement goals, and altering them as necessary, like Hoppe's subjects did, puts individuals in control of their successes and failures. The net effect for Hoppe's subjects was that their aspirations spiraled upward just ahead of current achievement levels, but not so far ahead that their temporary goals could not be reached and surpassed through persistent effort and practice. As a result, Hoppe's subjects were challenged to perform at their current maximum. Feeling in control of one's own progress was the key to this positive dynamic in Hoppe's day, more than a half century ago, and it remains so today.

Hoppe's Legacy

Perhaps the most enduring legacy of Hoppe's research is the recognition today that judgments about success and failure, as well as feelings of confidence or despair and optimism versus pessimism, are all creatures of a subjective world of the individual's own making (Carver & Scheier, 1986). Truth and falsity aside, reality has little standing here. What counts are beliefs and appearances. For instance, by shifting one's aspirations, even slightly, students can create a new round of successes or plunge themselves into a downward, irreversible spiral of failure. Naturally, the expectations of others, including parents and teachers, set limits on the freedom of children to maneuver. The finely tuned balance of successes offsetting failures enjoyed by Hoppe's subjects can quickly be overturned if individuals accept as their own the inappropriate standards imposed by others. But, then, there may be little choice. In a competitive environment there is continual pressure on students to raise their aspirations, irrespective of their ability and past performance, and often severe sanctions against lowering them.

The insights inspired by Hoppe's research provided most of the essential principles necessary for the development of modern theories of achievement motivation. Basically, all that was lacking were assumptions about the *why* of achievement – the reasons that arouse people to action. And, even here, Hoppe (as reported in Barker, 1942) came close with the speculation that aspirations represent a compromise between two opposing tendencies, one involving the need to strive for something better and the other, the need to avoid repeated failure.

NEED ACHIEVEMENT

To overcome obstacles, to exercise power, to strive to do something well and as quickly as possible.
Henry Murray

Approaching Success versus Avoiding Failure

John Atkinson's theory of achievement motivation (1957, 1981, 1987) built on Hoppe's earlier, brilliant speculations. According to Atkinson, all individuals can be characterized by two learned drives, a motive to approach success and a motive to avoid failure. These two opposing motives are viewed as relatively stable personality characteristics. Psychologically speaking, the approach mode is defined by a *hope* for success or, as Atkinson (1964) put it, "a capacity to experience pride in accomplishment" (p. 214). The anticipation of success and its emotional correlates of pride and exhilaration combine to produce a trust in the future and in life generally.

By contrast, the motive to avoid failure is described as the capacity for experiencing *humiliation* and *shame* when one fails. According to Atkinson, this emotional anticipation produces a tendency *not* to undertake achievement-related activities. In fact, given a free choice among assignments that vary from easy to hard, failure-avoiding individuals should choose none of them – not even the easiest – unless extrinsic incentives such as money or the threat of punishment are introduced to overcome their resistance.

This brief description underscores the basic feature of Atkinson's need achievement model, namely the assumption that the driving force behind all noteworthy accomplishments in school and beyond is emotional anticipation. Simply put, persons high in the need to achieve anticipate pride in their accomplishments, a feeling that propels them toward further successes. On the other hand, persons low in need achievement anticipate shame (caused by failure) and attempt to avoid its noxious effects by withdrawing or not trying.

Atkinson's longtime associate and collaborator, David McClelland, put an additional spin on the meaning of the need to achieve by describing it in competitive terms, competition against either highly demanding, absolute, or self-imposed standards of excellence to which many might aspire but against which only a few will prevail, or competition *among* individuals for a limited number of rewards (Combs, 1957; Greenberg, 1932). As to the winners, McClelland (1955) had in mind individuals imbued with an entrepreneurial spirit – someone driven to produce change, relentlessly, often without consideration for others and typically for personal gain. McClelland's notion (1955) neatly captures an unmistakable Protestant work ethic – the haunting fear that someone, somewhere, may be standing idle, and elevating the stoic virtues of independence and autonomy.

Just so there was no mistaking his point, McClelland (1961) likened the essence of achievement motivation to the mythological figure of Hermes. Recall the precociously gifted and ruthless Hermes – born in the morning, inventing and performing upon a lyre at noonday, and yet with enough energy left over to steal cattle from his older brother, Apollo, in the evening. Hermes conveys perfectly a tense, dynamic restlessness, an energy source always on the move, in a hurry, for the purposes of material and intellectual self-advancement, even at the expense of one's own family. Subsequent research confirms the broad outlines of this description. For instance, upwardly mobile boys appear more willing than those rated low in mobility to leave home in search of jobs, even though such a move might threaten family unity (Rosen, 1959). Moreover, persons high in need achievement tend to view time as a commodity – to be brought, sold, or saved – and perceive time as passing so rapidly that the future is "always here before we know it" (Knapp, 1960).

The Hermes myth also reveals a darker, brazen, more troublesome side of the motive to achieve which McClelland (1961) not only recognizes but appears to savor. "Above all else Hermes was dishonest. He lied outrageously to his brother Apollo and his father

Zeus; he stole his brother's cattle; he wore special sandals back-wards to try and conceal the way he had really gone; he boasted un-truthfully of his exploits. And in all he was a pretty unethical trick-ster and thief" (p. 329).

Thus, according to McClelland, the achievement archetype is not above flattery, trickery, and bluffing. Given these parameters, we can imagine an updated schoolboy counterpart of the ancient Her-mes – the ruthless student who gains competitive advantage by stealing assigned readings on reserve in the library or who studies secretly, hoping his intense effort will go unnoticed in the event of failure so that his reputation for brilliance will remain intact.

Actually, more recent research softens considerably McClelland's harsh portrayal of the success-oriented individual (Covington & Roberts, 1994). Although it is true that some success strivers are fiercely competitive, what emerges as the dominant characteristic of this group is an unquenchable desire to learn and improve, but not necessarily at the expense of others.

But are students either just success-oriented or failure-avoiding, and to the extremes described so far? Obviously not. Students are more likely to share these characteristics to one degree or another, a circumstance that creates an almost endless variety of motivational patterns within the same classroom. Atkinson acknowledged this reality by suggesting that the motive to approach success and the motive to avoid failure are separate, *independent* dimensions. This simply means that where individuals find themselves on one di-mension, say, high on the approach dimension, does not depend on their placement on the avoidance dimension. This independent re-lationship is portrayed visually in Figure 2.1. It permits us to de-scribe four different types of students, each of which represents a distinctly different combination of achievement motives.

First, there are those students who are characterized by a combi-nation of high approach, low avoidance – those persons falling in quadrant B whom we will refer to as *success-oriented* pupils. Second, we can also identify the opposite combination of low-approach, high-avoidance students falling in quadrant C whom we will de-scribe as *failure avoiders*. Third, pupils falling into quadrant A are characterized by a combination of high approach, high avoidance.

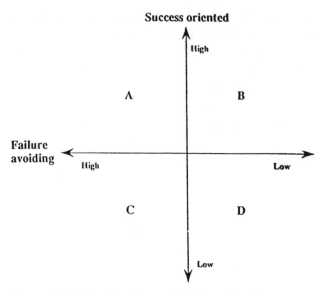

Figure 2.1. Quadripolar model of need achievement.

Source: Covington (1992).

These individuals, whom we will label *overstrivers,* illustrate the importance of independent dimensions. Independence allows us to characterize the achievement process as a conflict of opposing forces. Common sense as well as the observations of many clinical psychologists, including Sigmund Freud, suggest that individuals can be simultaneously attracted to and repelled by the same situation. Such a conflict reflects the essential nature of overstrivers. Finally, the assumption of independence also allows for a fourth type: students found in quadrant D reflect the relative absence of both hope and fear (low approach, low avoidance). In this case any conflict (and therefore arousal) is minimal, and as a result the chances of these individuals learning very much are minimal, too. We will refer to these students as *failure acceptors.*

Now, let's consider these four groups in more detail, using four different case studies. Although each is only a hypothetical figure, many readers will recognize at least some of their own reactions to school.

Losa: Success Striver. Losa Wu, a high school freshman, easily fits the description of the prototypic success-oriented student, that is, a youngster who possesses a great capacity for intrinsic involvement and a restless curiosity. The immigrant Asian culture stresses upward mobility and self-improvement through hard work, a heritage that began for Losa's family three generations earlier when her great-grandparents emigrated from China. Losa's parents expected her to excel and she was groomed for high achievement right from the beginning, almost before she could walk. After school and on Saturdays her "free" time was filled with various extracurricular activities – dancing and music lessons and family outings to museums or concerts. As Losa grew older she was permitted greater freedom in deciding what activities to pursue – music, photography, and biology became her favorites – but the high expectations remained and any success was quickly acknowledged. As the years passed Losa developed into a self-sufficient, resourceful, and self-assured young woman who now stands on the threshold of a highly promising academic career.

John: Failure Avoider. In contrast to Losa, for John, a high school senior, avoidance tendencies outweigh the anticipation of success. John can be characterized by a single phrase – able but apathetic (Beery, 1975). He describes his feelings toward school and life in general as continual boredom. John appears listless much of the time and he is vaguely apprehensive. Not that John was ever in academic trouble; in fact, to all outward appearances his academic record proclaims John to be a good if not a superior student. But he has always figured out the easiest way to get a good grade and relies heavily on a last-minute surge of studying to make up for weeks of neglect, procrastination, and disinterest in his classes. In view of how little interest John shows in school, these strategies have worked well – well enough, in fact, to earn him a place in the freshman class at a prestigious four-year college beginning next September.

John's passive, ambivalent reactions to school stem not so much from indifference, that is, a relative absence of the motive to achieve, but rather from excessive worry about failure and its im-

37

plications that he is not able enough. In such cases fear is most typically avoided by escaping the threat, either actually dropping out of school or by means of psychological withdrawal. In the psychological realm, the implications of failure can be avoided through the use of defensive, magical thinking by which John sometimes denies the meaning of impending failure or by which he minimizes the importance of assignments he is in danger of failing. Not surprisingly, John feels somewhat guilty and anxious about his accomplishments, worrying secretly that he is somehow a fraud, not really as knowledgeable as his grades reflect and bothered that someday he will be found out. John shares much in common with those individuals described as "anxious-defensive" (Wieland-Eckelmann, Bösel, & Badorrek, 1987) who repress or disregard threatening messages and react to stressful events by withdrawing (Depreeuw, 1992).

Amy: Overstriver. Overstrivers are at once drawn to and repelled by the prospects of achievement. In self-worth terms, these individuals attempt to avoid failure by succeeding! This reason for achieving is eventually self-defeating because its purpose is basically defensive, even though in the short run it may lead to extraordinary successes.

Amy, a black sixth-grade student, typifies the plight of the overstriver. Amy is a teacher's joy – bright, hard working, compliant, and seems especially mature for her young years. Whenever possible she does far more than her assignments require and when school work is not challenging enough, which is usually the case, she sets additional goals for herself by negotiating extra-credit assignments with her teacher. Amy's parents have high expectations for their only child, perhaps too high, and they are willing to sacrifice everything – their time, attention, and meager resources – in the hope that she will become a "somebody" in the mainstream world of white America.

To all appearances, Amy is an exemplary student, but like John with whom she shares intense doubts about her adequacy, things are far from well. Amy's slavish commitment to work often drives her to the edge of exhaustion. And for the last month she has been battling a painful case of the hives. There are also ominous signs of a preulcerous condition which has been diagnosed as psychosomatic.

Ralph: Failure Acceptor. Individuals falling in quadrant D of Figure 2.1 are identified as failure acceptors. Failure acceptors remain basically indifferent to achievement events, as reflected by the relative absence of both hope and fear. But indifference is open to several interpretations. We have already considered John's passivity as a kind of motivated inaction that allows him to avoid making mistakes and looking stupid. But indifference can also mean genuinely not caring, as when, for example, the lessons to be learned in school hold no relevance for one's life. Indifference may even reflect hidden anger, as when one is forced to conform to middle-class values that hold no attraction. This latter kind of indifference has often been attributed to minorities and poor white children. Finally, indifference may also reflect resignation and loss of hope. In self-worth terms this means giving up the struggle to avoid the implications of failure and in the process concluding that one is not bright enough to succeed in school (Covington & Omelich, 1985).

This slide into self-despair and resentment is illustrated by Ralph, a displaced middle school youngster from Appalachia. There was never any doubt in Ralph's mind that he would become a coal miner like his father – no doubt, that is, until his father's job was lost to automation. To make ends meet, Ralph and his three older brothers and sisters were sent to live with relatives. Sadly, Ralph never felt welcome in his new school. He was an instant outsider, a dumb "hillbilly" to hear malicious classmates describe him. Although Ralph tried hard at first, he could not keep up with the assignments. His name began to appear more and more frequently on the list of homework delinquents on the chalkboard. Ralph was angry at himself for feeling stupid and resented his classmates for making him feel that way. Ralph's frustration was often expressed in a wild, impetuous flurry of attention getting, which also had the effect of keeping others from learning – throwing erasers during silent reading or making armpit farts when the teacher's back was turned. Ralph's dreams were quickly evaporating. To work in mining, Ralph's generation will need to operate computers and other highly sophisticated equipment. But unless Ralph acquires the basics he will only carry a shovel, what his father before him referred to derisively as "an ignorance stick."

Risk-Taking Preferences

Is this all there is to Atkinson's need achievement model? Not quite. The quadrant in which a person falls (see Figure 2.1) is only one factor in determining how students will react to the learning game. For example, sometimes failure-oriented students like John will perform just as well or are just as willing to perform as are success-oriented students like Losa. Why should this be? Atkinson added two more factors to his model, which, when combined with approach–avoidance tendencies, determine who will be aroused to achieve, to what degree, and in which specific situations. First, all students will be aroused or not depending on the *attractiveness* of the achievement goal. Second, students also will be aroused depending on their *expectation* of attaining the goal. Taken together, these two statements lead to the commonsense observation that all persons will be stirred to action if there is a reasonable chance that they will get something they want. Likewise, as the expectation of achieving a desired goal – like doing well on a test – decreases, so will the individual's efforts to attain it, even though the goal may actually become more attractive because of its elusiveness. This observation reminds us once again that inaction does not necessarily mean a student is unmotivated. In fact, students can be highly motivated, but there may simply be no opportunity to do well. Finally, it does not matter how available or easy a goal may be. If it holds no attraction, it will be ignored.

Now, how do these dynamics apply specifically to success-oriented students like Losa? Simply put, Losa is not attracted to goals for which success is guaranteed. Although people rarely tire of success, it is not the "easy victory" that fully motivates us: as human beings, we quickly become bored with the sure thing. This is especially true of success-oriented persons. For them the attraction of achieving comes from the prospect of overcoming a manageable challenge in which there is some risk of failing. For Losa, and success-oriented persons like her, the optimal level of challenge is in the intermediate range – namely setting one's goals just high enough to provide some satisfaction should she succeed, but not so high that success is unlikely. By comparison, we would expect success-oriented individuals to lose interest quickly in exceedingly difficult assignments, and to reject altogether a simple assignment as unworthy.

Now consider the risk-taking preferences of failure-avoiding individuals like John. In the context of fear, the attractiveness of a task is defined in negative terms – how noxious failure will be if it occurs. From this perspective, the easy assignment is preferred because the chances of failure are low and the anticipation of shame is minimized. Hence, in theory at least, it appears that failure-avoiding individuals are the exception to our observation that humans shun the certainty of a sure thing. By similar reasoning, very difficult assignments should also prove attractive to failure-avoiding individuals because no one feels very bad when they fail at a task for which the odds against success are exceedingly long.

These predictions have received broad empirical support. For example, in one ring-toss experiment McClelland (1958) found that kindergarten children as well as third graders rated high in achievement motivation more often set their aspirations in the middle range of difficulty. They also pitched the rings from modest distances. On the other hand, children low in achievement motivation tended to make extreme choices, either standing right on top of the pegs to ensure success or so far away that success was virtually impossible.

Future Time Perspectives

Several other investigators have given a futuristic twist to Atkinson's original concepts. J. R. Nuttin and Willy Lens (Nuttin, 1984; Nuttin & Lens, 1985) argue that one's future goals and especially one's subjective notions of time are the basic motivational space within which all humans operate. Professor Lewin (1948) anticipated this same point years earlier when he remarked that "the setting of goals is closely related to time perspective. The goal of an individual includes his expectations for the future, his wishes, and his daydreams" (p. 113).

In effect, people translate their needs and desires into specific time-bound goals. Some goals involve satisfaction in the near term, as, for example, when one anticipates the taste of a candy bar as the wrapper is being removed; other goals involve planning within an intermediate time frame, as when a child begins saving his weekly allowance for ice skates next winter; and yet other goals like becoming a physician can preoccupy one's attention for years, even decades. In addition to this *time hierarchy,* goal striving can be distinguished by the number of intervening subtasks or steps that must be completed successfully on the way to a goal – a kind of *task hierarchy* (Raynor, 1969; Raynor & Entin, 1982). Thus future time perspective can be characterized by its extension or length, and by its density (the number of steps in a certain future time interval).

According to Lens, success-oriented individuals like Losa aspire to more complicated, distant goals than do failure-threatened individuals (DeVolder & Lens, 1982), and they are highly adept at arranging small steps of intermediate difficulty so that the chances of moving successfully from one to another, like stepping-stones, are good. A special characteristic of such plans, what Joel Raynor (1982) calls "partially contingent paths," is also the province of success-oriented persons. Here success in a step guarantees the opportunity to continue, but failure has no direct bearing on future striving. This is because success-oriented persons are forever hedging their bets by having backup plans. They also entertain alternative goals should the original objective prove impossible to reach.

This futuristic extension of Atkinson's model holds powerful implications for educational practice. For one thing, it suggests that the ability to plan is a part of motivation. Indeed, later in Chapter 7 we will consider the possibility that *motives* are actually just *plans* by a different name. This suggests that teaching students to be more planful will actually enhance their willingness to learn, and for the right reasons. For another thing, believing oneself to be, in the words of Richard de Charms (1968), an "origin" – that is, feeling in personal control of future events (as contrasted to feeling like a pawn) – is the key to all noteworthy achievements. Ellen Skinner and her colleagues (Skinner, Wellborn, & Connell, 1990) explain it this way: "When children believe that they can exert control over success in school, they perform better. . . . And, when children succeed in school, they are more likely to view school performance as a controllable outcome. . . . children who are not doing well in school will perceive themselves as having no control over academic successes and failures and these beliefs will subsequently generate performances that serve to confirm their beliefs" (p. 22).

The legacy of Atkinson's model is clearly evident in these comments as well as in some recent attempts to conceptualize student achievement motivation. For example, Paul Pintrich (1988; 1989) and his colleagues (Eccles, 1983; Pintrich & De Groot, 1990) propose three factors essential to task involvement, which are also linked to realistic goal setting and to the effective monitoring of one's plans: (1) an expectancy factor, which includes beliefs about one's ability to perform successfully ("Can I do this task?") – what James Connell (1985) calls "capacity" beliefs; (2) a value component, which includes the reasons for being involved (in other words, "Why am I doing this?" or "Of what importance is this to me?"); and (3) an emotional component ("How do I feel about this task?").

EDUCATIONAL IMPLICATIONS

Atkinson's model of achievement motivation provides several significant insights into the direction that responsible educational change must take. The first implication concerns the reasons behind ethnic differences in achievement motivation; and the second, the relationship between various child-rearing practices and the quality of later achievement striving. A third implication involves the question of whether skills associated with achievement motivation like realistic goal setting can be enhanced through classroom instruction.

Ethnic Differences in Achievement Motivation

Initially, investigators paid little attention to ethnic differences in achievement motivation, because the early research found the entrepreneurial spirit of Hermes among a wide range of cultural groups including the Japanese, Israelis, Europeans, and East Indians (Biaggio, 1978; Hayashi, Rim, & Lynn, 1970; Singh, 1977). But what was not fully appreciated at the time was that most of these groups either came from cultures that held values similar to those of middle-class Americans or were recent immigrants to America – the so-called immigrant minorities. These groups share little in common with American-born *castelike* minorities who according to John Ogbu (1978) were incorporated originally into our society against their will: Mexican Americans through colonization of the Southwest Territories, Puerto Ricans following the American takeover from Spain, blacks through slavery, and American Indians through the dispossession of their tribal lands. These groups were relegated by virtue of birth to the lower rungs of the economic ladder and were traditionally exploited as cheap labor.

What about the need achievement patterns of these so-called castelike groups? Black Americans typically score lower on traditional need achievement measures than do white Americans (Adkins, Payne, & Ballif, 1972; Cooper & Tom, 1984; Graham, 1984a). Native Americans and Spanish-speaking Hispanics and Latinos also exhibit these same reduced patterns (Ramirez & Price-Williams, 1976; Sanders, Scholz, & Kagan, 1976). Does this mean that black and Hispanic students lack the need to achieve? No, it is not a matter of a deficiency, but of how the need to achieve is expressed. Achievement differences among ethnic groups are reflected in the different goals to which they aspire. This emphasis on differential goals explains why only westerners are so intent on climbing Mount Everest. As an achievement goal this conquest is irrelevant to the Tibetans and Nepalese who live around Everest (Maehr & Nicholls, 1980).

Different goals also explain the remarkable academic accomplishments of Ernestino, a recent refugee from Nicaragua (as reported in Suarez-Orozco, 1989). On the face of it, Ernestino should have become just another nameless statistic in America's sad litany of crime, poverty, and personal failure. By fleeing to America, Ernestino barely escaped the random draft and military service in Nicaragua that had left two of his brothers dead and his father crippled. But Ernestino's escape had left him both traumatized and brokenhearted; not only had he left his mother behind, but his cultural heritage as well. Pushers regularly peddled drugs within a two-block radius of his new American school, violence and petty theft were rampant on campus, and prostitutes routinely paraded their wares nearby. Additionally, Ernestino worked forty hours a week as a dishwasher in order to support himself and other members of his extended family in America. But despite it all, Ernestino graduated from high school with an overall GPA of 3.8 and now attends a four-year college.

By any commonsense reckoning, Ernestino is a highly ambitious achiever. Yet, according to Suarez-Orozco who interviewed dozens of similar Central American refugees, need achievement concepts are inadequate to explain Ernestino's unique motivational dynamics. Obviously, like traditional entrepreneurs, Ernestino's basic purpose was to "better himself" – to become a doctor, an attorney, or an engineer, but not (in the spirit of Hermes) for the purpose of self-indulgence or personal gain. Ernestino's goals revealed a different ethos, one of nurturing and cooperation. He was driven first to rescue his mother left behind in Nicaragua who had sacrificed so much for his sake, and then more generally to convert his successes into help for others of his people who had been devastated by war. Nor do Ernestino's achievement goals suggest that he will become a "somebody" at the expense of breaking family ties or denying his heritage in a search for liberation and new freedoms.

Research indicates that, like Hispanic American children, black Americans also favor achievement goals that benefit their families (as opposed to individual benefits) and from which they would gain family recognition (Castenell, 1983; Ramirez & Price-Williams, 1976). As one example, researchers assessed the meaning of some six hundred concepts among adolescent males from some thirty language groups worldwide (Fyans, Maehr, Salili, & Desai, 1983). Terms like "independence," "competition," and "hard work" were

45

most closely associated with notions of success among white Americans and West Germans. These same terms were least salient for black Americans. Instead, for many of these latter youngsters, the most prominent associations with feelings of success were "family," "cooperation," and "tradition." Finally, not only were terms like "competition" and "champion" less salient in the minds of black students – words that represent major preoccupations among most middle-class whites – but, worse yet, for blacks they were often associated with feelings of failure and defeat, and sometimes even with images of death!

These findings suggest why some minority groups are placed at particular risk in school. First, for many youngsters the primary goals to which they aspire – assuming adult work roles and caring for others – lie outside the more traditional realm of academics, which favors competition and autonomy. As a result, these goals are not particularly honored or encouraged in many schools. Second, given the mainstream emphasis on competitive values, and on the scramble for improved social status, minority students are being deprived of their preferred means to achieve their objectives, which is through cooperation, sharing, and close social cohesion. Finally, to make things even worse, these youngsters must play by competitive rules, if they are to play at all – rules that are often alien, frightening, and confusing. Given these handicaps, we should not be surprised by the shocking rate of school dropouts found in the ghettos and barrios of America.

Just why academic competition represents a special threat to minorities, especially black youngsters, is a topic for later discussion (Chapter 4). In the meantime, the larger policy implications of this research seem clear. We must arrange school learning so that it encourages more varied achievement goals than the narrow set of values often associated with competitive excellence and high standardized test scores at all costs. We must also learn to respect alternative ways for attaining excellence – for the sake of the group, for tradition, and for honor. Moreover, these changes must be made without doing violence to the fundamental academic mission of all schooling, that of providing students with the subject matter skills necessary to thrive, not merely survive. Finally, in the process of reform, we must not ask students to give up their cultural and ethnic identities.

The history of research on need achievement provides an important perspective on this challenge. Scholars have moved, initially, from viewing ethnic differences in achievement motivation as a matter of *inferiority* for some groups, and *superiority* for others, to seeing the issue in terms of *diversity*. Deficiency explanations are generally unsatisfactory because they divert attention from one constant feature of underachievement among ethnic minorities, that is, the inability of the educational system to take account of the particular needs of these children. As Dennis McInerney (1988) points out, "When educators place the blame for minority children's poor achievement on factors for which the school cannot be held responsible, particularly such factors as children's innate lack of ability, or inappropriate cognitive style, then there is little perceived need for major alteration in the organizational structure or policies in school" (p. 33).

Child Rearing and Achievement

A second implication of Atkinson's need achievement model concerns the fundamental nature of need achievement and the question of whether changes are possible in what is often thought to be a basic, traitlike personality dimension. According to McClelland, the characteristic way in which individuals resolve the inherent approach–avoidance conflict posed by achievement situations depends largely on childhood experiences. Subsequent research has borne this out. Several aspects of child-rearing practices appear especially relevant to later achievement striving.

First, parents of success-oriented children expect their youngsters to achieve notable successes. As a result they encourage their children to try new things, to explore options, and to exercise independence, and such parents start at an early age compared with parents whose children are relatively lower in the need to achieve (Winterbottom, 1953).

Second, these same parents also provide an uncommon amount of nurturing so that their children will also acquire the skills necessary for independence. This point is illustrated by the work of Bernard Rosen and Roy D'Andrade (1959). These researchers administered problem-solving tasks to two groups of young boys, one of which was rated high and the other low in achievement motivation. In one test the boys were blindfolded and asked to build a tower using oddly shaped blocks. Parents could encourage their sons in any way they wished as long as they themselves did not touch the blocks. The parents of the high-striving boys provided far more encouragement, usually in the form of task-oriented tips about how to proceed (e.g., "Put the larger blocks on the bottom") and expressed more praise when the task was finished. Moreover, as in the Winterbottom study cited earlier, these parents also expected more of their children and were also more optimistic that their sons would not disappoint them. These same findings have since been confirmed for both boys and girls in the Netherlands (Hermans, ter Laak, & Maes, 1972).

A third line of research initiated originally by Virginia Crandall and her colleagues (Crandall, Katkovsky, & Crandall, 1965; Crandall, Preston, & Rabson, 1960) suggests that patterns of parental rewards and reprimands are also critical to the development of positive and negative attitudes toward achievement. The parents of high-achieving youngsters tend to reward praiseworthy accomplishments, yet ignore disappointing performances, a pattern well illustrated by Losa's parents. This pattern is essentially reversed when it comes to the parents of failure-avoiding youngsters like John (Teevan & Fischer, 1967). Here disappointing performances are seen as violations of adult expectations, and punished accordingly – usually severely – while success is met with faint praise and sometimes even indifference.

The research cited so far is based largely on observations of children and their parents. But do these same family dynamics hold as children grow older, even into young adulthood? Apparently so, if one can judge from the results of research conducted by me and my colleague, Kumiko Tomiki (Covington & Tomiki, 1996; Tomiki, 1997). We asked college students to describe retrospectively the quality of the achievement climate in their homes. Success-oriented students perceived their parents as employing praise more often in success and punishment less in failure compared with the reports of failure-prone students, who recall the opposite pattern. These and other results closely paralleled the findings of Virginia Crandall and her colleagues whom, it will be recalled, studied youngsters in the earlier years of family life. Given the apparent consistency of such child-rearing practices over time as well as their early onset, one gains the impression that the tendencies to approach success and to avoid failure found among adults likely reflect fundamental personality structures laid down at the deepest levels.

Recently researchers have isolated several other devastating parental reactions to failure, one of which is inconsistency – a tendency to punish failure sometimes and at other times to disregard or even reward poor performances (Kohlmann, Schumacher, & Streit, 1988; Tomiki, 1997). These reactions have been implicated in the development of "learned helplessness," a topic to be considered in the next chapter. Here learners give up trying because they come to believe, often rightly so, that they have no control over their own destiny (Mineka & Henderson, 1985; Mineka & Kihlstrom, 1978). Eventually profound depression, anger, and overwhelming feelings of anxiety can result. This description fits Ralph, the youngster from Appalachia, in most respects.

Research conducted by Walter Krohne at Mainz University (Krohne, 1990; Krohne, Kohlmann, & Leidig, 1986) suggests that such generalized anxiety reactions can also be triggered by another different combination of child-rearing strategies. In this particular case, parents provide neither consistent standards by which children can judge their performances nor the intellectual support necessary to develop effective coping skills.

Another disastrous pattern involves aggressive, often overbearing parental demands for excellence, but with little or no guidance for how to achieve it (Chapin & Vito, 1988; Davids & Hainsworth, 1967). Here the child hopelessly outclasses himself by maintaining unrealistically high goals, yet has no way to attain them. This discrepancy between *hoped-for* and *expected* outcomes has been associated with the phenomenon of "underachieving" (Bricklin & Bricklin, 1967). Underachievers perform at levels far below their capacity because, as the prevailing argument runs, if they were to try hard

49

and fail anyway – a virtual certainty given such high standards – their self-esteem would suffer. By refusing to try at all, these individuals deftly sidestep any test of their worth.

The overstriver also shares this same ideal–actual discrepancy (Martire, 1956). Rather than avoiding a test of their worth, however, these students, like Amy, are driven to avoid failure by actually living up to their overly demanding ideals. The parents of overstrivers demand excellence, and typically nurture the proper intellectual tools to insure success, but in the process overzealously pressure the child by also punishing failure.

If we can hazard any single, overall generalization regarding the quality of child rearing and later achievement, it is that youngsters raised in *authoritative* homes – homes in which parents respect their children's ideas, and act in accepting ways – are likely to do better in school than youngsters raised in *authoritarian* environments, which stress obedience and conformity to adult authority (Baumrind, 1991). However, if this is true, then why should Asian American children, whose home life is rated relatively high in authoritarian characteristics, tend to perform better academically than any other ethnic group? And, conversely, why should African American children, whose homes are generally characterized as authoritative, tend to perform relatively poorly in schools? Lawrence Steinberg and his colleagues (Steinberg, Dornbusch, & Brown, 1992) suggest that peer-group dynamics may explain these apparent contradictions. Peers who value doing well in school reinforce one another in positive ways academically, so that Asian youngsters whose parents and peer groups both push them in the same direction academically perform well in school. In contrast, other minorities, mainly African Americans and Hispanics, have relatively less peer support academically and as a consequence are less likely to do well in school despite warm parenting styles. Thus, according to Steinberg, in order to thrive academically, many minority youngsters must go outside their primary peer affiliation for support, thus splitting their allegiances. We are reminded of Amy, our young overstriver, who will be confronted increasingly as time passes with the need to balance an acceptance of dominant white academic values against the prospects of being rejected by her peer group.

Findings such as these, embracing as they do ethnic considerations, child-rearing practices, and peer dynamics, illustrate the complex challenges that confront educators. Effective reform is never easy. So many cross-cutting issues must be dealt with. Nonetheless, one overarching observation emerges from these findings. The mission of schools will be best served, motivationally speaking, if we modify the rules of the learning game so that teachers and students become allies, not adversaries, with teachers acting as coaches, mentors, and resources for students as they prepare for their futures. As we will see, this shift in the role of teachers requires a change in the prevailing way schools view the task of motivating students.

Motivation Training

If the quality of early child rearing contributes to later achievement styles in the ways described here, then cannot negative dispositions such as failure avoidance be reversed or at least moderated, and positive reasons for learning encouraged through systematic instruction once students enter school? Research with adults does suggest that intense skill training can increase the quality of entrepreneurial activities, and for at least several years after instruction (Aronoff & Litwin, 1966; McClelland & Winter, 1969). Typically such training involves using problem-solving games to teach realistic risk appraisal. For example, in the "business game" (Litwin & Ciarlo, 1961) players calculate how many toy rockets they can assemble in a given amount of time. If players overestimate how much they can accomplish and buy too many parts, they will lose money. But if too few parts are requisitioned, players will end up with time on their hands.

If realistic goal setting can be encouraged in adults, then why not in children? Given the importance of this question, it is surprising that more is not known about the answer. However, what little evidence we do have is promising (McClelland, 1972). It suggests that positive changes are possible, not only in those behaviors associated with a success orientation such as realistic goal setting and inde-

pendence of judgment, but also in improved school grades and reductions in absenteeism and dropout rates (de Charms, 1968, 1972;
Ryals, 1969). We will consider the wider educational implications of
this kind of research in Chapter 7.

CONCLUSION

In this chapter we have considered the proposition that the driving
power of motivation comes from emotions such as pride in success
and shame following failure. This perspective has allowed us to ex-
tract a number of powerful implications for educational change. In
the next chapter we will consider a rival proposition that it is
thoughts, not necessarily emotions, that drive achievement. If we
begin with the idea that thoughts are the basic building blocks of
achievement motivation, then additional prospects arise for educational practice and theory.

SUMMING UP

1. Success and failure are psychological concepts; they mean different things to different people. Judgments of success and failure depend less on the individuals' actual levels of attainment
   than on whether they achieved their goals.
2. When individuals are free to choose their own goals, they typically minimize failure by lowering their aspirations when they
   fall short. When individuals exceed their goals, they experience
   feelings of success and tend to raise their aspirations.
3. Atkinson's theory of achievement motivation states that all persons can be characterized by variations in two learned drives, a
   motive to approach success and a motive to avoid faliure.
4. For individuals characterized by excessive worry about failure,
   the implication that they are not able (hence unworthy) can be
   avoided through defensive, magical thinking that denies the
   meaning of failure or minimizes the importance of the failed task.

5. Although all ethnic groups are motivated to achieve, how this motive is expressed often differs from the white majority both in terms of the goals to which minorities aspire and the means by which they achieve these goals.

6. Child-rearing practices influence later achievement striving. The parents of success-oriented children expect their youngsters to achieve notable successes; they also provide guidance and reward successes while ignoring or minimizing their children's disappointing performances.

7. Many of the behaviors associated with the need to achieve, including realistic goal setting, can be encouraged through systematic instruction.

ACTIVITIES

Activity 1: Repeating Hoppe

Demonstrate the dynamics of individual goal setting by reproducing Ferdinand Hoppe's experiment described at the beginning of this chapter. You will need a large container (a wastebasket will do) and ten balls (paper wads are fine). Assemble a group of four or five players. Work with each player one at a time. To begin, ask the player to stand at a distance from the wastebasket of his or her choice. Ask the player to indicate how many balls out of ten he or she hopes to toss correctly from the chosen distance. Then let the player toss the ten balls, one at a time. Repeat this sequence several times in a row for the same player, say, five times (for a total of fifty throws). Always begin each repetition of ten throws with an opportunity for the player to change distances and to indicate, once again, how well he or she hopes to do. Record each player's aspirations at the beginning of every repetition, how well each player actually does, and the approximate distance each stands from the target.

Whether or not you actually conduct this demonstration, take a few minutes now to make a list of questions about achievement dynamics and goal setting that you might answer using these data. What other data might you wish to collect, and what additional questions might they answer? Finally, what parallels do you see between Hoppe's experiment and the kinds of learning games played in school?

If you do conduct this demonstration, did you find any evidence of the "check and balance" mechanisms proposed by Hoppe, and do your data support the theory that people define success as exceeding their aspirations and failure as falling short?

Activity 2: Reinventing Hoppe

Instead of having individuals set goals around tossing rings, as Hoppe did, think about how these same principles of goal setting could apply to school learning.

Design a teaching sequence in which students set achievement goals before each test as they progress toward mastery of a subject-matter concept, say, learning long division. Also, according to Hoppe's research, what might be some advantages, motivationally, of adding such a goal-setting component to the regular curriculum?

When you finish you may wish to compare your ideas with those of Alfred Alschuler (1969) who transformed a previously uninspired fifth-grade mathematics curriculum into a highly rewarding experience by introducing a simple goal-setting component (Appendix B).

Activity 3: Personalizing Hoppe

Three of the motivation principles introduced at the beginning of this chapter are listed here. Take this opportunity to personalize them around your own experiences.

Creating the Right Level of Challenge. As you know, when individuals are free to choose, they often set their goals so that the chances of success are balanced closely against the chances for failure. Think of a time that you, a friend, or a student achieved such a balance regarding schoolwork. What was the result? Or, perhaps there was a time when someone set their sights too high and failure was the result. Why do you think this imbalance occurred? What was the reaction to failure?

54

Merit-Based Standards. Kennedy and Willcut (1964) have shown that when individuals are held to a well-defined, merit-based standard of excellence – for example, in the case of qualifying for a driver's license – people persist longer and try harder compared with those cases in which success is defined competitively. Does this generalization make sense in your experience? As a follow-up to your answer, think of several different kinds of accomplishments besides acquiring merit badges that are couched in merit-based absolute terms. When you have exhausted your own ideas, you may wish to consult an extensive list found in Appendix C.

Success and Self-Confidence. As we now know, the event of success alone is not enough to enhance a sense of self-confidence. The causes of one's successes must be right, too. One of the most troubling doubts that often nags students even when they succeed is that, like John – our failure-avoiding student – they secretly worry that they are somehow frauds and not really as skilled or able as their good performances indicate. Have you, or a friend, or student of your acquaintance ever felt this way? What kinds of steps might be taken by teachers to help students take ownership of their successes?

Activity 4

Briefly review the case studies of Losa, John, Amy, and Ralph. Do any of these four hypothetical individuals remind you of any real-life students of your acquaintance? In which ways are they alike? Finally, in what ways might the analysis of student life in terms of the two motives of approaching success and avoiding failure help you understand the behavior of these real-life students?

3

MOTIVES AS THOUGHTS

I would say only that if some of my judgments were wrong . . .
they were made in what I believed at the time to be in the best
interest of the nation.
                    Richard Nixon, August 1974

Accoupling to Fritz Heider (1958), each of us, including
ex-presidents, searches ceaselessly for ways to create meaning
in our lives. Heider proposed that this process is guided by the principles of attribution theory, which means ascribing causes to our actions and to the actions of others. Clearly this is what Richard Nixon
was doing in his resignation speech as president of the United
States, trying to make comprehensible his questionable actions during the Watergate scandal. These same dynamics are also illustrated by the schoolchild who frets over a failing grade. Was failure the
result of incompetency, he wonders, or the fault of the teacher for
not better explaining the assignment?

Attribution theory is central to the topic of achievement motivation because in the early 1970s cognitive psychologists led by
Bernard Weiner proposed a radical reinterpretation of Atkinson's
need achievement model (Weiner, 1972, 1974; Weiner et al., 1971). As
will be recalled, Atkinson proposed emotional anticipation as the
basic driving force behind all achievement behavior, and defined the
motive to approach success as "a capacity to experience pride in accomplishment." Weiner transformed Atkinson's definition with an
intriguing substitution: "a capacity for perceiving success as caused
by internal factors, particularly effort" (Weiner et al., 1971, p. 96).

This is a fascinating assertion. Can it really be that all noteworthy
accomplishments depend on the meaning individuals ascribe to
their successes and failures? For instance, was Richard Nixon's
slow, painful rise out of genteel poverty to world prominence basically a matter of a lifetime habit of positive self-talk that extolled the

56

virtues of hard work? It is certainly true that Nixon's career embodied the spirit of Hermes to an extraordinary degree – his concern for the unique accomplishment, the restless energy, his entrepreneurial activities (in his early years Nixon pioneered the marketing of frozen orange juice) and his now-famous opportunistic style of leadership, which at times involved (allegedly) breaking rules and even illegal activities. According to psychologists David Winter and Leslie Carlson (1988; also see Winter, 1987), who analyzed the content of the first inaugural addresses of all U.S. presidents, Nixon scored near the top on achievement striving (trailing only Herbert Hoover and Jimmy Carter). It is also the case that Nixon's autobiographical statements are filled with references to hard work and persistence as the reasons for turning potential crises to his advantage (Nixon, 1962).

Although we must leave Nixon's motives as well as his cognitions to the verdict of history, there can be little doubt that the way individuals perceive the causes of their actions plays an important part in their lives, whether these perceptions are accurate or distorted. If we begin with attributions as the basic building blocks of achievement behavior, new prospects arise for educational theory and practice that do not readily flow from Atkinson's model. For this reason, it is important that we become better acquainted with Weiner's attribution model and with the research inspired by his proposed reformulation. What, then, is attribution theory? And what are the implications of attribution theory for educational reform?

COGNITIONS VERSUS EMOTIONS

Emotions are thoughts with feelings attached.
Spinoza

Weiner suggested that it is the naturally occurring attributional process that controls achievement behavior, not emotional anticipation. In making this declaration, Weiner is not denying the fact of emotions. Our daily experience confirms that emotions happen and that they can be vivid, intense, and sometimes inescapable. But attribution theorists doubt whether emotions – which besides being intense are also vague and often diffuse – are specific enough to guide behavior in the precise ways prescribed by Atkinson's model. It is one thing to become aroused emotionally, but then, once aroused, quite another to direct one's actions in finely orchestrated ways toward specific goals.

Attribution Theory

Weiner proposed four different reasons that individuals might offer to explain their successes and failures: ability, effort, the task at hand, and luck. First, consider success. Doing well can be attributed variously to ability ("My ability carried me through"), effort ("I worked hard"), an easy task ("Anyone could have done it"), or good luck ("I was fortunate"). Correspondingly, failure can be attributed to a lack of ability ("I'm not very smart"), inadequate effort ("I didn't try enough"), a hard task ("No one could have done it"), or bad luck ("I was unlucky"). Weiner designated ability and effort attributions, for both success and failure, as *internal* causes since they presumably reflect inherent characteristics of the individual. He further portrayed task difficulty and luck as *external* factors since both are beyond the individual's control.

Now, how do these attributions relate to Atkinson's need achievement theory?

Attribution theorists contend that success-oriented persons, like Losa, and failure-prone individuals, like John and Ralph, harbor different explanations for their successes and failures, and it is precisely these differences that are taken to be the essence of individual differences in achievement motivation. Generally speaking, persons motivated to approach success are thought to attribute their failures to internal factors – chiefly to a lack of effort – and their successes to a combination of high ability and effort. By contrast, failure-threatened persons are said to ascribe their failures to a lack of ability rather than to insufficient effort. Additionally, they attribute their successes, should any occur, to external factors such as luck or the help provided by others.

Clearly, the attribution pattern associated with success-oriented individuals is positive and uplifting. Because Losa believes herself capable of success, when failure occurs (which is rare) she concludes that she had not tried hard enough nor perhaps in the right ways. This interpretation robs failure of much of its threat. Failure no longer implies incompetency, but rather merely ignorance – simply not knowing or understanding, something that can be corrected by redoubling one's efforts. On the other hand, failure-prone individuals, like Ralph, find themselves caught up in a catastrophic situation. They take little credit for their successes (which are rare enough anyway) because they don't feel worthy of it, and they blame themselves for failure by reason of being stupid.

Now, how do these attributional patterns fit into the larger achievement process? Once again, consider Losa and John.

Losa: Success Striver. Recall that Losa is a high school freshman on a college preparatory track. Yesterday she took a sample geometry test for advanced placement on the college entrance boards. This was the first of several practice tests scheduled over the next few weeks. This arrangement suited Losa fine. She relishes a challenge, and the prospect of doing well always excites her. In fact, Losa's enthusiasm for this particular challenge carried her along despite her having scored only at the 85th percentile on the first try, clearly a disappointment in her mind. But why shouldn't Losa's enthusiasm be dampened by this presumed setback, and why is she likely to do better the next time?

The answers depend on Losa's attributions. Losa attributes her personally disappointing performance to inadequate study, a conclusion that in turn arouses feelings of self-reproach for not having attended all the review sessions provided by the geometry teacher. Feeling guilty for not having studied enough the first time around ensures that Losa will now take things more seriously and study harder for the next time. This chain of mental events can be diagrammed as follows: inadequate study (attribution) ! guilt ! adequate study. For Losa, then, emotions such as guilt or remorse, although clearly unpleasant, can ultimately work to her advantage by mobilizing her considerable talents.

A somewhat different scenario would apply if Losa's initial score on the practice test had placed her at the 96th percentile – an unqualified success even for Losa. In this case she would likely attribute this extraordinary performance to a blend of skillful effort and ability, a conclusion that leads both to pride and to increased confidence in her ability do well in the future.

John: Failure Avoider. Now consider the same attribution model as it applies to failure-threatened individuals, like John, our self-doubting, apathetic high school senior. Last year John also took the same advanced geometry course and, like Losa, went through the gauntlet of practice tests. As luck would have it, John's initial performance was identical to that of Losa's. He, too, scored at the 85th percentile and his sense of disappointment was equally keen. But the meanings that John and Losa attributed to these identical outcomes were worlds apart. For John, his performance raised anew lingering doubts about his ability. Whenever John does worse than anticipated, his first reaction is to attribute his failures to not being bright enough. These doubts elicit feelings of shame, an emotion that leads to poorer performance the next time around largely because shame distracts John and causes his mind to wander during study.

These same inability attributions also cause John to view his future prospects pessimistically, a judgment that also undercuts his next performance. If students expect to fail, they likely will. Thus we see how easy it is for John to become trapped in a reverberating cycle of plunging expectations, diminishing resolve, and increasing self-doubt, test after test.

And even if John was able to defy the odds and perform better on the next practice test – recall that he excels at turning defeat into victory at the last moment – John will nonetheless continue to doubt himself and worry about being found out as a kind of high-achieving impostor. In effect, high grades offer John little assurance. This is because success, when it does occur, is discounted by failure-threatened students, and attributed to factors beyond their control. For example, John might believe he simply had the good fortune to study for the right test questions. John's future prospects remain dim because he does not believe himself capable of repeated excellence even though he somehow always manages to come through in the end.

Note, once again, that all this mental anguish can occur despite a perfectly reasonable, even an outstanding record of achievement. From this perspective, the gravest danger to American education is not necessarily slumping achievement scores. John can always be coaxed, cajoled, or otherwise pressured into performing just a little bit better, or so the advocates of an intensification policy would have us believe. Actually, the greatest danger concerns the issue of *choice*, which according to the need achievement model (Chapter 2) is influenced by the motives that drive students, not necessarily by one's grade point average. One choice always available to students is whether to continue in school or not. John is at far greater risk for quitting school or dropping out mentally than for literally failing geometry. Moreover, poor academic potential is not as critical to this choice as the public believes. In fact, contrary to the popular view, dropouts are not always the poorest students. According to one estimate (Fetterman, 1990) nearly 30 percent of all school dropouts in America would test out as gifted.

So, for the moment, John will continue to cope marginally, even though he is performing well above average. In the words of Richard Beery (1975), John is "afloat but drifting" (p. 192). John hovers between hope and despair – a precarious balance that may soon be destroyed by the added stresses and dislocation of college life. Increased fears of being discovered as incompetent and mounting anxiety may soon exhaust, then overwhelm, John's natural resiliency and erode his undoubted academic talents.

Now that the main features of the attribution model have been presented, how do sex and ethnic differences fit in? For example, do males exhibit attribution patterns uniquely different from those of females? And, do minority groups differ from the white majority in their causal perceptions of the world?

Sex Differences

Although the evidence on sex differences is far from complete, and the findings occasionally mixed, it appears that on balance women and girls are more likely to express negative, failure-prone attributions than are men and boys. For example, females are more prone than males to cite inability as the cause of their failures. And, compared with boys, girls see ability as less important to their successes (Parsons, Meece, Adler, & Kaczala, 1982).

Several explanations for these differences have been offered. One is that girls and women simply mirror a dominant perception in our society, erroneous as it is, that females are less able intellectually and therefore their successes are more properly attributed to hard work and compliance (Etaugh & Brown, 1975; Heilman & Stopeck, 1985). It has also been suggested that the exercise of intellectual ability may be seen by many females as less role appropriate (Nicholls, 1975). For example, women readily express failure-prone attributions but only when the partner with whom they are in competition is a male (Stephan, Rosenfield, & Stephen, 1976). Another explanation is that privately males make the same attributions for their successes and failures as do females for theirs, but males are simply more defensive in their public statements owing to societal pressures to maintain an image of assertiveness and competency (Covington & Omelich, 1978; Snyder, Stephan, & Rosenfeld, 1976; Zuckerman, 1979). Whatever the causes of these sex differences, attempts at educational reform must be sensitive to the possibility that females may initially be more prone than males to discount themselves as agents of their own accomplishments.

Ethnic Differences

For the moment interest in the attribution patterns of different ethnic groups has far outrun the available evidence. We do know, of course, that many minorities, especially blacks and Hispanics, hold achievement goals that are not always shared by the white, middle-class majority. The goals of Ernestino and other Central American refugees attest to this (Chapter 2). It is also well established that many minority group members doubt that they will ever achieve satisfactorily in school. But the question is, Are the attributions these students make to effort and ability and to chance or luck responsible for their pessimism?

What we do know with some certainty is that most castelike minorities tend to exhibit an external locus of control. They feel like pawns of fate, buffeted by forces beyond their control. For example, in one study white elementary school students rated ability and effort as the most important causes of school performance compared with luck and task difficulty, whereas black youngsters tended to reverse these ratings (Friend & Neale, 1972). The tendency among blacks to discount themselves is thought to occur in large part because white America has long held low academic expectations for blacks and because blacks, as a result, have often come to doubt their intellectual potential (Fordham & Ogbu, 1986).

The prevailing reactions of native Americans, including the Plains and Pueblo Indians, are also consistent with external explanations for their achievements, likely because their cultural traditions emphasize humankind's dependency on nature, rather than its dominance over nature. Also, the tendency toward fatalism and a tradition of noncompetitiveness in the Hispanic culture can also be accounted for by this same reasoning (for a review, see McInerney, 1988).

Finally, the bulk of the evidence suggests that Asian youngsters – Japanese, Chinese, Filipinos, and Koreans – act in more success-oriented ways compared with the white majority as evidenced by their greater tendency to attribute academic success to effort (Hess, Chang, & McDevitt, 1987; Mizokawa & Ryckman, 1988).

EDUCATIONAL IMPLICATIONS

> The causes of events always interest us more than the events themselves.
> Cicero

The educational implications of attribution theory are central to our analysis of the current educational crisis. Four points are pivotal.

The Meaning of Failure

First, attribution theory provides an answer to the question of why failure that elicits shame and leads to lowered esteem among so many students can also mobilize other pupils to greater effort. Attribution theory teaches us that it is not so much the event of failure, or even its frequency, that disrupts performance as it is the meaning of failure. For students like Losa, who steadfastly interpret failure as the result of improper or insufficient effort, failure acts as a challenge – a goad to renewed striving. But for others, like Ralph, our displaced Appalachian student, who see failure as confirming suspicions of incompetency, failure can only be paralyzing. Likewise, it is now understandable why success does not always reinforce self-confidence, a point raised earlier in Chapter 2. If individuals believe their victories are the product of factors beyond their control – luck, chance, or the humanitarian impulse of a teacher – then there is little assurance that success can be repeated. This reasoning also accounts for why failure-prone students often prefer to explain their successes, infrequent as they may be, as simply a lucky break (Marecek & Mettee, 1972). Doing so also releases them from the obligation to repeat their successes, something they are doubtful of doing anyway.

The wider policy implications of these observations seem clear. One often-heard refrain in the chorus of reform proposals is the suggestion that teachers should arrange classroom learning so that students experience either no failure or as little failure as possible. This view assumes that failure per se causes loss of esteem and self-respect. Quite to the contrary, failure can act as a positive force so long as it is properly interpreted by the learner. Rather than focusing on failure as the culprit, educators should arrange learning so that falling short of one's goals, which inevitably happens to everyone, will be interpreted in ways that promote the will to persist.

The Role of Effort

Attribution theory also draws attention to the critical role that effort attributions play in achievement dynamics. For one thing, effort cognitions control one's expectancies for future success – if individuals, like Losa, can honestly attribute their failures to a lack of trying, then they are more likely to remain optimistic about succeeding later on. For another thing, effort cognitions shape emotional reactions to events – having tried hard increases one's pride in success and low effort triggers guilt in failure. And, perhaps most important of all, it is widely believed that student effort can be controlled by teachers.

The virtues of hard work have long been extolled in America. Nowhere is this more true than in schools. The paramount importance of a work ethic in the teacher's scheme of values has been convincingly demonstrated. In the typical study (Weiner & Kukla, 1970), teachers receive information about several hypothetical students including how well each one did on a school test (either excellent, borderline, or a clear failure), the amount of effort each student expended (either a lot or little), and the student's ability level (either high or low). Teachers then judged the performance of each student by providing varying amounts of rewards (in the form of gold stars) or reprimands (red stars). The results of the Weiner and Kukla study are presented in Figure 3.1.

To start, it is obvious that test outcome is the major determinant of teacher rewards and reprimands. Whether the student is bright or dull, motivated or not, teachers reward excellent performances and reprimand failure. At the same time, however, it is clear that teachers also reward effort. Students who studied diligently (the groups with solid black circles and squares) were rewarded more in success and punished less in failure than those who studied little (the groups with open circles and squares). Interestingly, information about ability level alone does not exert much influence on these evaluations. Everyone who tries hard is rewarded, irrespective of ability, although there is a slight tendency for teachers to reward less able students more than bright ones. This finding may reflect a disposition among teachers to compensate poorer pupils by focusing on their occasional successes. In fact, low-ability students who work hard (black circles) are evaluated more favorably than all others, even more so than high-ability students who also try (black squares)!

This pattern of teacher rewards and reprimands also varies for different kinds of students, like Losa, Ralph, and John. For example,

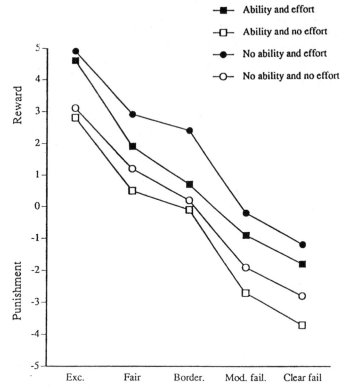

Figure 3.1. Evaluation (reward and punishment) as a function of pupil ability, motivation, and examination outcome.

Source: B. Weiner & A. Kukla (1970). An attributional analysis of achievement motivation. *Journal of Personality and Social Psychology, 15*(1), 1–20. Copyright 1970 by the American Psychological Association. Adapted by permission of the publisher.

notice in Figure 3.1 the decidedly positive teacher reaction to high-effort, high-ability students (black squares), basically those youngsters we have referred to as success-oriented, like Losa. In effect, students who succeed through a combination of high ability and hard work are rewarded generously, an action that reinforces their willingness to keep on trying. And, at the same time, in the rare event of a clear failure, these same students are among the least punished because they tried hard. This combination of praise for success and leniency in failure reminds us of those child-rearing patterns that encourage achievement motivation at home (Chapter 2).

A far less positive pattern of rewards and punishments applies to failure-avoiding students, like John – nominally, those youngsters in Figure 3.1 who are less likely to try, especially when they are judged by teachers to be able (open squares). This latter group includes underachievers who are known to be capable but unwilling to work hard (Bricklin & Bricklin, 1967). These students are praised less in success and reprimanded more in failure than any other type of student represented in Figure 3.1. Whether these teacher policies are helpful in reversing the negative dynamics of underachievement will be discussed later. Meanwhile, there is no denying that teachers as well as adults in general believe that the most effective way to promote learning is to provide rewards for increased effort (Boggiano, Barrett, Weiher, McClelland, & Lusk, 1987).

Learned Helplessness

One of the most important potential contributions of attribution theory to educational practice concerns the phenomenon of "learned helplessness" (Smiley & Dweck, 1994). Learned helplessness has been described as a state of depression or loss of hope which accompanies a belief that no matter how hard or how well one tries, failure is the inevitable outcome (Coyne & Lazarus, 1980).

Learned helplessness was first studied in research laboratories on the conditioning of fear in animals (Seligman, Maier, & Geer, 1968). In the first phase of these experiments, dogs were subjected to electric shock from which there was no escape. In a second phase, the dogs could avoid the shock by performing a simple routine, which under other circumstances they would have easily learned. Yet many of the dogs continued to endure the shock and exhibited symptoms of extreme withdrawal, passivity, and even yawning – reactions that had they occurred in humans would likely be construed as indifference or boredom. On the basis of these results, it was suggested that being exposed to an uncontrollable, aversive outcome in the first phase of the experiment rendered these animals helpless to act in their own behalf later on (Seligman, 1975; Seligman, Maier, & Solomon, 1971). Once punishment was accepted as beyond their ability to control, positive coping strategies disappeared. In short, it was not the aversiveness of the shock, but rather its uncontrollability that caused helplessness.

This same experimental paradigm (minus the shock, of course) has been used in research with human subjects (e.g., Abramson, Seligman, & Teasdale, 1978; Dweck & Reppucci, 1973). These procedures often form an uncomfortably close parallel to regular classroom learning. As a first step, students are given a series of problem-solving tasks that unbeknownst to them are unsolvable. Next, once a pattern of failure is well established despite the best efforts of the children to succeed, they are given simpler solvable versions of the same failed tasks. In this second phase the children often fail to solve problems known to be well within their capabilities. Such impotence is often accompanied by feelings of despair, frustration, and hopelessness, and in some cases even anger and hostility (Gatchel, Paulus, & Maples, 1975).

From an attribution perspective such outcomes are quite understandable. If I believe studying will help my grade, then I'm more apt to study. But if I believe my grade is the result of factors beyond my control, such as a teacher's whim or just plain luck, then there is really no point in studying at all. As just noted, the logic of this position suggests that despair is a reaction to the uncontrollable nature of the situation. If true, the culprit would seem to be the vagaries of school achievement including unfair tests, teacher bias, or institutional indifference, but not necessarily personal limitations. However, this argument appears to violate common sense. Why, as Lyn Abramson and Harold Sackeim (1977) ask, should people feel responsible for events beyond their control, especially if they have tried their best? The answer is found in the fact that the main trigger for a sense of despair is not necessarily that the individual tried hard and failed anyway – that is, of not being in control – but rather the implication that one is incompetent (Covington, 1985).

Accordingly, we can conclude that a sense of helplessness occurs when one repeatedly ascribes failure to stable, internal causes – in attributional terms, to low ability. And, as we have seen, with these attributions come despair and even self-loathing. This is a perfect description of Ralph.

Helpless children differ from success-oriented youngsters not only in the attributions they make, but also in the kinds of strategies they employ when confronted with failure. In a study by Carol Diener and Carol Dweck (1978), both helpless and successful children were trained to solve a series of visual discrimination tasks. By the end of training both groups were equally proficient. In a second phase of the experiment, similar but unsolvable visual discrimination problems were introduced, and students were then asked to verbalize their thoughts as they worked. As soon as the failure phase began, helpless children behaved as though their prior successes had never occurred. They showed a decrease in the use of reasonable strategies such as hypothesis checking and began engaging in irrelevant, stereotyped activities, such as making random choices. Classic statements of helplessness were also much in evidence (e.g., "nothing I do matters"). By contrast, during this failure phase, success-oriented children employed the same and on occasion even more sophisticated strategies than they had learned in the initial training session. They also tended to attribute failure variously to a lack of personal effort or to increasingly difficult problems. But, most important, they were less concerned about dwelling on the causes of failure than they were with discovering remedies for failure.

The true insidiousness of this helplessness dynamic and its pervasive, negative influence on all aspects of achievement was demonstrated in a companion study by Diener and Dweck (1980). After helpless students had experienced repeated failure, they were asked to reflect on their earlier successes during the training phase. These youngsters revised their earlier attributions, which initially had been quite positive, so that in retrospect they no longer recalled having felt competent. On the other hand, success-oriented youngsters remained steadfast in their positive recollections. Finally, the helpless children systematically underestimated the number of problems they had solved correctly in the first phase and recalled more failures than had, in fact, occurred. We know that the meaning individuals attribute to their past successes and failures can influence the future. In addition, we now know that for some individuals the present can also reach back and distort the past, to the detriment of the future.

Attribution Retraining

The practical implications of the learned helplessness paradigm have not been lost on researchers. If it is true that the essence of learned helplessness, or what might be called a "motivational deficit," is the belief that one is unable to control events for lack of ability, then perhaps teachers can promote a renewed sense of hope by encouraging students to change their explanations for failure from being the result of low ability to being a lack of effort.

This reasoning has given rise to a body of research referred to collectively as "attribution retraining." These retraining procedures generally involve giving failure-threatened students repeated practice in verbalizing effort-oriented explanations for their failure (e.g., "I failed because I did not try hard enough"). For example, Gregory Andrews and Ray Debus (1978) worked with sixth-grade boys who routinely attributed their failures to low ability. Some of these youngsters were randomly assigned to a control group that received no training. The remaining boys were assigned to one of two training conditions in which the experimenters reinforced the boys with either tokens or verbal praise whenever they gave a low-effort explanation for failing to solve various geometric puzzles; high-effort explanations were likewise reinforced whenever the boys succeeded. The findings from this study form part of a consistent pattern of results shared by several studies (e.g., Chapin & Dyck, 1976; Perry & Struthers, 1994; Wilson & Linville, 1985; Zoeller, Mahoney, & Weiner, 1983). Following attribution retraining, otherwise demoralized individuals tend to persist longer in their work on school-related tasks, and in some cases there is evidence that the *quality* of persistence also improves.

The effectiveness of attributional retraining will likely depend on where in the downward spiral of demoralization students find themselves. If, for example, students are already convinced of their

70

incompetency (failure acceptors, like Ralph), then they may be unable to accept success as caused by their own efforts (Marecek & Mettee, 1972). This perception occurs because success implies an obligation to succeed again in the future, something for which these self-doubters may not feel capable. By contrast, other students may not yet have completely internalized their failures, and hence remain uncertain about their ability status. These students, failure avoiders like John, are more likely to embrace success as evidence that their self-doubts are unfounded after all (Coopersmith, 1967).

The effectiveness of attributional retraining may also be greatest among younger children, and for several reasons. For one thing, trying hard is consistent with adult values, and it is the young child who is most willing to accept adult authority. For another thing, as we will see in Chapter 4, effort is associated in the young child's mind with increasing competency. On the other hand, adolescents have reason to doubt the benefits of effort not only because they are more likely to reject adult values. There is also the dawning recognition, beginning in late childhood, that effort and ability are separate, essentially independent contributors to achievement, and that trying hard can compensate only so much for a lack of ability. For these reasons, demands by teachers (or even by researchers in the laboratory) to try harder may do little to improve the performance of older students, especially if they already feel themselves incompetent.

In Chapter 7 we will explore more recent approaches to attribution retraining, which hopefully will largely avoid these obstacles. They involve ascribing one's failures to inadequate learning strategies – in short, focusing on the poor *quality* of one's effort, not just on inadequate *amounts* of effort. The concept of learning strategies bridges the domains of effort and ability, so that trying hard, but in sophisticated, strategic ways, is tantamount to increasing one's ability to learn. In this sense, the conviction among children that ability is perfectible through effort may be less naive than might be first thought (Chapter 1). As we will see, this perspective ushers in quite different ways of thinking about the educational enterprise.

71

CONCLUSION

We have reached an important juncture in our analysis of achieve-ment motivation. We are now familiar with the broad historical per-spective that envisions motivation as a learned drive, whether such drives are thought of as unresolved emotional conflicts arising from early childhood or the result of the attributions made to one's suc-cesses and failures. We have also discovered much that will be use-ful in crafting our recommendations for educational change. To mention only a few critical points: the importance of early child-rearing practices; the notion of future time perspective; and a rec-ognition that the meaning individuals attribute to life events – like failure – is often more important, motivationally speaking, than the event itself.

Yet despite these potentially valuable observations there is an im-portant sense in which, if we are not careful, the lessons of the learned-drive tradition can thwart effective reform and, worse yet, even perpetuate wrongheaded proposals for change. If motivation is thought of largely as a matter of internal arousal, whether such arousal is characterized variously as needs, feelings, or effort attri-butions, it then becomes all the more reasonable to assume that the current crisis in schooling can be overcome by pressuring or arous-ing students (and teachers) to greater effort through "*more* hours in school, *more* homework, and *more* tests." In effect, the learned-drive tradition lends plausibility, and even a measure of scientific justifi-cation, to a policy of intensification. Support for such a policy is growing nationwide and has been endorsed at the highest levels of government. At least this seems to be what George Bush, our ex – "education" president, had in mind when he remarked during the 1989 Education Summit of Governors that "educators should not worry about *resources*, but rather *results*" (emphasis added). If it is results America wants, then one sure way to get them, the argument runs, is to increase student motivation – arouse youngsters to greater effort through the judicious application of positive rewards like good grades and the withholding of negative reinforcers, like poor grades. And then there is the additional, typically unspoken assumption that these grades should be distributed on a competitive basis, with the best performers receiving the most rewards. Similar remedies have just recently been proposed by President Clinton on the occasion of the 1996 National Education Summit (for a critique see Covington, 1996).

Intensification policy also implies the need to raise academic standards. But this solution by itself is surely incomplete and also too facile. Veteran poker players know what is likely to happen when the table stakes are increased. Far from clarifying one's mind, increased pressure is likely as not to encourage irrational risk taking and even cheating. Because we will soon liken school achievement to a special kind of competitive game, this poker analogy becomes quite compelling. The counterproductive aspects of an intensification policy are not limited to poker play, nor are its potential ironies lost on the business community. A leading industrialist was recently overheard to say, "If I had a situation in which one-third of my products [students] fell off the assembly line along the way [referring to the national dropout rate prior to high school graduation] and two-thirds of those remaining did not work right in the end, the last thing I would do is speed up the conveyor belt!"

Not only is the ultimate goal of intensification policy too narrowly focused – merely raising standardized test scores – but the means to this restricted goal are incomplete as well. Every time a crisis boils over, we hear renewed calls for higher standards. But the fundamental issue is not really a matter of increasing academic standards. Nor can we any longer afford the kind of cheap rhetoric that reinvents higher standards from time to time for political gain. Actually, standards of excellence have never really been forgotten. For years teachers have struggled to maintain high academic standards and also to lament, often alone and unheeded, the slow erosion of the quality of academic life in our schools. Clearly, maintaining high standards is vital; if we expect little of our children, little is what we will get. But more is needed. The pursuit of high standards must also be safe and free from the fear of failure.

The proper question is how to revitalize a commitment to excellence, and learned-drive formulations do not provide the key to this process. If merely intensifying student effort were the answer, then the current crisis should never have occurred. As we know, teach-

73

ers already reinforce effort. Moreover, when elementary school children are placed in the role of "proxy" teachers, they dispense and withhold rewards in essentially the same ways as do adults (Weiner, Heckhausen, Meyer, & Cook, 1972). This means that students get the message starting in the earliest years: America values achievement through effort. Youngsters quickly become aware, often painfully so, of the consequences of not trying. On the basis of these pervasive reinforcement patterns, attribution theorists have concluded that students should come to value effort as a major source of personal worth, and, to the extent that students do not comply with this work ethic, they will experience guilt and remorse.

There is little doubt that students experience guilt when they do not try (Covington, Spratt, & Omelich, 1980). But do they also come to value effort? Not always. But why not? If teachers are so generous in their praise of effort, then why is it that so many students do not try, often giving themselves up to inaction and failure? And why do other students hide their effort or refuse to admit they have studied at all?

These questions indicate that something more is going on in the achievement process than can be accounted for easily by cognitive reinforcement principles. Basically, we need to know more about achievement dynamics than cognitive attributions alone can tell us. In order to get to the heart of the matter we must understand the *reasons* students study or not, not just *how much* they study or their explanations for success and failure.

In summary, for all the conceptual benefits of the attribution approach – and, as we have seen, they are substantial – it is nonetheless important to continue our search for a fuller understanding of achievement dynamics elsewhere, elsewhere being the domain of self-worth theory.

SUMMING UP

1. Attribution theory suggests that whether individuals typically approach success or avoid failure depends on the causes they ascribe to their achievements.

2. Persons motivated to approach success attribute failure to a lack of effort, and their successes to a combination of high ability and effort. Failure-threatened persons ascribe their failures to a lack of ability, and their successes to luck or the help of others.

3. Men and boys express failure-prone attributions less than women and girls probably because males are more defensive owing to societal pressures to maintain an image of competency.

4. Many minority youngsters exhibit an external locus of control, that is, they feel like pawns of fate, buffeted by forces beyond their control.

5. Attribution theory teaches that it is not so much the event of failure that disrupts academic achievement as it is the meaning of failure. Thus, rather than minimizing failure, educators should arrange schooling so that falling short of one's goals will be interpreted in ways that promote the will to learn.

6. Teachers reward students who study hard, irrespective of their ability, and reprimand those students the most who study little or not at all. This formula should cause students to value effort and hard work in school. But not always. Why not?

ACTIVITIES

Activity 1: Posing Puzzles

Chapter 3 ends on a puzzling note: "If teachers are so generous in their praise of effort, then why is it that so many students do not try, often giving themselves up to inaction and failure? And why do other students hide their effort or refuse to admit they have studied at all?"

Drawing on your own classroom experiences, think of some possible answers to these questions. Doing this will make your reading of Chapter 4 more meaningful.

Activity 2: Altering the Meaning of Failure

Attributing failure to low ability can destroy the will to learn, but attributing failure to inadequate or improper effort can actually motivate students. How might teachers arrange the "rules of the learning game" so that failure will more likely be seen by students as the result of poor planning or of setting unrealistic goals – mistakes that can be corrected – and not necessarily the result of inadequate skills or ability?

Richard de Charms, a noted psychologist, changed the rules of the traditional spelling bee from a highly competitive game to one in which the ability to spell became less important for success and making good judgments about the right level of spelling challenge more important.

Think of different ways he might have done this. Before turning to Appendix D for at least one answer, you might wish to review the way Ferdinand Hoppe set up his ring-toss experiment (in Chapter 2) for some inspiration.

Activity 3

Now that you have the benefit of de Charms's ideas, choose a school assignment other than spelling that you believe depends heavily on specific kinds of abilities, or on skills that may not yet be well developed among some youngsters at a given grade level. Modify this assignment so that doing well depends as much on students' choosing a realistic level of challenge for them as it does on ability, on present skills, or on past experience. Share your ideas with another student or colleague.

4

SELF-WORTH AND THE
FEAR OF FAILURE

> Almost every man wastes part of his life in attempts to display
> qualities which he does not possess, and to gain applause
> which he cannot keep.
>> Samuel Johnson

IN THE PRECEDING CHAPTER WE EXPLORED THE PROPOSITION THAT passion – or, put more sedately, motivation – is the by-product of cognitive (rational) processes, and that emotions such as shame and pride depend on the meaning that individuals attach to their successes and failures. The guiding metaphor of this view is that of the "intuitive scientist" (Kelley, 1971a), who ceaselessly analyzes information in order to master himself and his environment. The principal values associated with this quest are rationality, consistency, and accurate self-knowledge. Obviously, these attributes are critical to survival. Accurate self-knowledge enables individuals to credit their talents fairly, as well as to recognize their shortcomings; as a result, they can avoid those tasks that exceed their present skills, yet, when possible, seize the moment and take advantage of unexpected opportunities that fall within the scope of their abilities.

In this chapter we will examine the alternative view that motives drive thoughts and alter, even distort, the meaning of success and failure (Kunda, 1990). The essence of this complementary argument is reflected in another metaphor, that of the "intuitive politician" (Tetlock, 1985). This metaphor implies that life, like politics, requires the reconciliation of many contradictory demands, a process that involves compromise and concession. What are these potentially contradictory demands? First, as just noted, there is the need for accurate *self-knowledge*. Second, there is the need for *self-validation* – the need to gain the approval, love, and respect of others, and, when necessary, to disassociate oneself from those events like failure that might cause disapproval or rejection. This disposition to establish and defend a positive self-image is the *self-worth motive.*

SELF-WORTH THEORY

Rationality, even now, is a promise waiting for fulfillment.
Reuven Bar-Levav

Self-worth theory (Covington, 1992; Covington & Beery, 1976) assumes that the search for self-acceptance is the highest human priority and that, as applied to schools, one's worth often comes to depend on the ability to achieve competitively. In our society there is a pervasive tendency to equate accomplishment with human value – put simply, individuals are thought to be only as worthy as their achievements. Because of this, it is understandable that students often confuse ability with worth. For those students who are already insecure, like John, Amy, and Ralph, tying a sense of worth to ability is a risky step because schools can threaten the belief in one's ability to achieve. This is true because schools typically provide insufficient rewards for all students to strive for success. Instead, too many children must of necessity struggle simply to avoid failure. In essence, then, self-worth theory holds that, psychologically speaking, school achievement is best understood in terms of maintaining a positive self-image of one's ability, particularly when risking competitive failure.

There is compelling evidence that students value ability, sometimes above all else. For instance, among college students a reputation for sheer brilliance is the most important contributor to feelings of academic pride, far more important than the individual's grade point average (Covington & Omelich, 1984). This suggests that, at least among older students, ability alone defines worth, even in the absence of solid accomplishments. Additional research on student preferences confirms these findings. Students prefer

78

low-effort explanations for failure over low-ability explanations (Brown & Weiner, 1984). This makes sense not only because low ability is predictive of future failure, but also because failure does not necessarily imply low ability, if one does not try. Correspondingly, in the case of success, high-ability explanations are preferred over low-ability explanations; however, successes achieved without much effort are valued even more, indicating once again that a reputation for brilliance – succeeding without really trying – is of paramount importance to a positive self-definition.

But why should students be concerned with ability at all, given the universal pattern of teacher reinforcement that favors a work ethic? Basically, the answer is that the importance of effort in the teacher's value scheme is limited to the teaching context. When the job is to help students learn, teachers recognize the importance of hard work and reward pluck and energy accordingly. When the focus shifts, however, from learning per se to predicting those students who will most likely succeed in prestigious occupations, teachers weigh ability as the more important factor (Kaplan & Swant, 1973). This distinction between ability as a predictor of future occupational success and effort as a necessary ingredient for learning is not lost on students and places them in a cruel bind. Despite the undeniable benefits of trying hard, students must also face a competing need: the protection of a sense of competency.

From this perspective, ironically enough, trying hard puts students at risk because a combination of studying hard and eventual failure is compelling evidence for low ability (Kun, 1977; Kun & Weiner, 1973). And, there is the obvious corollary: by not studying, the causes of failure become obscured.

Several points have been made so far in outlining the broader self-worth position. First, self-perceptions of ability depend on the circumstances of failure. For example, a combination of high effort with failure implies *low* ability. Second, self-perceptions of incompetency trigger feelings of shame and humiliation. Third, by not trying, or trying with excuses, individuals are able to minimize information about their ability should they fail and thereby avoid these destructive emotions. Fourth, student preoccupation with ability status and the teacher's understandable tendency to reward effort set the stage for a conflict of classroom values between ability and effort. Each of these four points can be demonstrated in a single experiment.

Dynamics of Failure

My colleague, Carol Omelich, and I (Covington & Omelich, 1979) asked college undergraduates to imagine how they would feel if they failed a test that most of their classmates passed. These students reported that they would feel most incompetent if they had studied hard yet failed anyway and, as a result, would also experience considerable shame. In contrast, when these same students imagined themselves failing but without having studied much, they reported feeling far less stupid. Because failure was now attributed to a lack of trying, not to inability, these students also experienced less shame. This reaction is just the opposite of what one might expect in a society where honest effort counts for something. Effort – even losing effort – should compensate somewhat for the sting of failure, but it clearly does not in the school setting. Actually, it makes things worse. The reason for this curiosity seems clear. These students were interested not so much in the consolation that honest effort brings to a losing cause as they were in avoiding the implication of failure – that they lacked ability. One of the best ways to avoid this conclusion besides not trying is to have an excuse for not trying. When excuses were made available to these same students for why their studying didn't pay off – "the test emphasized things you did not study for" – their burden of shame and distress was lifted dramatically.

Little wonder, then, that excuses are such a permanent part of the school scene: students blame tests, arguing that the questions were not the kind one could study for; shrewdly attack grading as unfair; and sometimes even complain that they were penalized by the cheating of others. Despite some truth in each of these allegations, when used repeatedly by the same individuals these arguments are likely to be rationalizations, a defense mechanism well known to psychologists in which individuals create false but plausible explanations to justify or excuse their behavior. In this particular case these students are attempting to avoid the implications of poor performance.

Distressing as the results of this research study were, worse was yet to come. In another part of the experiment, these same undergraduates were also asked to play the role of teachers and reprimand students for failure. Interestingly, the results were identical to those presented previously in Chapter 3. These proxy teachers reprimanded most those failures caused by lack of studying, and punished students least when they studied hard but failed anyway. Here is clear evidence of a clash of classroom values. Teachers punish least precisely those circumstances (high student effort) that trigger the greatest shame in students should they fail. Conversely, teachers strongly discourage precisely those situations (not trying) that provide students the greatest protection from the negative implications of failure.

There emerges from this impasse an optimal survival formula for failure-prone students when risking failure. It is a strategy designed to avoid personal humiliation, on the one hand, and to minimize teacher punishment, on the other: try, or at least appear to try, but not too energetically, and with excuses always handy. It is difficult to imagine a strategy better calculated to sabotage the will to learn and derail the pursuit of personal excellence.

This research indicates why simply increasing the pressure on students to try harder in the face of failure invites disaster. The basic premise of the policy of intensification is flawed. It assumes that teachers can encourage achievement by rewarding hard workers and punishing the indifferent. Yet what is most meaningful to many students is not necessarily receiving rewards for trying hard, but finding ways to avoid the implications of *too much* effort when risking failure.

Changes over Time

Recall from the preceding chapter what attribution theorists originally predicted – that if teachers encourage effort, students should

81

internalize a work ethic. We now know that, at least among older students, the need to protect a sense of worth can override these otherwise straightforward reinforcement mechanisms. For young children, however, the original prediction is essentially correct. Primary grade youngsters value trying hard far more than do college adults or even high school students. Young children believe that hardworking, compliant pupils are more likely to succeed and, as a result, are more worthy of praise and admiration. Thus early in the developmental sweep of events, teachers and students find themselves truly in agreement – effort reigns as the supreme classroom virtue. But, obviously, this alliance is only temporary. Somewhere along the line teachers and students part ways. For example, teacher praise for trying hard, which in the primary grades conveys the impression of competence (Meyer et al., 1979), just a few years later in the junior high years, comes to imply the opposite – a lack of ability. Indeed, among these older students praise for trying hard is seen as one way that teachers attempt to encourage pupils of low ability (Graham, 1984b).

What do we know about this shift? How and why do these changes occur? Basically, the answers depend on the child's changing view of the nature of ability.

The developmental timeline proposed by John Nicholls (1978; 1984) provides the best way to track these changes. Beginning in the early and middle elementary years, effort emerges in the minds of children as the most important cause of success – the harder one tries, the better children at this stage believe they will do. This kind of reasoning is basic to the so-called *incremental* theory of intelligence in which young children believe ability is a process that is expandable through hard work and experience (Chapter 1). Indeed, they believe that by trying harder they can actually increase their ability – or, as one first-grader remarked, "Studying harder makes your brain bigger" (Harari & Covington, 1981).

As children enter the late elementary years, however, they begin to view ability as separate from effort and as an independent cause of achievement. As a result, ten- to twelve-year-olds begin to think in terms of compensation; that is, by this age students are able to understand that increased effort can make up for low ability and that high ability permits a relaxation of effort. At the same time, students begin to view ability not only as independent of effort, but also as a fixed, stable factor. This development corresponds to the onset of *entity* beliefs about ability (Chapter 1).

Finally, with the rise of entity beliefs, beginning roughly around twelve years of age, the perceived importance of effort wanes, and is replaced by the conviction that ability alone is sufficient for success. In short, ability becomes the limiting factor in achievement, or, as stated emphatically by an eleventh-grader, "When people who are not smart study, they still do not do very well" (Harari & Covington, 1981). In other words, without ability, the benefits of effort are seen to be only marginal. This pessimistic assessment stands in stark contrast to the buoyant, optimistic view of ability held by the younger child as knowledge well and wisely used.

Having established this series of developmental anchor points, we can now answer the earlier question of why a work ethic declines as students grow older. It is not merely that effort is seen by young people as progressively less important to success – which is true – but also because the child's conception of intelligence changes so that needing to try hard in order to do well comes to signify lesser ability, whereas trying hard for kindergarten youngsters is taken as clear evidence of ability, or as one first-grader confided, "Smart students try, dumb ones don't" (Harari & Covington, 1981).

Thus by the high school years, it is having to work hard that leads to doubts about one's ability. Not surprisingly, the self-serving advantages of little or no effort also become increasingly clear. As already noted, achieving with little or no effort enhances a reputation for brilliance, while not exerting effort also obscures the causes of failure, should it occur – according to one twelfth-grader, "If he does not try, you don't know how smart he is" (Harari & Covington, 1981).

As the child grows older, protecting a sense of worth defined by the ability to achieve competitively becomes increasingly more important. Some of the many self-aggrandizing strategies used for this purpose are discussed next.

AN ARSENAL OF EXCUSES

> We have good reasons for *our* bad performances; other people
> give excuses.
>   C. R. Snyder

Excuses have been a part of the human scene ever since Adam first
blamed Eve, and Eve blamed the serpent. In school, as we have
seen, excuses moderate the conflict of classroom values. They allow
students to repackage otherwise questionable actions, like not trying, in a more flattering, less blameworthy form (Snyder & Higgins,
1988).

Getting Along, Going Along

Actually, many of the ploys used in this self-protective drama are
not ability excuses at all. They are simply ways to avoid revealing
one's ignorance because students don't always do every homework
assignment nor do they always listen when directions are being giv-
en. At their most innocent, these tactics form a cherished part of
childhood lore. Everyone recalls those desperate classmates who
scrunched down in their seats, trying hard to become the smallest
possible target as the teacher scanned a sea of anxious faces searching for a victim in the game of "question and answer." Above all,
eye contact with the teacher was to be avoided. Other good advice
at times like this included, "Look busy!" Then there was the outra-
geous business of waving one's hand wildly in response to the
teacher's question – *not* knowing the answer, of course, but hoping
against hope that he or she would call on someone else who appeared less well prepared. And there was, and still is, the universal
strategy of responding to the teacher's questions in as vague a manner as possible, vague enough to hedge against exposing a mistake
or revealing that one just plain does not know the answer. The student who hesitates in answering or gives only a provisional answer
can often count on the teacher for help (Dillon & Searle, 1981). This
cat-and-mouse game often involves what Ulf Lundgren (1977) has
called "piloting." Here the teacher unwittingly leads the student

84

toward an answer until the correct response is virtually assured. The teacher may derive considerable satisfaction from such an exercise, assuming that the student knows something but is simply too nervous to express it. Obviously, the student *has* learned a lot, but likely more about how to control and "pilot" the teacher toward the right answer than anything about the topic in question.

There is also the strategy of simply not trying, of avoiding work that is not absolutely required, or of doing as little as possible and assuming somehow, magically, that this lack of participation would be overlooked or forgiven. By remaining silent or at least uncommitted, the student is operating on the principle that it is better to be thought a fool than to open one's mouth and remove all doubt. Yet blatant noninvolvement is risky because teachers *do* expect students to try. For this reason, students often combine outright refusal with other more subtle ploys, including the ruse of "false effort," or what Donald Hansen (1989) refers to as "lesson dissembling." This involves appearing to be interested in one's schoolwork, but in reality using a cloak of apparent commitment to dodge the teacher's wrath. Here the gambits are almost endless: giving the outward appearances of understanding, while not really understanding at all; posing a pensive, quizzical look – too busy thinking to be interrupted; asking questions whose answers are already known; or copying from a neighbor's paper, and perhaps adding a unique touch.

This drama admits to many other subtle variations as well. For instance, indifferent students can sometimes redeem themselves in the eyes of teachers and generate considerable sympathy if they occasionally undergo a flurry of activity at the last moment just before an assignment is due. Teachers judge these erratic performers to be more prone to discouragement than diligent students, because when they do try, their reward is often another failing mark. As a result teachers are more likely to reward these marginal workers, hoping to encourage more effort next time (Covington et al., 1980). They often do try harder, but largely in the interests of perfecting their strategies for dissembling with scarcely any attention given to the assignments themselves.

Unfortunately, all too often, not really trying takes a more ominous turn. Now, instead of merely avoiding being seen as unprepared – for instance, not knowing a particular answer – the struggle is to escape being labeled as stupid. Ignorance and stupidity are not the same. Ignorance can be corrected but, presumably, not stupidity. Certainly, as we have seen, this is what many older youngsters believe. So riskier defenses are called for, riskier because they are more likely to undermine the will to learn by causing the very failures that students are attempting to avoid. These tactics can be divided into two broad categories: self-handicapping strategies and techniques designed to guarantee success.

Self-Handicapping Strategies

Self-handicapping involves the creation of some impediment to one's performance – either imagined or real – so that the individual has a ready excuse for potential failure. For instance, Steven Berglas and Edward Jones (1978) have proposed that some people may use alcohol or other drugs to protect their self-image. If one is drunk, performing well may be seen by others as quite remarkable, whereas failure is more readily explained, if not always excused. In a similar fashion, some students may use excuses like a narcotic, addictively, and to excess, in order to defend against the pain of academic failure. Unfortunately, although the pain may be relieved, relief is only temporary, and in the process, the likelihood of chronic failure increases.

Procrastination. One of the most universal self-handicapping strategies involves procrastination – universal and decidedly contemptible as well if Thomas De Quincy's famous nineteenth-century epigram is any indication: "If once a man indulges himself in murder, very soon he comes to think little of robbing; and from robbing he next comes to drinking and Sabbath-breaking, and from that to incivility and procrastination." Today some experts believe that at the college level a near majority of students procrastinate as a way of life (Rothblum, Solomon, & Murakami, 1986; Solomon & Rothblum, 1984).

Putting things off – postponing until tomorrow what one might do today – sometimes makes sense. Many politicians and bureaucrats have built successful careers on little more than the clever application of this wait-and-see strategy. But when it cannot be justified, postponement becomes stalling and a way to sidestep failure. By studying only at the last minute, procrastinators can hardly be blamed for failure – they simply had too much to do, and not enough time. Moreover, if these individuals are successful, a reputation for brilliance will be assured because they will have succeeded with so little effort. Thus, in one sense at least, procrastinators have little to lose and much to gain. Indeed, the temptation of succeeding with little apparent effort is often too much for some students who become "closet achievers." Closet achievers are those students who complain about not having had enough time to study for a test but who, in reality, secretly spend the weekend in an isolated part of the library. Such students will appear unusually capable if they succeed, but also will have protected a reputation for brilliance if they should fail.

A subtle variation on the procrastination theme involves apparently genuine attempts to keep busy, very busy – in fact, too busy but with little to show for it. The student who can never get beyond rewriting the introduction to her term paper in an endless succession of polishing and tinkering illustrates this point. So does the behavior of the student who spends endless hours collecting references for his paper so that in the end nothing ever gets written. This illogical use of one's time and resources allows a variety of explanations for eventual failure, including the often-heard refrain, "I ran out of time," and its implied corollary, "Given enough time, I could have done much better." Then there are those students who take on so many jobs that they can never devote enough time to any one project. The resulting work may be uniformly mediocre, but at least they score big on being involved and energetic. Busyness also has the added advantage of making one feel important. If these individuals can't do everything they should, then – the implied argument runs – they must be doing something important.

Unattainable Goals. The trauma caused by failure can also be minimized by pegging one's achievement goals so high that failure is virtually assured – for instance, aspiring to a straight A average while carrying a double major in college and two part-time jobs. This apparently irrational behavior makes perfectly logical sense when viewed from a self-worth perspective. Failure at an exceedingly difficult task reveals little about one's ability since success is beyond all but the most capable or energetic of students. If virtually everyone else fails, too, then the problem resides not in us, but rather in the goal. And even if the failed task is in reality not very hard, we can still easily convince ourselves of its inherent difficulty. Just how this neat trick is accomplished is illustrated by the research of David Bennett and David Holmes (reported in Snyder, 1984). These investigators informed one group of students, falsely, that they had failed a vocabulary test, while another group was provided no test feedback at all. The first group estimated that a near majority of their friends would also fail the same test, while the second group estimated that most of their friends would pass. As Snyder points out, "misery loves company," which is what the alleged failure group arranged – lots of company – and now we understand why. It is because the collective failures of the many obscure the individual failures of the few.

Underachievers. Chronic underachievers avoid any test of their ability by refusing to work, thereby maintaining an inflated opinion of themselves. In order to justify this deceptive cover, underachievers often make a virtue out of not trying. They may take a perverse pride in their unwillingness to achieve by downgrading the importance of the work they refuse to do, or by attacking others who do try as hypocritical, foolish, or stupid. Underachievers may even convince themselves that failure is a mark of nonconformity and evidence of their individuality. Naturally, this kind of uniqueness is more piteous than admirable, because it originates more out of a fear of inadequacy than out of any high moral conviction. Experts agree that underachievers not only believe that their worth depends on succeeding, but on succeeding perfectly and against virtually unattainable standards of excellence (Bricklin & Bricklin, 1967). For underachievers, this gap between their "ideal-self" (as they think they *ought* to be) and their "actual-self" (as they perceive themselves to be) produces an intolerable situation (Higgins, 1987). Often the result is self-rage for not achieving perfection, and anger toward others who would insist on perfection. These "others" are typically parents who expect too much, too early in childhood without the guidance necessary for such idealistic performances (Davids & Hainsworth, 1967). From this perspective, there are also other advantages to be gained by not trying. Underachieving students can punish parents by not living up to their expectations.

The Academic Wooden Leg. The final example of self-handicapping involves a kind of self-worth plea bargaining. Here the individual admits publicly to a minor personal weakness or handicap, the proverbial wooden leg, in order to avoid disclosing a far greater imagined weakness – in this case, being intellectually inadequate and hence unworthy. One of the most convincing of these handicaps is anxiety. By arguing that their poor performance is the result of test-taking anxiety, individuals reason that it is better to appear anxious than stupid and, in the process, they can convert ridicule and scorn instantly into sympathetic, solicitous concern.

Actually, test anxiety is far more than a convenient excuse; it is real enough, and its disruptive effects on school performance are well documented (for a review, see Covington, 1992). Still, from a self-worth perspective, anxiety is the near-perfect alibi. Test anxiety is not a reprehensible shortcoming, and everyone has experienced it enough to know that anxiety is legitimate, unlikely to be feigned, and often beyond the control of the individual. The test-anxious student is the perfect blameless victim. For these reasons, we would be surprised if students did not occasionally use symptoms of anxiety to self-serving advantage. In fact, the evidence suggests that they probably do (Smith, Snyder, & Handelsman, 1982).

Guaranteeing Success

Another group of self-serving ploys involves a frontal assault on failure – avoiding failure by succeeding! These fear-driven successes can be extraordinary. Many failure-threatened students are merit scholar finalists, class valedictorians, and National Science Fair winners. However, despite such outward signs of success, being driven to succeed out of fear may be the ultimate academic ordeal. The individual's sense of worth comes to depend to an increasingly perilous degree on always succeeding, relentlessly, and against lengthening odds. Moreover, because such successes are essentially defensive in nature, they do little to help individuals shake their suspicions of worthlessness. The textbook example of this predicament is the overstriver.

Overstrivers. According to our analysis of Atkinson's need achievement model (Chapter 2), overstrivers reflect an intense desire both to succeed and to avoid failure (high approach, high avoidance). On the hopeful side, overstrivers, like Amy, describe themselves as being highly qualified academically; but on the fearful side, they worry that they are not really as smart (and worthy) as their outstanding record would seem to indicate.

This hybrid quality of hope and fear conspires to drive overstrivers to greater and greater accomplishments through a combination of high ability, meticulous attention to detail, and extraordinarily effective study strategies (Covington & Omelich, 1987). Indeed, ironically, overstrivers are often *too* effective because in the long run their successes become an intolerable burden. No one can avoid failing forever, despite Herculean efforts to do so. Eventually, failure is assured because human beings cannot remain satisfied for long; the next obstacle must be more difficult, more of a challenge than the last if success is to retain its allure. We know from Ferdinand Hoppe's research more than half a century ago that raising one's aspirations after success is a perfectly natural reaction, part of the "typical shift" phenomenon (Chapter 2). But for the overstriver, setting one's sights higher and higher, success after success, becomes an obsessive ritual. Overstrivers cannot moderate their self-demands since perfection is their goal. As a result they experience no grace in failure, nor can they exercise self-forgiveness. This predicament is analogous to the tightrope walker who must perform increasingly more daring feats, at ever dizzying heights, to ensure that the circus crowds will return. But it can be a long way down for overstrivers. Just how far down, and how devastating the fall, is reflected by the fact that overstrivers are risking failure under the most threatening circumstance of all: failure after having tried hard. In effect, slavish preparation strips the overstriver of most potential excuses. Overstrivers rarely procrastinate; in fact, they are among the first to begin studying and among the last to stop, often grudgingly putting away their study notes just as the test is being passed out in class. Nor do overstrivers settle for utterly unattainable goals, because they are betting on success, not excused failure as the way to prove their worth.

Low-Goal Setting. Another success-insuring strategy involves setting one's academic goals so low that there is little or no chance of failing. In its most sophisticated form this tactic involves the manipulation of what Robert Birney and colleagues (1969) call the "confirming interval." This is the interval between the lowest performance an individual can attain without experiencing discomfort and the best he or she can hope for. Performances that fall within this range are met with a sense of acceptance. By extending this interval – for example, by dropping the lower bounds of what one will accept – students can continue to evade feelings of failure, sometimes indefinitely. The student who publicly announces before an examination that he or she will be satisfied with just a passing grade is taking crafty advantage of this strategy.

Naturally, however, there are trade-offs. Low-goal setting eventually leads to inadequate performances. Students do only as much as they expect of themselves. When they expect more, they deliver more; when they expect less, as in this case, they deliver that, too (Locke & Latham, 1984). At the same time, success that is virtually assured becomes predictable and loses any intrinsic value associated with challenge and uncertainty. Since there is no real challenge, there can be no genuine pride in accomplishment, only boredom.

Chronically low aspirations create a dull, protracted mediocrity where success is defined only by not losing. Students may occasionally find some thin satisfaction in such marginal successes, be-

91

cause, as it has been observed, at least mediocre performers are *always* at their best. Still, they have constructed an illusion for self-respect based on a life of underachievement.

Academic Cheating. Cheating in school has long been a topic of concern, and sometimes moral outrage. Some investigators have interpreted chronic cheating as a sign of stress and misplaced coping, whereas others see cheating as further evidence of a general ethical decline in our society. And there are those who believe cheating to be the result of bankrupt educational policies that encourage deception and fraud. Whatever the validity of these various interpretations, it is abundantly clear that cheating also qualifies as a highly tempting way to avoid failure by appearing to succeed (Aronson & Mettee, 1968; Monte & Fish, 1989).

From the self-worth perspective, cheating qualifies as part of the unhealthy legacy that results from having tied one's sense of worth to achieving competitively. Students themselves contribute poignantly to our understanding of the stakes involved. In one informal study middle school youngsters who were caught cheating were asked to write an essay explaining why. Several of their replies are presented here (as reported in Covington & Beery, 1976, p. 55):

> Kids don't cheat because they are bad. They are afraid that they aren't smart and what will happen if they don't do good. People will call them dumb or stupid.

> If you cheat you will not know how to do the lesson right. You just put off flunking until later. It is scary.

> Sometimes teachers don't see cheating. But something terrible will happen to cheaters anyway. They will pay for it. Maybe they will get sick. Or maybe they will have to explain their right answers in class.

> I know someone who studies hard for tests and cheats too. They feel really bad but it is better than being yelled at for bad grades.

> People cheat because they are afraid of doing poorer than other kids and feeling miserable for being different and behind. Some do it to be the best in class or move to the next group.

Naturally, we must view these confessions with caution. What-ever they may reveal about the stresses of school life, they are also self-serving. No one likes to cheat, but being caught is even more hateful, and it is important to cast such wrongdoing in as positive a light as possible. Nonetheless, the intensity of these confessions, their emotionally charged content, and, above all, their expressions of fear, self-loathing, and anger indicate something of the extent to which students are haunted by the fear of falling behind, of being compared unfavorably with others, and of the persistent, often overbearing demands of others. Also, there is a rueful awareness of the true horror of cheating that has all the classic elements of a Faus-tian bargain. By trading on their integrity, cheaters may gain some measure of relief from the prospect of failing. But the respite is short-lived, since this ill-starred postponement creates new, greater fears: of being unable to repeat one's successes, and of being found out.

Minority Dynamics

The failure-avoiding strategies described so far are largely the prop-erty of middle-class white students, and of those minority young-sters, represented by Amy – our young, black overstriver – who ac-cept traditional schooling in the competitive spirit of Hermes. If Hermes is the archetype of achievement motivation, as McClelland argued (Chapter 2), then Hermes is solidly middle class, as reflect-ed in his impatience to get ahead and the lengths to which he will go to stay ahead or at least not fall behind.

But, as we have seen, thanks largely to the research of Suarez-Orozco (Chapter 2), Hermes is largely a stranger in the barrios and urban ghettos of America. Castelike minorities tend to strive for dif-ferent goals and prefer different ways to achieve those goals. They reject competitive advantage within their group, strive for honor, and prefer the cooperation that comes from tight-knit family or neighborhood traditions. But these youngsters must still operate in schools dominated by middle-class values and ways of doing things. What does the self-worth perspective reveal about the spe-cial problems that face minority youngsters who choose for the moment to play the middle-class school game or at least pretend to play?

Esteem and School Performance. To start with, we are now in a position to explain a puzzle of long standing. Although the academic performance of blacks and Hispanics is lower on average than that of whites, these minority youngsters nonetheless often rate themselves relatively high on measures of well-being and ability (e.g., Franco, 1983; Hare, 1985; Healey, 1970; Rosenberg & Simmons, 1973). But if poor school performance is associated with low levels of self-esteem and inadequate ability in the minds of middle-class whites, which it is, then why should minorities buck this trend and hold themselves in higher self-regard than their grades would indicate?

The answer is that feeling able and worthy among many castelike minorities depends less on performing well in school than it does for middle-class whites. Rather, these minority youngsters are more likely to find their worth in peer acceptance and being cooperative (Hare, 1985). Also, minority youth tend to view ability differently. In the contemporary black community, for example, ability is typically measured in a broader, more practical, everyday context than in the narrow academic sense in which being bright means getting good grades. Ramah Commanday (1992) found that black family members judge the ability of children with reference to concrete actions. Thus, "My boy is so smart he can help me fill out job application forms," or "My granddaughter is able to go to the pharmacy for me all on her own." Being able also means mastering the rules and facts of survival: knowing, for example, whose turf is whose and who is likely to back up his demands with violence. In such an earnest, often dangerous, world, aggrandizing ability as an academic credential scarcely seems relevant. As one of Commanday's exceptionally bright fifth-grade ghetto informants explained: "I know I'm smart so I don't have to prove it in school." If ability is equated with effective coping and survival in the ghettos and barrios of America, then the reports of high self-perceived ability among minority children are neither puzzling nor inaccurate.

Disidentification. Not surprisingly, minority children often reject the dominant academic values of middle-class schools, especially competitiveness, thereby distancing themselves from what they see to be a losing battle. Recall from Chapter 2 that many black adolescent males associate concepts like "champion" and "competition" with failure and death (Fyans et al., 1983). This self-distancing process has been referred to as "disidentification" by Claude Steele (1988). Simply put, individuals devalue that which threatens their sense of well-being. We have already met the white version of this conflict-management technique as practiced by John, our college-bound high school senior. John routinely minimizes the importance of his occasional academic disappointments, thereby becoming less vulnerable to personal devaluation. For minorities, too, like the white majority, rejection and withdrawal are typical protective tactics.

These same disidentification dynamics also operate in the case of poor, white youth. But the problem for blacks is compounded and their predicament intensified by the burden of stigmatization (Steele, 1989a). Stigmas arise when a person's actions violate social expectations. For example, a student's blackness may be stigmatized and the child held up to ridicule if he or she does well in school, since many whites refuse to acknowledge that black Americans are capable of significant intellectual accomplishments. Such biases are well illustrated by the black fifth-grade student described by Dorothy Gilliam who was questioned about whether he had really written an outstanding essay without help, an episode that ended when the teacher gave him a grade that clearly showed that she did not believe the boy's outraged denials of plagiarism (reported in Fordham & Ogbu, 1986, p. 176). It is the accusation, tacitly implied by this example, that black Americans are inferior – inferior simply because they are black – that has helped relegate them to the sidelines of American life. All children worry about not being good enough, but it is principally blacks who, in the words of Shelby Steele (1989b), "Come wearing a color that is still, in the minds of some, a sign of inferiority" (p. 50).

Under the circumstances it is easy to see why many young

blacks and Hispanics are driven into such potentially destructive pursuits as ganging, which, although it may provide a means for self-affirmation and peer acceptance, nonetheless places children on the wrong side of the law at increasingly early ages and at risk for drugs, violence, and death. Yet withdraw as they might, minority youngsters must eventually come to terms with traditional, mainstream American values in order to make a living, even a marginal one. The fact that fewer than 20 percent of all black families in American have incomes above the poverty line attests to the difficulty of this task.

This need for survival places castelike minorities in a tortuous bind. On the one hand, they must function at least minimally in the larger society to make ends meet, yet at the same time to protect their sense of group identity they must hold the values of this same society at arm's length. Here, once again, we are reminded of dilemmas. We have considered the effort-avoiding dilemma facing many white and middle-class students who struggle to maintain a balance between too much effort, at the risk of being judged incompetent should they fail, and too little effort, at the risk of incurring teacher displeasure. Now we suggest a special dilemma for minorities, which can best be described as an allegiance-avoiding dilemma – accepting dominant white values just enough to get along, but not enough to incur the wrath of one's friends and family. This dilemma is brought to an exquisite level of torment for those minority students, like Amy, who struggle at least in the beginning to succeed in a white world.

Acting White. According to Signithia Fordham and John Ogbu (1986), this struggle inevitably involves blacks taking up the burden of "acting white," which means, among other things, speaking standard English, working hard to get good grades, going to museums, and having parties with no music. These behaviors invite anger and resentment from both blacks and whites. On the one hand, by doing well academically – a domain of excellence long forbidden to blacks – the black child is often met with hostility and mistrust from a large cross section of the white community. On the other hand, upward-striving blacks risk rejection from their own peer group

96

and sometimes even their families, as betrayers of their cultural heritage.

From this perspective, then, black underachievers may be thought of as youngsters who have the ability to do well in school but choose, consciously or unconsciously, to avoid the costs of acting white. And the pressures to give up on school are enormous. For example, there is the fear that performing well will bring on additional responsibilities and problems. Shelvy, an underachieving black girl in the eleventh grade, expresses it this way: "because if you let . . . all your friends know how smart you are, then when you take a test or something, then they are going to know you know the answer and they are going to want the answers. And, if you don't give them to them, then they're going to get upset with you" (Fordham & Ogbu, 1986, p. 191). Also, those minority students who persist in attempts to better themselves academically become a *target* in the experience of Kareem Abdul-Jabbar, one of the great athletes of this century:

> When the nuns found this out [being able to read with proper inflection] they paid me a lot of attention, once even asking me, a fourth grader, to read to the seventh grade. When the kids found this out I became a target. . . . I got all A's and was hated for it; I spoke correctly and was called a punk. I had to learn a new language simply to be able to deal with the threats. I had good manners and was a good little boy and paid for it with my hide. (Abdul-Jabbar & Knobles, 1983, p. 16)

The key to academic survival for gifted minorities in such a climate is to conceal their ability from peers – ironically, exactly the opposite tack taken by many middle-class whites who typically seek to aggrandize and flaunt their ability as a mark of superiority. Basically, concealing means drawing as little attention to one's achievements as possible – in effect, cloaking one's ability or sabotaging one's successes in order to remain part of the group. Kaela, a brilliant black teenager, carried this later strategy to perfection: she did well on all her course examinations but, by not attending classes on a regular basis, she forced her teachers to give her F's. By putting "the brakes on," according to Kaela, she was also able to avoid the eventual frustrations of being overqualified for the low-status job for which she believed herself destined (Fordham & Ogbu, 1986).

Another strategy for maintaining a low academic profile, one especially favored by young, aspiring black males, is called "lunching" (Fordham & Ogbu, 1986), that is, becoming a clown or buffoon who achieves well despite his bungling, often manic ways – feigning surprise at receiving high grades, disrupting the class with jokes, or making strange facial grimaces during silent reading. Yet behind this facade of apparent disinterest and ineptitude stands a serious student who often attends classes faithfully and completes most homework assignments. Other bright students survive by choosing friends – sometimes hoodlums and bullies – who will protect them from hallway violence and fights in exchange for favors, like helping with homework or taking tests for them.

Although bright black males are more likely to draw attention to themselves as a way to disguise their ability, high-achieving black females typically work to maintain a low profile. Fordham and Ogbu (1986, p. 196) describe the plight of Katrina, a brilliant straight-A math student, who arranged with her physics teacher not to be chosen as one of three students to represent her school in a television competition, even if she qualified for the team. As things turned out, Katrina was the top qualifier, but because of the prior arrangement she was made an alternate member of the team.

Given the burdens of acting white, we can only worry at the future prospects for Amy, our young black overstriver, who for the moment is uncritical in her acceptance of middle-class values, loyalties that in time, however, may bring her into increasing conflict with the countervailing values of many youngsters in her immediate peer group.

Failure-Accepting Students

Even though one's failures may be well defended for a time by a bodyguard of alibis and excuses, these self-serving explanations eventually lose their credibility, and vague doubts about one's worth become virtual certainties. This collapse of defenses has been studied in classroom settings where unremitting failure is a natural, albeit unfortunate occurrence. In one study researchers tracked students who fell short of their grade goals on each of several successive tests, thereby enduring repeated feelings of failure (Covington & Omelich, 1981). The degree of shame following a first failure depended largely on the individual's initial self-estimates of ability – the lower one's estimates, the more one experienced shame and feelings of hopelessness. Then as one failure followed another, these feelings intensified, driven by two interlocking processes. First, as self-serving excuses for failure became increasingly implausible, estimates of one's ability steadily deteriorated. Second, these failures were increasingly attributed to a lack of ability. In other words, as failures mounted, these students rated themselves lower and lower on the very factor – ability – that was emerging in their minds as the most important ingredient to success. This dual process, akin to a kind of double jeopardy, was most pronounced among those students who initially held the lowest self-concepts of ability.

The research of Ralf Schwarzer and his colleagues (Schwarzer, Jerusalem, & Schwarzer, 1983; Schwarzer, Jerusalem, & Stiksrud, 1984) is consistent with this "double jeopardy" interpretation. They proposed that a first failure, especially if unexpected, represents a *challenge* to be overcome. However, subsequent failures, particularly as they become anticipated, elicit anxiety caused by increasing attributions to low ability, until finally – after repeated failures – individuals may experience feelings of a total loss of personal control over events. In order to test these predictions, Schwarzer tracked the relationship between test anxiety, feelings of helplessness, and school grades for German high school students over a two-year period. Of special interest was the identification of a substantial subsample among these students whose level of anxiety progressively decreased over time only to be replaced by an increasing sense of hopelessness. This process appears akin to a state of resignation that may share much in common with the lack of emotions and unresponsiveness of those individuals identified as failure acceptors in American samples (Covington & Omelich, 1985).

Having given up the struggle for approval via high achievement, failure-accepting students naturally search for alternative sources of worth. The evidence suggests that at least some of these individuals come to embrace the socially rewarding values of diligence, punctuality, and hard work, a strategy that is especially favored by women and girls (Covington & Omelich, 1985). For other students, most likely men and boys, failure acceptance means the rejection of both effort and ability as sources of worth, which may lead to dropping out of school or simply refusing to cooperate.

CONCLUSION

In this chapter we have explored the dynamics of classroom achievement from a self-worth perspective. School learning has been described as involving a profound conflict of values between ability and effort. By this analysis, failure-prone students, especially middle-class white youngsters, are condemned to thread their way between the threatening extremes of trying too hard (for fear of being revealed as incompetent should they fail) and of exerting too little effort (for fear of teacher reprimand). For those minority students who struggle to succeed in a white world, the situation is further complicated by the need to maintain an ethnic identity that may not always be compatible with mainstream values.

We have also cataloged many of the ruses and artful dodges employed by students who struggle to preserve a sense of dignity in school. Despite the complexities involved, these dynamics reflect a primordial struggle for self-protection so elemental that many students are prepared to sacrifice even good grades for the sake of appearances.

The vision of school life conjured up by self-worth theory is disturbing. The kinds of motivational dynamics revealed here portray a far more troubling picture than the idealized account of schools in which "teachers gladly teach, and students gladly learn." All too often, in reality, classrooms are battlegrounds where the rules of engagement favor deception, sabotage, and lackluster effort.

This self-worth analysis gives further reason to doubt the wisdom of implementing a policy of intensification as the best way to meet the current crisis in education. Increasing the pressures on students to work harder may prove effective for a time, especially in the earliest years of school when students value effort and respond eagerly to effort-based rewards. But, according to the evidence presented here, this policy becomes progressively bankrupt as students grow older, until eventually intensification becomes part of the problem, not part of the solution.

Needless to say, motivating students to try harder is critical if we are ever to reverse the shameful statistics that place American students as second best in the academic sweepstakes among the leading industrial nations. But our attempts to mobilize student involvement and effort will remain counterproductive and an undiminished threat, as long as effort is viewed as a commodity to be aroused, managed, and manipulated through competitive incentives.

SUMMING UP

1. Self-worth theory assumes that the search for acceptance is the highest human priority and that, in many schools, one's worth comes to depend on the ability to achieve competitively.

2. In these schools success is defined in terms of outperforming others, and the reasons for learning involve bolstering one's reputation for ability or trying to avoid failure, which implies low ability.

3. In such circumstances, failure-prone students must make their way between the threatening extremes of trying too hard – with the prospect of feeling shameful if they fail – and exerting little or no effort at all, which results in teacher punishment.

4. Numerous self-serving strategies are employed by students to preserve a sense of competency, even though they may lead to the very failures that these students hope to avoid, including procrastination, underachieving, and striving for unattainable goals.

5. The effectiveness of these strategies is short-lived. Eventually, excuses lose their credibility, and then doubts about one's worth become virtual certainties. The collapse of these defenses leads individuals to feel hopeless and betrayed, angry at themselves for feeling stupid and resenting others for making them feel that way.

6. Even though many minority and impoverished youngsters may reject the white, middle-class mentality that defines success as winning at the expense of others, they are nonetheless caught in a cruel dilemma. They must accept the dominant mainstream values enough to acquire the skills necessary for economic survival, but not necessarily so much that they become rejected by peers as betrayers of their cultural heritage.

ACTIVITIES

Activity 1: Posing More Puzzles

Now you are in a position to explain the following classroom puzzles. You may wish to compare your explanations with those found in Appendix E.

1. Why is it that for some students, like overstrivers, getting high grades does not necessarily lead to a sense of pride and personal satisfaction?

2. Why is it that for some students who have always done well in school, one single failure can be so devastating to their sense of worth?

3. Why should failure-prone students sometimes actually perform better when they have excuses to explain potential failure, or when the odds against their succeeding are great?

Activity 2: Encouraging Multiple Abilities

Not only do schools sometimes inadvertently perpetuate a view of ability as a fixed, immutable capacity, they also promote a narrow view of ability as well, something limited largely to verbal, abstract, and logical reasoning. Fortunately, teachers and researchers alike are beginning to appreciate that there are many kinds of ability, not just a few. The more students are able to represent their knowledge using alternative kinds of ability, the more they will feel in control of their learning.

Make a list of abilities that students might draw on to express their ideas and thoughts. Then create a second list, this time consisting of classroom activities that might make use of each of these different modes of ability. For example, if you include spatial ability on your list, then drawing a map would be one way to express what a student has learned. When you finish your lists, you may wish to compare your ideas with those of Howard Gardner, a leading advocate of a multiple-abilities approach to learning (Appendix F).

Activity 3: Identifying Tests of Self-Worth

Recall the four students introduced in Chapter 2: Losa, John, Amy, and Ralph. From a self-worth perspective, each of them, like all of us, struggles to maintain a sense of personal value. But each has chosen different ways to judge self-worth, with dramatically different results.

1. Review briefly the earlier descriptions of Losa, John, Amy, and Ralph. How do success-oriented individuals, like Losa, measure their worth differently from failure-threatened students, like John and Ralph?

2. How might teachers help students like John, Amy, and Ralph to find better, less threatening ways to prove their worth and value both to themselves and to others?

5

THE COMPETITIVE
LEARNING GAME

Learning is an exciting adventure – unless, of course, we go out
of our way to make it unpleasant.
John Krumboltz

WHAT IS IT ABOUT SCHOOL LIFE THAT DRIVES THE HURTFUL, DE-structive dynamics that subvert the joy of learning and cre-ates such a profound conflict between ability and effort as sources of worth? Many answers have been offered, but none comes as close to the mark as that implied by John Krumboltz's mocking challenge (1990): "Imagine how we would go about designing an education-al program if our purpose were to make students hate to learn." First, Krumboltz suggests, "we would not involve them [students] in establishing the purposes of their class." Second, "we would re-quire them to perform some impossible tasks – for example, to be perfect in everything they do. Third, when we discovered that the students were failing to master the impossible tasks, we would ridicule them and report their mistakes, failures and shortcomings to their friends and relatives."

It is hard to improve on this formula if the purpose is to make learning unpleasant, yet ironically – and, of course, this is Krum-boltz's point – these are precisely the circumstances that prevail in many schools today and help explain why children become alienat-ed from school, hate teachers and learning, vandalize school prop-erty, and drop out as soon as they can. But no one wants to make learning unpleasant, not deliberately anyway. So why do we treat children this way? According to George Leonard (1968), a longtime education critic, it is not for the purpose of helping "students to learn other subjects, but to teach competition itself" (p. 129).

But is the competitive spirit of Hermes so important that we must promote it directly in schools? Certainly there can be no mistaking the unique American commitment to competition, a commitment that is summed up perfectly by football coach Vince Lombardi when he commented, "Winning isn't everything, it's the only thing." In later years Lombardi regretted his comment: "I wish to hell I'd never said the damn thing. I meant having a goal." Misunderstood or not, Lombardi's remark neatly illuminates the competitive side of American society, which is perpetuated by a powerful set of claims. First, there is the assertion that teaching competition prepares students for the rigors of economic survival in later life, and that to downplay competition in school is to prepare children for a world that does not exist. Then, second, there is the argument that academic competition is the most efficient – some would say even the fairest – way for society to allocate talent proportionally across the available jobs, some jobs being more prestigious and sought after than others.

These powerful arguments must be addressed and unmasked for what they are – appealing but basically misleading articles of faith – before we can take seriously the kinds of changes to be proposed in coming chapters. These two particular arguments will be rebutted in the final chapter. Meanwhile, there are several other reasons thought to favor competition that are best examined now because they concern the mission of schools more directly. First, there is the widespread belief that competition motivates students to do their best, and that for the mass of dispirited, listless students competition is the only way to ensure a minimum level of competency. The second belief is that achieving under adversity (competition) builds character and enhances a sense of self-confidence. In this chapter we will present evidence to the contrary, and document the enormous costs associated with arranging schools around a competitive ethos.

THE STRUCTURE OF LEARNING

The literature on school achievement makes clear that different kinds of incentives call out different student behavior. Every classroom reflects some type of reward structure within which all academic work is embedded. It is this structure that conveys information to students, explicitly or implicitly, about how they are to be evaluated and what they must do if they hope to be successful (Doyle, 1983). Alfred Alschuler (1969, 1973) likened these dynamics to a game, albeit a serious game. For instance, in what Alschuler called failure-oriented (competitive) classrooms, the rules of the learning game require that an inadequate supply of rewards (e.g., good grades) be distributed unequally with the greatest number going to the best performers. This arrangement amounts to a zero-sum scoring system. When one student (player) wins (or makes points), other students must fail (lose points).

Social scientists have studied the effects of such competitive power games on learners, especially the impact of rewards insufficient for the number of players. For example, Linden Nelson and Spencer Kagan (1972) awarded young students prizes (attractive toys) if they cooperated in their work on a problem-solving game. The children did in fact cooperate as long as everyone received a reward. However, when fewer rewards were provided than players, the children became antagonistic. In fact, some even forfeited their own chances to win by sabotaging the game in order to deprive others! This research tracks a vicious cycle: inadequate rewards create competition, which in turn discourages cooperation, and competitive pressure further diminishes the likelihood of rewards through sabotage and cheating. Moreover, as scarcity increases, the more important these fewer rewards become as evidence of one's ability to get them. Incidentally, of all the groups investigated by Nelson and Kagan, the most antagonistic were middle-class whites. Mexican American youngsters from low-income families were far less competitive (Kagan & Knight, 1981; Knight & Kagan, 1977), but not necessarily because of their ethnic background. Middle-income Mexican American youngsters also proved to be highly competitive, suggesting that competition is mainly a characteristic of the middle classes.

Student versus Student

Aggression and resentment toward one another is the inevitable result of the kinds of competitive dynamics set in motion experimen-

106

tally by Nelson and Kagan. These destructive impulses can take many forms. Overtly hostile expressions include spying and tattling. If Susan can get Heather into trouble, even though the transgression is minor and the purpose of the accusation transparent – "It hurts me to say this, but I saw Heather talking" – then Heather's status as a rival will be diminished. Also there is the merciless laughter at someone else's mistakes and those delicious opportunities to provide answers for other children who cannot get the problem right themselves.

Student versus Teacher

In the competitive learning game, teachers become the gatekeepers of success and approval, which puts a powerful weapon in their hands. Teachers may use the dynamics of scarcity to ensure good behavior, or at least to create the impression that classroom activities are organized around some kind of plan. Or teachers may introduce competition to divide and subdue students, a strategy born of the fear, often justified, that students will otherwise unite against them in open revolt and rebellion. Teachers often imagine that particular students cannot be controlled and will always remain wild and undisciplined. Such fears hang over many ghetto schools like a shroud.

For some children, especially the young, the compliant, and the middle-class, the use of competition by teachers for self-protection works well most of the time. Many of these students react docilely, giving teachers what they want for fear of offending them. Unfortunately, this scarcity of rewards also discourages intellectual risk taking by placing a premium on conformity and submissiveness. In its more extreme manifestations, submissiveness sets the stage for what Jules Henry (1957) calls the "witch-hunt syndrome" – a devastating confection of student docility, boredom, feelings of vulnerability, and fear of punishment. Witch hunts allow teachers to mobilize and direct student anger inward, toward themselves and each other in a perpetual search for wrongdoers. A critical part of this process (in fact, the culminating act) involves the confession by those who would violate the rules, however minor the infraction –

107

whispering in line and the like. In this drama of total submission to teacher authority, the teacher decides what type of confession he or she wishes to hear and what the resolution should be. Children eagerly throw themselves into the role of both the hunter and the hunted in an effort to placate the teacher: first come the hunters – resolute in their defense of the realm – followed by the hunted, with their confessions of weakness and statements of contrition.

Mostly, the dynamics just described, including docility and submissiveness, are found in white, middle-class schools where children are well versed in the rigors, techniques, and importance of deciding who are the winners and losers. On the other hand, these controlling tactics are less effective among minority students, especially blacks and Hispanics, who, being more cooperative, are more likely to band together against the authority of the teacher (Erickson & Mohatt, 1982; Foster, 1974).

Alschuler (1973) has identified some of the basic tactics involved in a game in which teachers and students are pitted against one another. The teacher is clearly savaged by the apparent need to resort to the following tactics:

1. Waiting, staring (stops lesson)
2. Tunnel vision (ignores disruption or does not see it)
3. Making rules (orders student to "stop")
4. Sarcasm, belittling ("Do you think you can remember if I tell you a fifth time?")
5. Minilecture on good and bad behavior and its consequences ("She wouldn't be bothering you if you did not turn around")

According to Alschuler's estimates, a teacher spends an average of some 22,000 minutes per school year in reproaching, rebuking, nagging, and otherwise punishing students in this fashion. The students – who obviously lose out too because they fail to learn – are occupied by their own routine:

1. Getting up (to sharpen pencil, to throw something in wastebasket, to get paper from desk . . .)

108

2. Noise making (tapping foot, drumming desk, playing imaginary harmonica, banging teeth with pencil . . .)

3. Solitary escape (daydreaming, combing hair, pretending to do work, sleeping)

4. Forgetting or not having materials ("My mother tore it up by mistake")

Even at the best of times, the relationship between students and teacher is remarkable for its complexity and potential dangers. As already noted, many students, especially white, middle-class pupils, value ability and prefer to be seen as succeeding by reason of brilliance. But in a climate of scarcity, few students are consistent winners. And, at the worst of times, teachers face sullen, suspicious groups of students – an "absent audience," as Herbert Kohl (1967) describes them – or children who chatter away, oblivious to the pleas of the teacher. Such outcomes represent a breakdown in the teacher–student relationship.

SCARCITY OF REWARDS

The game is on again. . . . The winner takes it all. The loser has to fall.
>   Abba

Specifically, what is it about the competitive learning game that sets up these conflicts? Basically it is a *scarcity* of rewards such as approval, recognition, and personal satisfaction caused by the fact that in competitive climates those students who perform best are rewarded most. In fact, ironically enough, it is scarcity, the very factor thought by many to arouse student effort, that actually subverts it.

The devastating consequences of this competitive mentality have been demonstrated in a series of experimental laboratory studies conducted by Carole and Russell Ames (for a review, see Ames & Ames, 1984). These investigators observed elementary school students working in pairs on a common task (typically solving puzzles) under either a competitive condition (e.g., "the one who solves the most puzzles will be the winner") or a condition of individual goal setting (e.g., "solve as many puzzles as you can"). Under both conditions one student in each pair solved most of the puzzles (success) while the other student solved only a few (failure). This success–failure manipulation was accomplished by assigning students to work on puzzles that, unbeknownst to them, were either easily solvable or completely unsolvable.

When conditions of scarcity prevailed – that is, when only one player could win – failure was more likely to be interpreted by the loser as a matter of personal incompetency, while the loser's few successes were typically seen as the result of luck or good fortune. This pattern of attributions is reminiscent of that associated with failure-avoiding students, like John (Chapter 2). Also, when children succeeded competitively they were more likely to perceive themselves as smarter than their companion (adversary). As a result, the winners engaged in more self-praise at the expense of their failing competitor who was seen as less deserving. As to the losers, competitive failure created self-loathing, especially among those students who were high in self-perceived ability. This suggests that under competitive goals, individuals are likely to continue striving only for as long as they remain successful. No one wants to continue if the result is shame and self-recrimination.

School as an Ability Game

First and foremost, scarcity turns learning into an ability game. The fewer the rewards available, the more ability becomes a factor in attaining them. And the fewer the rewards, the more valued they become, too, because if only a few can win, then success becomes all the more convincing as evidence of high ability; conversely, if many succeed then, attributionally speaking, the task will be considered a relatively easy one, certainly not requiring any great talent. And if success becomes inflated in its importance, the meaning of failure likewise becomes distorted. Not surprisingly, in an ability game most students are unable to explain how failure might be useful in the process of learning (Covington & Beery, 1976). These children, it seems, rarely ascribe to Alexander Pope's observation that being

110

wrong is but another way of saying that the individual is wiser to-day than yesterday.

This reluctance to appreciate the value of mistakes goes deeper than simply not understanding that failure is an important part of all problem solving. In the minds of children, help seeking tacitly implies that one is stupid (Graham & Barker, 1990; Karabenick & Knapp, 1988). These youngsters have confused ignorance – that is, a temporary lack of knowledge, for which seeking help is one cure – and stupidity or being dumb, with the likelihood that they will remain both ignorant *and* stupid. Interestingly, help seeking as a cue for low ability seems especially strong when children are working for extrinsic payoffs like praise or a grade compared with those times when they are pursuing some independent line of inquiry for no other reason than to satisfy their curiosity (Nelson-Le Gall, 1985; Newman, 1990; Newman & Goldin, 1990).

Unidimensional Classrooms. All these sources of distortion are present in those classrooms defined by Susan Rosenholtz and her colleagues as *unidimensional* (Rosenholtz & Rosenholtz, 1981; Rosenholtz & Simpson, 1984). Unidimensional classrooms are those in which students perceive themselves as being segregated mainly by ability, with a specific emphasis on *verbal* ability as the single most important dimension compared to visual, artistic, or spatial ability. Such a narrow focus can lead to a great inequity in feelings of worth, beginning in the earliest grades. Susan Harter, a psychologist who studies social development in children, estimates that "by the second or third grade children know precisely where they stand on the 'smart' or 'dumb' continuum, and since most children at this age want to succeed in school, this knowledge profoundly affects their self-esteem" (quoted in Tobias, 1989, p. 57).

Rosenholtz argues that one of the main reasons for the drift toward unidimensional dynamics is the seemingly innocuous practice of assigning a single task to all students or of assigning students in the same class to different reading and math groups based on ability. Such within-class grouping invites students to think of ability in narrow, fixed terms and encourages the view that ability or a lack of ability is the dominant cause of success and failure, respectively (Rosenholtz & Wilson, 1980; Weinstein, 1981). By contrast, when students work individually on different tasks or participate in groups not necessarily defined by ability, then perceptions of ability become less salient to achievement. Another aspect of unidimensional dynamics involves the perceived boundary between academic and nonacademic work. Whenever this line becomes sharply contrasted and what counts as academic assignments narrows to only a few activities or skills, the likelihood of ability stratification increases. On the other hand, if students have some choice over what they learn, and when and how they learn it, the distinction between academic and nonacademic work will likely blur.

Ability stratification also affects the quality of classroom social relationships. Given its valued status, ability commands power and prestige far beyond academic matters (Botkin & Weinstein, 1987). For instance, good readers tend to be accorded positions of leadership in group decision making even when the problems under discussion are unrelated to reading (Morris, 1977; Stulac, 1975). As a result, many students experience feelings of powerlessness and isolation, and those who suffer from a low self-concept of ability are likely to rate themselves as lazy and mean, basically a moralistic, self-censoring reaction to school.

Ability Tracking. Another form of grouping – ability tracking – involves assigning students to whole classrooms on the basis of their ability or achievement scores. For example, an elementary school might have a high fifth grade, an average fifth grade, and a low fifth grade, while at the high school level students might be tracked into either vocational, general, and college preparatory courses. Although this is the most frequent kind of grouping in American schools – by one estimate 25 percent of all first-grade classrooms are tracked – there is no evidence that doing so accelerates student achievement compared with what one would expect from students in mixed-ability classrooms (for reviews, see Oakes, 1987, 1992; Slavin, 1987). Actually, if anything, ability tracking seems to accentuate initial differences among students with those youngsters placed in the top tracks excelling, partly because better teachers are attracted to these more able students, while lower-track students

112

fall progressively behind. Moreover, the evidence does not support the belief that slow students suffer emotional strains when enrolled in mixed-ability classes. Actually, just the opposite has been found. Rather than helping students feel better about themselves, the tracking process seems to foster unreasonable aspirations, lowered self-esteem, and negative attitudes toward school (Alexander & McDill, 1976).

Ability tracking also leads inevitably to a watered-down curriculum for those students in the lowest groups which often simply reflects the school's minimal expectations for these youngsters (Rosenbaum, 1980). When teachers expect little from students, they are usually not disappointed – the minimum is what they get. And, typically, because these students are in the lower track to begin with, teachers sometimes attribute their unresponsiveness to a lack of ability. This reaction is understandable. No one wants to accept responsibility for the failure of others. Teachers tend to take credit for their successful students, but are reluctant to shoulder the blame for mediocre ones (Felsenthal, 1970; Omelich, 1974). Better to attribute student failure to factors beyond one's ability to control, such as student indifference, idleness, and depravity.

Quite often, however, these explanations are without foundation. Take, for example, the experiences of those recent refugees from Central America described earlier in Chapter 2 (Suarez-Orozco, 1989). Far from being marginal students, many of these youngsters came to America with outstanding academic backgrounds, having excelled in schools that in some cases were superior to those in which they found themselves in America. Also, contrary to conventional wisdom, the parents of these children *do* care about education and often made considerable sacrifices to see that their children stayed in school. They saw America as giving their children a chance for advancement not available to them in their own homelands. But these parents were rarely consulted by schools because, according to Suarez-Orozco's convincing documentation, the school staff routinely presumed that these new arrivals lacked the intellectual potential necessary for college. Time and again, counselors saw their primary duty to enroll these Hispanic students in programs that would simply graduate them from high school with no thought of preparing them for college entrance. As one teacher, herself a Hispanic, told Suarez-Orozco, her primary job was to "housebreak the little immigrants who come down from the Central American mountains" (1989, p. 10). Another counselor dismissed a student's request for an advanced algebra course since he had already completed the beginning class back in Nicaragua by explaining that algebra in his country is "different from American algebra" (Suarez-Orozco, 1989, p. 5).

The expectation that few if any of these immigrants are "college material" is one form of inadvertent tracking, or, as Suarez-Orozco calls it, "gatekeeping." This process of segregation based on dubious ability rankings sets the stage for the phenomenon of self-fulfilling prophecies.

Self-Fulfilling Prophecy. The concept of self-fulfilling prophecy has been a powerful conceptual tool for understanding classroom achievement dynamics ever since Robert Rosenthal and Lenore Jacobson (1968) first attempted to demonstrate that the expectations teachers hold for their students influence the student's future performance. These researchers informed teachers at the beginning of the school year that several of their students had shown potential for considerable academic growth based on the results of a written examination. In actual fact, these students were selected randomly. By the end of the school term some of those students for whom teachers held artificially high expectations enjoyed significantly greater IQ gains than did other students in the same classrooms. These findings were said to demonstrate the operation of a self-fulfilling prophecy, which has been defined as a "false definition of a situation [telling teachers that selected students would improve] that evokes a new behavior [from teachers] which makes the original false conception come true" (Merton, 1949, p. 423).

In schools the process of self-fulfilling prophecy involves several steps. First, teachers anticipate that certain students will succeed in school, while others will not (as with the Hispanic examples just described). Second, these expectations invariably influence the ways teachers relate to students. For example, teachers spend less time with students whom they believe are less likely to succeed (Alling-ton, 1980). Not only are these interchanges fewer, but they are of dubious educational value. Investigators report a tendency among some teachers to supply answers impatiently to children of lesser ability, thereby depriving them of the chance to think through and formulate their own ideas (Brophy & Good, 1974; Brophy & Mc-Caslin, 1992; Rowe, 1972). Given this kind of treatment it is not surprising that students of whom little is expected, and little help given, will fall progressively behind and, in effect, complete the third step of the prophecy cycle – by acting in ways that fulfill the teacher's initial predictions of incompetency.

Ray Rist (1970) provides the classic example of how the dynamics of self-fulfilling prophecy can shape the lives of children, in this case a group of ghetto youngsters just entering kindergarten. Covington and Beery (1976) take up the story from its beginning:

After the first eight days of school, the kindergarten teacher identified the "fast" and "slow" learners in the group and assigned them to different work tables. Rist convincingly demonstrates that these placements were made not so much on the grounds of academic potential – no test scores were available to the teacher – but, in reality, according to social class differences within the group. Children who best fit the teacher's middle-class "ideal" (e.g., neat appearance, courteous manner, and a facility with Standard American English) were seated at Table 1, while everybody else was relegated to an inferior status. Predictably the teacher spent the majority of her time and energy on the students at Table 1. Just as predictably, this led to a lack of interest and restlessness at Tables 2 and 3, so that when the teacher *did* attend to these students, it usually took the form of reprimands for misconduct ("sit down"). From the lack of attention and teaching, these students made little or no progress, which further convinced the teacher of the correctness of her original judgment that these were indeed nonlearners. Sensing the teacher's low regard for these children, the students at Table 1 began to ridicule them ("I'm smarter than you"; "The answer is easy, stupid"). The youngsters at Tables 2 and 3 reacted by withdrawal, self-blame, and hostility directed within their own group. In effect, these children were internaliz-

115

ing what the students at Table 1 were saying about them. The label of "fast" and "slow" learner was reinforced throughout the kindergarten year, first by the teacher and then by the students themselves, so that when it came time for first grade, these labels, which were originally informal, took on an official character in the form of cumulative records. Acting on these evaluations, the first grade teacher assigned the children to *new* reading groups but in predictable ways. No child who had sat at Tables 2 or 3 in kindergarten was placed in the top group; conversely, with the exception of one student, no one from Table 1 was placed in the middle or low reading groups. Later, when these same students entered second grade, the names of the reading groups changed once again, but the pattern of placement remained virtually the same. (pp. 78–79)

Rist (1970) summarizes his three years of observation: "No matter how well a child in the lower reading groups might have read, he was destined to remain in the same reading group. This is, in a sense, another manifestation of the self-fulfilling prophecy in that a 'slow learner' had no option but to continue to be a slow learner, regardless of performance or potential. . . . the child's journey through the early grades of school at one reading level and in one social grouping appeared to be pre-ordained from the eighth day of kindergarten"(p. 435).

Rhona Weinstein and her colleagues (Brattesani, Weinstein, & Marshall, 1984; Weinstein, 1985; 1993) add fresh insights to Rist's earlier observations with research that focuses on those parts of the self-fulfilling cycle in which children evolve from bystanders to participants in the process. Besides the use of particular seating arrangements, teachers convey their expectations that some will succeed while others will not by means of behavioral cues to which most students are very well attuned. For example, children believe that when teachers expect a lot of a particular student, especially if he is a male and is also given special privileges, then he must be bright. On the other hand, those students who are subject to the greatest teacher surveillance, often males as well, and who receive fewer chances before being reprimanded are believed by other students to be among the least bright in class.

116

Twenty-five years have passed since Rist published his findings. One would hope that with the passage of time and with an increased sophistication among teachers that Rist's observations would be a thing of the past. Unfortunately, not always (R. S. Weinstein, personal communication 1996). Whole generations of new students continue to get the message that they are educational discards and untrainable. In fairness, most teachers are quite aware of the negative potential of self-fulfilling prophecies. Indeed, some teachers even attempt to compensate for any unconscious biases they might be harboring by deliberately lavishing greater praise on students of lesser ability whenever they succeed and by downplaying their failures (Fischer, 1982; Smits & Meyer, 1985). There is some evidence that this is especially true for teachers of minority students (Kleinfeld, 1972).

Ironically, however, praising students for success on relatively simple tasks – those that are more likely solved by children of lesser ability – and withholding blame for failure can actually convey the impression that teachers expect little academically from these youngsters (Graham, 1984a; Rustemeyer, 1984). This seeming paradox occurs because withholding comment in the case of failure suggests that the cause was not insufficient effort; otherwise the teacher would have reprimanded the student. Therefore, by the process of elimination, the cause must be low ability! This is the psychological basis for the so-called paradoxical effect of praise and blame. These compensatory efforts by the teacher may fail for other reasons as well. Although teachers praise hard work, effort alone may not be sufficiently rewarding for the failure-prone student who is just as likely to judge himself or herself inadequate when measured by the stringent, competitive standards of the peer group. When such discrepant evaluations occur, teacher praise is unlikely to increase student self-confidence (Covington & Beery, 1976).

At times it must seem to teachers that they cannot win, no matter what they do to help students. Once again, however, it must be noted that things often go badly because, in a competitive climate, the efforts of teachers to help may be interpreted incorrectly by students. The paradoxical effect of praise and blame is proof of this.

Learning to Lose

A scarcity of rewards also fuels unrealistic aspirations. Once students realize that the prevailing standards of excellence are set by the performance of top students, many lose control over their own learning, and instead must scramble to keep pace with ever accelerating demands that grow increasingly beyond their reach. In effect, scarcity causes a collapse of those self-protective mechanisms originally described by Ferdinand Hoppe (Chapter 2). In the face of scarcity, students are no longer free to lower their sights after failure, as they were in Hoppe's ring-toss game, or to adjust their aspirations in ways that balance the likelihood of succeeding equally against the chances of not succeeding. The true insidiousness of this inflexibility is revealed by the fact that a pattern of "atypical shifts" is encouraged (Diggory, 1966). Atypical shift refers to the fact that sometimes students *raise* rather than *lower* their expectations after failure. Although this phenomenon is rare – hence the term "atypical" – it is actually quite adaptive in the circumstance. For one thing, there are serious sanctions against ever lowering one's aspirations, even in failure; in effect, no one likes a loser, especially those who back away from a challenge. For another thing, the mere statement of a worthy goal, unattainable as it may be, can become a source of personal gratification.

Albert Bandura and his colleagues have studied the consequences of young children resolutely conforming to inappropriate goals (Bandura, 1971; Bandura, Grusec, & Menlove, 1967; Bandura & Kupers, 1964). In the typical experiment children watched adult models playing games of skill, including bowling in a miniature bowling alley. Whenever these adults did better than their publicly stated goals, they rewarded themselves generously with freely available toys and candy. But whenever they fell short – a deliberate part of the experimental design – the adults denied themselves these same rewards. After watching these proceedings, the young observers were then given a chance to play. Their behavior is troubling for several reasons.

First, these youngsters imposed upon themselves essentially the same standards they observed in the adult models, although the expectations could be so stringent that even the adults had difficulty achieving them. Second, the children clung rigidly to these inappropriate standards even after repeated failure. Third, once having adopted these self-defeating standards, children who rewarded themselves sparingly, if at all, transmitted these same unrealistic expectations to other children who had no part in the original experiment (Mischel & Liebert, 1966). Fourth, these unforgiving standards took on an existence of their own. These young subjects continued to punish themselves, days and even weeks later, for otherwise perfectly adequate performances and in the absence of the original cause, namely, the implied social pressure of an adult authority.

What is especially disturbing is the apparent ease with which these grievous dynamics can be established. Children, it appears, are especially vulnerable because they have little basis on which to make realistic judgments about their own capacity relative to the demands of the task. They rely heavily on adults to make these judgments for them, and, to make matters worse, they are subject to various kinds of magical thinking. All too often children believe that what they *want* to happen (getting a good grade) *will* happen, no matter how poorly they might have performed in the past.

If such self-destructive behavior can be initiated so quickly and easily in laboratory settings and sustained indefinitely, how much more dismal the prospects are for youngsters in regular classrooms where a whole host of factors continues to promote inappropriate standards relentlessly, year after year, including teacher preferences for superior achievement and the tendency for students to model themselves after other high-status pupils.

Little wonder that many children hold unrealistically high achievement expectations for themselves – unrealistic when compared with their actual records of past accomplishments. For instance, Esther Battle (1966) found that junior high school students usually set their *minimum* achievement standards (the lowest grade they could receive and still feel satisfied) higher than the grades they actually expected to get! It is likely that these unrealistic aspirations are partly the product of wishful thinking caused by an intense desire for acceptance and respectability (Sears, 1940).

119

Battle's research also indicated that such irrational goal setting is found among youngsters at all ability levels. Students tend to associate with other pupils of like ability and achievement. Within the context of their own particular group, even bright students can see themselves as relatively dull compared with their immediate peers. Moreover, when homogenous peer groups are artificially created, as in the case of ability grouping and tracking, the evidence indicates that students of lesser ability tend to hold themselves to standards of performance exhibited by pupils in more advanced, prestigious groups (Weinstein, 1976). As a consequence, these aspirations remain unfulfilled and frustration leads to deteriorating performance (Reuman, 1988). And, what is worse, teachers often mistakenly praise unrealistic aspirations as evidence of a student's willingness to try hard, and thereby unwittingly reinforce goals that are destined to be disappointed.

In sum, all the arguments marshaled so far suggest that achievement itself is the first casualty when students compete for diminishing rewards. Granted, scarcity may set students to scrambling at least for a time and especially among those who believe they have a chance to win. But in their scramble most students do virtually everything *except* learn in their attempts to avoid having fewer points than others. The futility of this dynamic is driven home by Alfie Kohn (1986): "How can we do our best when we are spending our energies trying to make others lose – and fear that they will make us lose?" (p. 9).

This is not to suggest that performance always suffers in the face of competition. Actually, when tasks are simple and mechanical or highly repetitive, as in the case of canceling letters in the alphabet as quickly as possible, then performance is promoted by offering prizes to the fastest workers (de Charms, 1957; Shaw, 1958). However, this competitive edge quickly disappears when the task requires that students come up with the best ideas for solving novel or complex problems of the kind found in human relations and conflict management issues (Deutsch, 1949).

It must be especially galling to advocates of competition to find that competitive rewards are most effective in situations that are of the least importance educationally. The advantage favoring cooperation over competition occurs because individuals, when they compete to solve complex problems, are less willing to share information (Miller & Hamblin, 1963) and may even try to hinder others (Shaw, 1958). On the other hand, when students cooperate they are less prone to make errors precisely because they do share information and act as vigilant monitors. When working toward a common goal, it is in the interest of everyone to correct errors. But when one is competing, it is best not to draw attention to the mistakes of others, at least not until it is too late. Not surprisingly, then, cooperating individuals feel less hostile than do competing individuals, show greater personal concern for one another, and even express greater interest in the task at hand (Raven & Eachus, 1963).

Rewards as Motivator

One final criticism can be leveled against competition as a means to promote learning. Competition threatens intrinsic task involvement. This is scarcely surprising. Whenever students are preoccupied with trying to make others lose, for fear that they themselves will lose, the joy of learning quickly dies. It is not only the economics of scarcity that is at fault here. The problem is also the *kinds* of rewards teachers often use and their *role* in competitive dynamics. First, competitive rewards tend to be tangible and extraneous – gold stars, stickers, and grades – extraneous in that they are unrelated to the process of learning itself. Second, as to their role, competitive rewards are seen by many educators as providing the major motive power for achievement. This is part of the myth of intensification: if we can only provide the right rewards and enough of them, so the argument goes, then we can arouse (drive) otherwise passive students.

Overjustification Effect. Rewarding individuals unnecessarily for doing something they already enjoy may undermine their interest in the task. This is said to happen because an already justifiable activity becomes suspect by the promise of additional rewards –

121

hence the term "overjustification," so that, in effect, the individual reasons, if someone has to pay me to do this, then it must not be worth doing for its own sake.

This phenomenon was first noted by Mark Lepper, David Greene, and Richard Nisbett (1973). These investigators found that a group of nursery school children who were rewarded extrinsically (given a "good player award") for drawing pictures – an activity they had previously enjoyed without rewards – were less likely to draw later during free play time compared with a group of youngsters who had not been rewarded for drawing.

Bribing or paying individuals to perform creates an extrinsic set that discourages intrinsic involvement. These detrimental effects take many forms, all of which cut directly at the heart of the educational mission. For instance, offering tangible rewards as inducements to learn causes students to select easier assignments over more challenging ones (Harter, 1974). Also, students are less persistent in their studies (Fincham & Cain, 1986) and less creative and flexible in their problem-solving efforts (Amabile, 1979, 1982). Additionally, students appear more willing simply to "guess" at correct answers (Condry & Chambers, 1978) and are less likely to remember information learned earlier (Grolnick & Ryan, 1986). Poor recall likely occurs because extrinsic rewards tend to distract the individual's attention during learning.

But, perhaps most troublesome of all, from the longer motivational perspective, is the fact that the preference for easier assignments just mentioned generalizes so that later, when tangible inducements are no longer available, students show no renewed interest in more challenging problems. Equally alarming is the fact that children who adopt an extrinsic mentality take on many of the characteristics we have associated with learned helplessness. They come to doubt their ability to complete the very kinds of assignments that they undertook successfully for rewards just a short time before (Boggiano, Main, & Katz, 1988). Also, they may believe that powerful others control their academic destiny (Boggiano, Harackiewicz, Bessette, & Main, 1985). This makes sense when we realize that the availability of extrinsic rewards often depends on factors that lie outside the control of students and may be quite unpredictable and quixotic, such as the teacher's mood. Yet despite this unstable source of rewards, or perhaps because of it, externally oriented children become more rather than less dependent on teacher opinion about how to approach schoolwork.

Behind this complex pattern of deterioration lies a single process. When students are offered rewards for good behavior and adequate schoolwork, they become expedient (Pittman, Boggiano, & Ruble, 1983). They attempt to maximize rewards for a minimum of effort, a work orientation referred to as the "mini–max" principle (Kruglanski, 1978). Learning becomes the way to obtain a reward, not a way to satisfy one's curiosity or to discover something of interest. The "mini–max" dictum may make a certain amount of economic sense in other contexts. Why spend more time at a task than is necessary? In school, however, coming to rely on extrinsic rewards creates impatience at best, and at worst induces instability in one's expectations, self-doubt, and eventual dependence on the judgment of others.

Grading Policy. These observations provide an important perspective on grading policy, and on how grades affect the reasons students learn, for good and ill. Grades are frequently defended on the grounds that they, like other tangible incentives, motivate complex learning, even though the evidence is solidly against this proposition. But still, should not grades make a difference in how hard students try? If they do not, we should find out; and we should also know *why* not. Some of the best evidence on this issue comes from the classic study by Louis Goldberg (1965) who attempted to alter student test performance by manipulating grading policy. One group of college students was graded severely – with only a few high grades awarded – on the theory that the group would be aroused, or driven, to try harder on the next exam. A second group was graded leniently on the theory that positive reinforcement would best motivate future achievement. Finally, for the third group, Goldberg gave a disproportionate number of A's and F's thereby creating a discrepancy for many students between the grade they expected and what they actually received. Presumably those students who did unexpectedly well would work harder to keep their high grade. Likewise, those students who were surprised by a poor grade would also work hard but, in their case, to improve.

Actually, no differences were found in average test outcomes among the three groups; neither did the performances of these groups differ from that of a fourth, control group, which was simply graded on a "normal" curve. Although we know that a specific grade given to a particular student can influence his or her subsequent achievement, sometimes dramatically, there is no guarantee that blanket, institutionalized grading policies of the kind featured in Goldberg's research will affect all students in similar ways. One reason is that grades motivate students differently. This much is clear from our earlier attributional analysis of success and failure experiences (Chapter 3). Recall that success-oriented individuals are driven to do better following failure because they attribute it to factors under their control. In contrast, failure-oriented persons are demoralized by failure because they feel inadequate to correct the situation. Similarly, an unexpected high grade – like some of those administered by Goldberg – may be met by failure-oriented students with disbelief because they may feel themselves incapable of achieving such a mark. In effect, and ironically, good grades tend to motivate those who need motivating the least, and further discourage those who need motivating the most. No wonder that the effects of a single, uniform grading policy on individual students is so unpredictable and, for some, may even be counterproductive. This includes not only poorer students but successful ones as well. For example, Ruth Butler (1988) has shown that a narrow preoccupation with grades can interfere with the kinds of higher-order thinking often associated with students of superior intellect.

In sum, grades, especially those that are distributed on a competitive basis, are apt to motivate marginal students but for the wrong reasons, and only temporarily, by arousing the threat of failing. At the same time, such grades foreclose the most able students from using their capacities to the fullest. And, tragically, the more students resist learning the more grades are justified by educators as a necessary, often last-ditch way to motivate the unruly and the uncontrollable. It is in this sense that teachers refer somewhat apologetically to grades as a "necessary evil." The threat of a poor grade is thought of as a weapon to overcome apathy. But we know better. Indifference is already a motivated behavior. Therefore, when students compete for limited rewards, grading will likely intensify avoidant behaviors, not reduce them, and in the process exaggerate the value of ability as a source of worth.

If there is so much wrong with extrinsic inducements, and in particular with grades, how can schools operate constructively within a wider, reward-driven world in which, "If you sell enough items, then you will receive a commission; if you succeed on the GRE, then you will be admitted to graduate school; if you publish enough research, then you will receive tenure" (Boggiano & Pittman, 1992). Fortunately, not everything about rewards is negative; they disrupt learning and inhibit creativity largely when they become scarce commodities in an ability game (Pittman & Boggiano, 1992). However, when properly employed, extrinsic rewards become part of the solution to school reform, not part of the problem, as we will see in Chapter 6.

COMPETITION AND MINORITIES

Many minority students and disadvantaged white youngsters are put at special risk whenever pupils are stratified and rewarded according to their perceived ability level. In our zeal to magnify differences among students rather than to seek out the common ground shared by all in matters of curiosity, enthusiasm and creativity, we unwittingly turn scores on achievement tests into self-fulfilling prophecies that favor some and damn others. Little wonder that many students quickly get the message that they are educational discards, untrainable, and, worst of all, unworthy.

The inevitable result of this sorting process is the "warehousing of children," a thoroughly distasteful but sadly accurate phrase. Warehouses are places to store goods – lumber, pork bellies, and machine parts – temporarily for safekeeping until they are needed in the future. But when children become goods, things to be shelved, isolated, and rendered inert, they are saved only from learning, cut off from proper intellectual development. As a result, they will never be ready in time for the future. In the circumstance, schooling becomes a vast bureaucratic maw into which countless children simply disappear without a trace, appearing only in record books as ciphers. Anonymity becomes a way of life. The individual student is too often forgotten; as it was poignantly expressed by one young black, "somebody is in charge of everything at the regular high school – attendance, schedules, lunch. But nobody is in charge of caring" (Epstein 1989, p. 36). In short, a vast underclass of children have become damaged goods generation after generation, increasingly held down against their will and increasingly disenfranchised.

For many disadvantaged students, school is an endless daily cycling through crowded, decaying classrooms managed by overburdened teachers who serve up listless, make-work assignments with little or no hope that these youngsters will even catch up and escape an adult life limited to dead-end, marginal jobs. These students are rarely exposed to what has been called "high-status knowledge" (Tobias, 1989), the kind of knowledge that might be useful in college such as reasoning and decision-making skills (Davis, 1986; Trimble & Sinclair, 1986). Instead, according to Jeannie Oakes (1985), a researcher concerned with classroom inequality, low-track classrooms typically focus year after year on basic arithmetic facts and rarely, if ever, move beyond simple measurement skills, such as converting English measures to metric. This kind of functional literacy is not functional at all. It provides students with neither relevance nor rigor. No one would deny the need for such arithmetic skills, not as ends in themselves, however, but rather as stepping-stones. But these youngsters are destined simply to repeat the steps, with little forward progress. In the absence of at least some formal academic training worthy of the name, tracking formalizes a caste-like system, engenders ethnic and class humiliation, and leads to questions about what schools can do to improve the lives of its clients.

The seeds of doubt and failure begin remarkably early and often innocently enough – triggered, for example, by the mere fact that simple number concepts may remain a mystery for a second-grader. This youngster is likely to be judged "backward," a bureau-

126

cratic label that will probably stick as demonstrated earlier by the dynamics of self-fulfilling prophecy. This label is profoundly unfair and wasteful of human talent, a predictable consequence of the widely held view among students that it is ability, not effort, that counts the most. And, as we know, ability status counts for more and more in the minds of children as they grow older, magnified by competition, by the demise of intrinsic task-involvement, and by the fact that more and more course work is grouped by ability. As Oakes (1985) points out, by the ninth grade, 80 to 90 percent of all students are in separate classes determined by whether they are judged to be "fast," "average," or "slow."

So far we have described the problems faced by many minority children who continue to endure the noxious gauntlet of competitive sorting year after year. But what of those students who drop out along the way, before high school graduation – by some estimates, up to 60 percent of all inner-city youngsters? There are many reasons for this exodus. Some students drop out simply for having no good reason to continue or because they are intellectually marginal. But dropouts are not necessarily the poorest students. In fact, the Houston school district, the fourth largest in the United States, has reported that 25 percent of all its dropouts scored above the 75th percentile on standardized reading and mathematics tests (Maugh, 1987).

Why do such promising individuals quit? Kathryn Epstein (1989) conducted extensive interviews with some twenty high school dropouts from inner-city neighborhoods in Oakland, California – youngsters who subsequently returned to alternative schools to complete their degrees and then, in many instances, began college. The reasons given for having dropped out originally are surprising. Such factors as economic hardship and family problems were rarely mentioned. Feeling unfairly treated in school and saddled with a sense of boredom were far more frequently cited. Raymond, a gifted black student, captures perfectly the essence of such complaints. Although he eventually completed several years of college, he refused to sit through his high school classes because, he said, "Nothing happens. It is totally pointless for me to be there" (Epstein, p. 39). A lack of caring and anger at being treated as a nameless cipher also figured prominently in the complaints of Epstein's youngsters. Another black informant put it this way:

> I was invisible, man. I knew it. I sat in those schools for two years. I sat in the back of the room and did nothing. I didn't speak to anyone and no one spoke to me. Nobody said, "Do your work" or nothing. Then one day I said it, "Man, I'm invisible here." I got up and walked out the door and I never went back. (Epstein, p. 1)

Although it is true that Epstein's interviewees were creating their own interpretation of events, and perhaps putting the best face on failure, still there is little here to support the traditional view of dropouts as incorrigible or marginal. It appears that dropping out for many students represents the failure of schools as institutions, and not simply the failure of families to provide encouragement, or of economic dislocation or of personal upheaval, including pregnancy or illness. In one recent nationwide survey of some fifty thousand high school students, the only major reason for dropping out that came close to reflecting personal circumstances was that of being offered a job (Jones, 1982).

Yet, in fairness to schools, the dynamics of self-fulfilling prophecy are subtle and difficult to combat once they are set in motion. Everything students do – or do *not* do, such as refusing to participate in class or ignoring homework assignments – simply reinforces the teacher's view that they are, indeed, unprepared, antagonistic, and marginal; and often teachers are right. But the conditions that create such underpreparation and anger in the first place are not right.

CONCLUSION

It has long been believed that the use of competition – in modest amounts to be sure, that is, *healthy competition* – guarantees the highest average performance for the group by maximizing the output of each individual member. Actually, as we now know, the facts do not support this contention. The notion of "healthy competition" is a contradiction in terms and cannot be justified, educationally, if it is meant to imply that competition in small, carefully administered doses will increase school performance. The evidence simply does not encourage such distinctions by degree. The introduction of competitive incentives, in any form or amount, produces a decrease, not an increase, in school achievement, at least among complex, meaningful assignments. And we have seen why. When students are busy avoiding failure, there is little to encourage true task involvement. So much for the argument, introduced at the beginning of this chapter, that competition enhances academic productivity. In reality, it is the presence of competition, not its absence, that threatens school achievement, and at all ability levels.

Likewise, the claim that achieving under adversity (competition) builds character is flatly contradicted by the evidence. In the process of scrambling, children learn that the purpose of school is to avoid losing – or, worse yet, to make others lose. Children quickly learn to cheat, lie, and become saboteurs. They band together, not for the purpose of learning, but in temporary alliances to keep others from winning or to avenge themselves for imaginary injustices. Where is the nobility of purpose here? Far from building character, it appears that competition in schools contributes to a breakdown of personal integrity and encourages a mentality that favors ganging and fractious rivalries.

Even among the winners, the psychological casualty rate is prohibitive, whether it be reflected in the young, upward-striving entrepreneur who sacrifices the joy of discovery for the sake of conformity, or the gifted child who amasses an enviable academic record as a way to offset persistent self-doubts about her worth, doubts that linger nonetheless. Also, the rewards of competitive success are often tarnished by the realization that one's pride is based on the ignoble sentiment of being better or more deserving than others. In effect, winning tends to breed feelings of guilt for having denied others success.

We have implicated a scarcity of meaningful rewards as a major cause of the current educational crisis. But to indict only the most blatant mechanisms of competition and scarcity such as grading on a curve or grouping by ability is to miss the larger point. Competition is more than a dubious way to arouse children to learn. Competition is also an ethos, a world view that determines the rules by which people relate to each other – in this case, rules that set person against person and discourage cooperation. Many beliefs and practices form this vanguard of competitive rivalry in schools, not the least being America's preoccupation with the sorting of children by ability, and the uncritical acceptance of motives as drives (inner states to be manipulated and aroused at will by others) and our tolerance of testing procedures that short-change children through the dynamics of self-fulfilling prophecy.

Thus not only must a specific set of practices be changed but also a broader philosophy as well. This extraordinary challenge is made even more difficult by the fact that not all of what has been criticized here is necessarily wrong. Consider, for example, the need to take account of ability. There can be no denying that ability is a major source of individual differences among learners, a reality that must never be forgotten by teachers. Indeed, as we know, the key to motivating students properly depends on providing instruction that is neither too easy nor too difficult for each individual (Chapter 2). Such fine-tuning requires that teachers know as much about how their students differ as the ways in which they are alike. But ability grouping is not the preferred way to achieve this balance. Grouping by ability comes to grief, not because the goal of providing instruction according to student readiness to learn is pedagogically unsound, but rather because when grouping is employed in a competitive atmosphere *differences* invariably become equated with *deficits*. We must seek ways to celebrate and encourage the special qualities of each student, while recognizing the fact that ability differences are, after all, part of that uniqueness.

Basically, this approach means encouraging beliefs about ability that empower students, not constrain them unduly. Suggestions made earlier for ways to halt the drift toward unidimensional classrooms are a case in point. However, the purpose of permitting students some choice over *what* they learn, and *how* and *when* they learn, and to participate in groups not always defined by ability is not to halt the formation of ability estimates among children. Children will inevitably compare themselves no matter what teachers do. Rather, the true purpose is to broaden student beliefs about the multidimensional nature of ability – including reasoning and visual and intuitive skills – and to increase an appreciation of the various ways that differing patterns of ability can be brought to bear on different problems. By recognizing that there are as many approaches to a task as there are problem solvers, perhaps a unidimensional view of ability and the social stratification that follows can be moderated. Whether these hopes are realistic is a question to be taken up in the remaining chapters.

We have now completed our analysis of the motivational roots of the classroom crisis in America, thanks largely to the theme of motives-as-drives. In the next chapter we begin considering recommendations for change that call for a different motivational metaphor. In preparing for this step, it is useful to ask once again if competition is not after all an unavoidable fact of life, or even basic to human nature. Is it in the nature of individuals to seek out inequality? Whatever the answer to this age-old question, one thing seems quite clear. Changing the way people behave will depend on more than simply exhorting them to exercise reason, cooperate, and act in good faith. Aggressive, authoritarian, and rebellious behavior is virtually assured in situations of inequality. Changing such behavior requires that we change the system in which the behavior occurs. R. Garry Shirts (1969) believes that "it would be possible to take a group of individuals [competing for insufficient rewards] and put them in a social system that rewards openness, honesty, warmth and tenderness and have them act entirely different; not because they are any better or worse as individuals but because they are operating in a different social system" (p. 19). What kinds of reward systems might these be, and if there are no losers, would it still be worth playing?

SUMMING UP

1. Every classroom reflects some kind of reward system that conveys information about what students must do if they hope to succeed.

2. These reward systems can be likened to a learning game. Some learning games are competitive in nature, which means there is an inadequate supply of rewards (e.g., good grades) that are distributed unequally, with the greatest number of rewards going to the best performers.

3. When rewards are scarce, learning is turned into an ability game. The fewer the rewards available, the more ability becomes a factor in attaining them.

4. In an ability game, children are busy trying to avoid losing or making others lose. As a result, competition contributes to a breakdown of personal integrity. Competition also threatens to destroy the love of learning.

5. An ability game encourages the expectation that some students are incapable of learning. Students from whom little is expected, and to whom little help is given, fall progressively behind and, in effect, fulfill initial predictions of incompetency.

6. The inevitable result of an ability game is that schools become a vast bureaucracy into which countless children essentially disappear without a trace, especially minorities, the underprivileged, the poor, and the disenfranchised. Many of these students are never exposed to the kinds of knowledge and skills necessary for a life beyond that of the barest minimum for survival.

ACTIVITIES
Activity 1: Revisiting Hoppe

Demonstrate how competition can affect an individual's achievement for the worse by repeating Ferdinand Hoppe's ring-toss game (see Activity 1 in Chapter 2). This time, however, instead of encouraging individuals to set their own goals, require these new players to compete with one another by announcing that "The player who gets the highest score will be the winner." Rotate turns among players with each player allowed one trial of five tosses, then on to the next player, and so on, until everyone has had four or five trials.

Before you start (and even if you choose not to play), make a list of the kinds of player behaviors that might illustrate the negative effects of competition. Do any of these behaviors have counterparts in school? You may wish to consult Appendix G to complete your list.

Activity 2: Anxiety and Individualized Testing

As we know, students often believe that their worth as a person is reflected in how well they perform on tests, especially tests that are competitive in nature. Test taking in this situation can cause great anxiety, and anxiety blocks out what students know.

Ms. Jefferson, a junior high school geography teacher, hopes to diffuse the test-taking anxiety she has noticed among many of her students. But she is not sure how to develop tests that will tell her how well her students understand what she has taught them without arousing the very feelings (anxiety) that undercut the ability of her students to demonstrate their knowledge. Fortunately, we know from the research of Ferdinand Hoppe (Chapter 2) that students are likely to feel more sure of their knowledge, and therefore less anxious, when they are allowed to demonstrate what they know by choosing a level of challenge within the range of their current skills.

How might Ms. Jefferson take advantage of this principle to restructure the way she tests her students? By reviewing your responses to Activity 2 in Chapter 3, you will give yourself a head start toward answering this question. After you gather your own thoughts, you might also wish to consult the additional possibilities presented in Appendix H.

6

MOTIVATIONAL EQUITY
AND THE WILL TO LEARN

Be happy in your work.
Colonel Situ

IT WAS INEVITABLE THAT COLONEL SITU'S ADVICE (IN PIERRE Boulle's *The Bridge over the River Kwai*) would fail to move the British prisoners under his control. After all, the work in question involved building a railroad bridge that would advance Japan's cause in World War II, and to comply – happily or not – would mean collaborating with the enemy. As a result, Situ had few motivational cards to play. Yet he needed British help. At first Situ sought to persuade the prisoners by increasing their food ration. Then later, when these *positive inducements* failed, Situ applied the principle of *negative reinforcement*. By resuming work the prisoners could escape brutal beatings. Still British cooperation was only halfhearted and punctuated by numerous acts of sabotage.

Situ's frustration compellingly illustrates what we already know about achievement dynamics: the quality of one's effort, whether it be enthusiastic engagement, timid reluctance, or active resistance, depends largely on the reasons for performing. Clearly, defiance and anger are a poor basis on which to build anything, not bridges, and certainly not the future.

In the first five chapters we explored the consequences of using competition as a means to motivate students, thanks to the perspective provided by drive theory. In essence, we learned that competition arouses short-sighted, divisive reasons to learn, namely, to win over others and, when necessary, to avoid losing. Competing in schools for limited rewards in a climate of scarcity, like Situ's cunning use of food as a bribe, arouses little in the way of true enthusi-

134

asm. Students no longer focus on learning, but only on gold stars and grades. Likewise, avoiding failure and ridicule (or beatings, in the case of the British prisoners), like other forms of negative reinforcement, cannot sustain task involvement. A competitive, ability-stratified environment provides few prospects for being happy in one's work.

In the remaining chapters we will consider the possibilities for reducing the threat to school achievement posed by competitive incentives and by the wrongheaded policy of intensification that focuses on performance, not necessarily on learning. To do this we must now shift our attention away from the metaphor of motives as drives, or forces that impel action, and consider instead motives as goals – reasons that draw or inspire individuals to action.

The kinds of goals we must foster in school are intrinsic in nature, that is, involving the desire to become more effective as a person or to perform actions for their own sake. Recall the properties of intrinsic goals. First, because intrinsic reasons are their own reward, the psychic payoffs for learning are not limited to a few individuals, but are open to all. Second, when the individual is intrinsically motivated, learning becomes the means to an end, not an isolated event whose only purpose is to get the right answer or to please the teacher. Where education is concerned, things go better when intrinsic motives predominate.

For this reason, the remaining chapters belong to Colonel Nicholson, Situ's counterpart, the highest-ranking British officer in the jungle prison camp. What Situ was unable to accomplish by cunning and brutality, Nicholson achieved by appealing to a higher purpose. Nicholson gave the men under his command a reason for living: to create something worthwhile, even though he could offer them little in the way of tangible rewards. But we are getting slightly ahead of our story.

Before proceeding, we need to pause briefly and take stock. It is essential that we be clear about the likely causes of the current crises in education, at least those that can be deduced from a motivational perspective. Then, after having targeted the problem, we will

135

draw together the many lessons learned so far into a single set of guidelines for change.

THE PROBLEM

Nothing is more despicable than respect based on fear.
Albert Camus

We will proceed by the process of elimination. What then are *not* the likely causes of the widespread failure to learn in our schools?

First, and fundamentally, the problem does not appear to reside in the process of learning itself. Nowhere in our review have we found any evidence to suggest that the act of learning is inherently abrasive. It is only when the egotistic goals of self-aggrandizement and status seeking predominate that the learning process becomes threatening. This suggests that the problem of student indifference lies as much in the kinds of goals that society chooses for its children as in the means by which these goals are achieved.

Second, the root cause of the educational crisis is not poor school performance; inadequate achievement is merely a symptom. The causes go deeper to underlying motivational concerns. Indeed, the logic of our position argues that an exclusive concern with improved test scores not only overlooks the real problem, but is also largely irrelevant to the solution. Better academic performance should not be the primary objective we seek. Actually, academic gains are the by-product of attaining other more fundamental objectives. As we have seen, a preoccupation with performance – and its handmaiden, ability – tends to inhibit the very excellence we hope to promote. Increasing test scores alone will not ensure future excellence as long as the pupil's sense of worth is linked to succeeding competitively. The student may improve, but then so will others, and the competitive race will simply escalate. Ultimately, it is the value and meaning of what is learned – more particularly, the sense of satisfaction arising from enhanced understanding – rather than accumulating knowledge for the sake of power or prestige that will determine whether the will to learn is maintained. This is not to suggest that achievement is irrelevant. It is through one's accomplishments that self-confidence is nurtured. But it is equally true that confidence depends on the reasons why students learn. In effect, competency and confidence must prosper together – in tandem, and for the right reasons – if either is to advance. Otherwise, the will to learn will suffer.

Third, we must also be wary of attributing the problem of school failure simply to inadequate motivation. Characterizing indifferent students as unmotivated does not explain the problem. Based on the research presented so far, it seems more reasonable to conclude that the failure to achieve is as much the result of students being *overmotivated*, but for the wrong reasons, as it is of their not being motivated at all. By this logic, preferred solutions to indifference involve altering the reasons for learning rather than simply arousing students to greater effort as is implied by intensification policy.

Fourth, and finally, the collective failure of will does not derive from the fact that the quality of school achievement depends heavily on academic ability or on the fact that children compare abilities, even though some observers have pointed to the "tyranny of intelligence" as a major culprit. Some reformers would suggest that schools treat all students more alike – in effect, encouraging a uniformity of achievement outcomes – thereby creating a kind of egalitarianism that is thought to produce a shared sense of dignity among all learners. However, these proponents do not understand what we have come to discover, namely, that dignity is achieved through striving for excellence, not equivalency. Bringing the achievement of all students to the same level will only result in mediocrity and, in the process, destroy the spirit of individual initiative so crucial to high accomplishment.

With these comments in mind, what is the central cause of the widespread deterioration of school learning from a motivational perspective? And in what directions might effective solutions lie? Fundamentally, the failure to learn arises whenever the student's sense of worth becomes equated with the ability to achieve competitively. Students who anchor their sense of personal value in ability are placed at considerable risk because schools, like the rest of life, cannot guarantee an unbroken string of successes. If pride in success and shame in failure depend largely on self-perceptions of ability, then one's involvement in learning will continue only for as long as the individual continues to aggrandize his or her ability. But, once failure threatens one's image of competency, with its legacy of shame and anger, students will likely withdraw from learning and may even make it difficult for others to learn.

What part do schools play in forging this potentially destructive ability–worth link? Basically, as we have argued, this linkage is strengthened by school environments that magnify the importance of ability and, as a result, tend to limit the supply of meaningful rewards. When schools provide insufficient incentives for success, many – if not most – youngsters must shift their achievement goals. They must now struggle to avoid failure and its accompanying sense of worthlessness. As we have seen, in a competitive climate the supply of meaningful rewards shrinks largely because students come to judge the value of their accomplishments relative to the achievements of others. For example, even though Gloria merits high praise for a job well done, she may still not feel successful because her efforts are less polished or less complete than those of others. Such harsh, self-imposed standards push the possibilities for genuine pride further and further out of reach.

An important proposition emerges from this self-worth analysis. The structure of classroom learning, and the educational goals implied by a particular incentive system, control the amount, duration, and quality of student involvement in learning. If this argument is correct, then we should be able to change both the number of failures and their meaning by restructuring the "rules of the learning game," to use Alschuler's (1969, 1973) phrase. This observation reminds us of our earlier contention that preferred solutions to the educational crisis lie in the direction of altering the reasons (or goals) for learning rather than increasing motivation (drive) per se.

SOLUTIONS

Colonel Nicholson had the sort of faith which moves mountains, built pyramids, cathedrals, or even bridges, and makes dying men go to work with a smile on their lips. They succumbed to his appeal that they should pull their weight. They went down to the river without a murmur. With this fresh impetus, the bridge was soon finished.

Pierre Boulle, *The Bridge over the River Kwai*

It was a proper bridge, too, not a shoddy, makeshift affair, but an accomplishment worthy of civilized men working in squalid places. For the sake of pride, dignity, and the awe of creation, Colonel Nicholson's men toiled, suffered, and occasionally died. Yet, curiously, they remained indifferent to the blows and curses rained down on them by Colonel Situ. Free men and slaves differ in their reasons for working. Slaves perform merely to avoid punishment; and, at their best, free men aspire to the goals of honor and excellence.

Likewise, in schools it is the reasons for achieving that control not only the quality of one's learning but, of equal importance, the meaning of one's accomplishments for the continued will to learn. As we have seen, some goals are unworthy and disrupt learning: avoiding failure, aggrandizing ability status for the sake of power, and gaining favor at the expense of others. By contrast, other goals encourage those behaviors associated with task engagement and creativity. We must identify these intrinsic goals and systematically reinforce them: *mastery* – becoming the best one can be; *helping others* – or, as defined more broadly by John Nicholls (1984, 1989), a commitment to solving society's problems; and, lastly, the satisfaction of *curiosity*.

Such goals promote *motivational equity* – equity in that the satisfaction that comes from the struggle to achieve them are within the reach of all students, irrespective of background or ability. These sources of equity are denied students when excellence is defined competitively.

139

How do we encourage these egalitarian goals? What guidelines emerge from the research reviewed so far? Five broad generalizations suggest themselves.

1. Provide Engaging Assignments

Schools must provide the opportunity for intrinsic goals to emerge in the course of daily work. In effect, when possible schools must turn "work into play," recalling Mark Twain's distinction between *work*, "whatever a body is obliged to do," and *play*, "whatever a body is not obliged to do." What, then, are the characteristics of tasks that promote a sense of playful involvement and personal commitment? Thomas Malone (1981) suggests four characteristics: manageable challenges, authentic tasks, curiosity arousal, and fantasy arousal.

Manageable Challenges. Tasks are engaging to the degree they challenge the individual's present capacity, yet permit some control over the level of challenge faced. So far Hoppe's ring-toss experiment has served as our prototype (Chapter 2). But there are many everyday examples as well. The childhood game of tag readily comes to mind. Tag permits each participant to adjust the level of challenge to his or her own physical abilities by choosing whom one chases and by modifying the distances to stay away from whoever is "it" (Eifferman, 1974). Such subtle adjustments create drama and excitement, which is to say that the outcome of each round is left in doubt.

Authentic Tasks. School tasks are engaging to the extent that they are personally meaningful and interesting (Deci, 1992). When interest in an assignment is high, students perceive grades as a positive motivator, that is, as inspiring them to do their best work. By contrast, when these same students have little personal interest in an assignment, they tend to view grades as a way for teachers to force at least a minimum of effort (Covington & Wiedenhaupt, 1997). Personal relevance is greatest when students practice thinking in the same ways as do real-life practitioners in the context of what Jean

Lave (1988) refers to as "authentic activities." Authentic activities, like serious games, have their counterpart throughout the real world, especially in the crafts and trade occupations – cooking, woodworking, gardening, and weaving. When individuals learn to perform authentic tasks, they become apprentices and enter into the life and community of the practitioner. Even highly formal occupations, including medicine and the law, are taught largely through a process of apprenticeship. As John Sealy Brown and his colleagues point out (Brown, Collins, & Duguid, 1989), graduate students in the sciences and the humanities refine their research skills by apprenticing to senior researchers, who themselves are working on authentic problems that require the resolution of ill-defined issues and the clarification of controversy, as contrasted to those kinds of well-defined workbook exercises that make up so much of school life.

In school, students are most often treated as novices or, worse yet, as supplicants in the most passive, infantilized sense of that term, whereas by contrast the expert is a practitioner. But beginners need not wait to become practitioners, despite their fledgling conceptual knowledge. They only need enter into a community of apprentices. Obviously, passing history or mathematics tests is not the same thing as entering into the world of the historian or the mathematician.

Curiosity Arousal. Assignments are also inherently appealing to the extent they arouse and then satisfy curiosity. The arousal of curiosity depends on providing sufficient complexity so that outcomes are not always certain. Complexity that stimulates rather than overwhelms can be introduced by providing for the possibility of multiple goals that emerge within the same task as work proceeds (Csikszentmihalyi, 1975). This process is described wonderfully by James Diggory (1966):

> [But] once this exploration ends . . . [the student] tries to produce a result as good as the last one, but quicker. Next, he may disregard time altogether and try to improve the product. Later he may concentrate on the smoothness of the process and attempt to

swing elegantly through a well-ordered and efficient routine. He may discover and invent new processes or adapt new materials or new methods of work. (pp. 125–26)

It is the natural progression of goals described here that maximizes playful involvement. Assignments that feature emerging, multiple goals can be contrasted to tasks that are dominated by one constant, overweening purpose, that of winning over others, or tasks characterized by rigid, fixed conventions. These latter instances offer little incentive to take the risks associated with discovering and overcoming challenges; one is too busy worrying about who is ahead and who is behind.

Fantasy Arousal. Assignments are inherently captivating to the extent they elicit fantasy. Here fantasy does not mean merely unbridled wish fulfillment or fairy tales, but rather the creation of imaginary circumstances that permit the free and unfettered use of one's growing abilities. The child who uses books as a medium of passage into new worlds of his or her own creation is but one example of this phenomenon. Such fantasizing stimulates the child to read more and better, thus closing the circle between self-reverie and competency.

The larger point is that if educators are clever enough they should be able to arouse students to greater involvement, and for the best of reasons – for the sake of satisfying curiosity, for the stimulation of personally valued imagery, and for meeting manageable yet challenging goals.

2. Reward Positive Reasons for Learning

Once a teacher arranges school assignments in ways that stimulate intrinsic engagement, the next step is to reward such behavior directly, as often as it occurs, and for anyone. For example, this might mean paying students for expressing curiosity, perhaps by giving them grade credit or recognition for each question they think of whose answer cannot be found in the reading assignment, and giving further credit for indicating where the answer might be found;

or, additionally, in the case of scientific investigations, where not all inquiries have ready answers, giving credit for designing experiments to provide the necessary answers. Likewise, a mastery motive can be reinforced by giving credit for improvement.

Notice that by tying rewards to specific, well-defined actions, the economics of competitive scarcity can be reversed so that success is within the grasp of all students, not just a few. We have already seen by example several ways in which such equitable reward systems can be established. The first of these involves changing the basis on which success is defined. Recall how Richard de Charms allowed students a virtually limitless supply of self-generated successes in what otherwise would have been the epitome of competitive contests – the spelling bee (Activity 2 in Chapter 3). Here success came to depend more on the students selecting realistic performance goals within their reach than on the ability to spell or to outperform others.

A second approach is what we have referred to as a merit-based system (Chapter 2). Here success depends on each student satisfying the requirements of a task, irrespective of how many others may also succeed – an approach we likened to the merit-badge system employed by the Boy Scouts of America. Many, if not most, school tasks can be cast in absolute, merit-based terms, and have numerous counterparts in the outside world. For instance, there is the eager sixteen-year-old preparing to pass his driver's license test, and the insurance executive studying to pass an examination that will certify her as a life underwriter. In effect, any number of merit badges can be awarded or driving tests passed. The struggle now focuses on the obstacles imposed by the difficulty of the learning task itself, and on the various levels of excellence required, not on competing with others for diminishing rewards. Naturally, not everyone is capable of becoming a life underwriter, nor should everyone try; it doesn't make economic sense. But when it comes to schooling, it *does* make sense for *all* students to master as many of the basic lessons as possible.

But isn't there a potential problem here? Haven't we argued against the use of external reinforcers like points, gold stars, or grades, and for several reasons?

Plentiful Rewards. For one thing, if there are enough rewards to go around for everyone, will not the value of these plentiful rewards be degraded? Will not students work less hard to attain them, especially if the rewards are no longer clear evidence of one's ability status? Not necessarily. It is largely when rewards (e.g., grades) are dispensed on a competitive basis that their value depends on scarcity. When rewards are distributed on a self-defined or merit basis, then pride in accomplishment depends more on whether students have improved, how hard they worked, or whether their work measures up to the teacher's standards, no matter how many other students may also do well (Covington & Jacoby, 1973).

Mini–Max Principle Revisited. For another thing, the research reviewed in Chapter 5 suggests that when we pay students to perform, they will do only as much as necessary to win the prize and stop. Here, too, this danger is greatest when rewards are defined competitively. In contrast, when rewards are distributed for merit, and when learning, not performance, is the goal, the evidence suggests that eventually the experience of learning itself will acquire intrinsic properties (Ames & Archer, 1987a). This transformation from extrinsic to intrinsic control of learning is well illustrated by the findings of Harold Cohen and James Filipczak (1971) who worked with delinquent boys. Tokens were dispensed as rewards for completing homework assignments and could be "spent" in various ways, including the purchase of items from a mail-order catalog. In the beginning, the mail-order business was lively. But eventually, as their school performances increased, the boys became dissatisfied with material rewards. They began to purchase library time and paid rent on study cubicles. In effect, the boys were willing to pay for the privilege of studying.

These findings are all the more remarkable for the fact that these boys had a history of bad experiences around learning. The positive changes occurred because, initially, tangible rewards kept the boys involved long enough for the process of discovery and self-improvement to take on rewarding properties of its own. Moreover, when students learn that knowledge, in addition to its intrinsically satisfying properties, also has relevance for improving their lives, they will be motivated all the more. For example, the teacher who illustrates the importance of diagramming sentences as a gateway to more satisfying future activities – such as expressing one's ideas sufficiently well to win an argument, or poetically enough to win the girl – is taking clever advantage of an instrumental connection between knowledge and one's goals. This link might be lost on young students who would otherwise see no majesty, no larger purpose, but only tedium in school. In effect, rewards for learning must be arranged so that the act of acquiring knowledge itself becomes a conditioned reinforcer, to use the terminology of behavior modification. Money is a common conditioned reinforcer. Clearly money itself is no good to eat or drink, nor does it provide entertainment (unless one is a Midas). But money will buy these things, and that is the source of its reinforcing value. Students must be taught the lesson that knowledge, too, like money, buys things of value.

Overjustification Revisited. All this may be true, but what happens when teachers begin rewarding students for what they are already doing spontaneously without pay, such as browsing through the library on their own or expressing personal interest in a current event? According to the overjustification hypothesis (Chapter 5), will not paying students turn play into work and stifle creativity?

Actually, tangible rewards need not interfere with intrinsic task involvement, and may even enhance it (Eisenberger & Cameron, 1996). It all depends on how extrinsic rewards are used. For example, it is when they are used as *motivators* to arouse greater effort that intrinsic involvement is most imperiled. But when rewards are used as *information* about how well students are doing or signal that a different approach is needed, then feedback messages can themselves take on intrinsic properties. Moreover, such feedback need not always be positive to be effective. For example, Ruth Butler and Mordici Nisan (1986) provided a group of sixth-grade students with feedback describing one aspect of a task that they had performed well and another aspect performed less well (e.g., "You thought of many ideas, but not many *unusual* ones"). These students continued to express interest in the task and improve their performance over several work sessions compared with another group that received feedback designed simply to arouse effort level – actually, a numerical score indicating how well each student performed relative to others. The performance of this latter group deteriorated over time because, as the children later explained in poststudy interviews, they were worried about failure and were trying to avoid losing. Clearly, then, the context in which feedback is provided, as well as its purpose, is important to continued striving. When rewards smack of surveillance, of being compared with others, or if they imply manipulation and control, even if it is thought to be for the student's own good, youngsters – like adults – are likely to respond with anger, resentment and fear (Boggiano et al., 1988; Deci & Ryan, 1987).

Minimal Sufficiency. As we just noted, sometimes tangible rewards are needed to keep students involved long enough, especially in the early stages of learning, for the process of self-improvement to take on satisfying properties of its own. But extrinsic rewards should be used sparingly and withdrawn as soon as skills are adequately mastered. This realization has prompted Mark Lepper (1981) to propose the principle of "minimal sufficiency," that is, teachers should rely on extrinsic rewards only as absolutely necessary, and no more: the less powerful the extrinsic controls employed by teachers, the more likely students will be to internalize what they learn and apply it spontaneously without being prompted to do so.

3. Put Students in Control

Obviously, plentiful rewards by themselves are insufficient to sustain the will to learn. Students must also come to interpret their newly won successes as caused by their own skillful effort. Gaining a sense of personal control over events involves strengthening the belief that effort, not just ability, pays off. This is no simple proposition. As we know, expending effort represents a potential threat to those students caught up in a competitive mentality. By shifting the focus from competitive goals to equity goals, however, teachers can encourage plausible interpretations of failure other than low ability. For example, if students are allowed to choose tasks within their level of competency – as was the case in de Charms's spelling bee experiment or in Hoppe's earlier ring-toss research – then good self-judgment becomes the main reason for success, and failure occurs because of unrealistic aspirations, a cause of failure within the power of students to correct. For this reason learning need no longer be so aversive, nor effort feared.

These observations take on special meaning in the light of David Mettee's (1971) answer to the question of how the cycle of despair might be broken for failure-prone students who deny success and, on occasion, even sabotage their own efforts. Mettee proposed that such individuals might eventually accept total responsibility for their successes if they first started by taking only partial credit – just enough to engender some pride but not enough to arouse fear. According to Mettee, as individuals become more comfortable with success and the sense of pride it creates, they will assume more of the credit. However, our self-worth analysis suggests a different approach. Overcoming fear of success is not so much a matter of growing accustomed to feelings of pride, but of restructuring the meaning of success. Failure-prone individuals do not accept credit for their successes because they are afraid that they will be unable to repeat them later. But if these students exercise proper task analysis and set realistic goals, then success is repeatable. Hopefully, these students will not only accept credit for their successes – and not just partial credit – but will also become increasingly confident about their future chances.

4. Promote Positive Beliefs about Ability

According to self-worth theory, a preoccupation with ability status is the central, oppressive reality of much of school life and must be dealt with constructively if we are ever to promote the will to learn. This cannot be done simply by dismissing the importance of ability

147

or ignoring individual gifts. Far from minimizing the importance of ability, teachers must, in fact, actively promote implicit theories of ability, but theories that are conducive to sustained motivation.

The key is to view ability as a form of strategic planning (Covington, 1986; Resnick, 1987). Here the notion of a *static* capacity gives way to a more animated, *plastic* view of ability as a repertoire of skills that can be improved and expanded through instruction and experience – the so-called *incremental* perspective. As will be recalled, those students who embrace an incremental view of ability are more likely to focus on the task at hand, display greater involvement, and are less preoccupied with learning as a test of their worth compared with students who hold an entity view. It is this incremental view of intelligence that must be fostered in schools, again, not to discourage peer comparisons, which are inevitable anyway, but rather to strengthen student beliefs about the true, multidimensional, dynamic nature of human talent.

Doing this means providing students with evidence of their own intellectual growth through time. For example, mentorship programs in which older children tutor younger ones offer an excellent vehicle for gaining the proper perspective, especially if teachers encourage mentors to compare their own, presently more sophisticated understanding of school subjects with that of their young clients, who, like the mentors themselves in an earlier day, are now struggling to learn. The difference between the first halting efforts of the novice and later secure knowledge represents more than just differences in age; these differences are largely the product of accumulated knowledge used wisely. Demonstrating progressive intellectual growth need not involve only comparing oneself with others, as in the previous example. Students can also be encouraged to gauge self-improvement against their own past. Consider providing the proper perspective by means of a spiral lesson plan, spiral in that the same problem is reintroduced from time to time, say, every year or two, so that children can judge for themselves how much better and more sophisticated their reasoning is now than before, with the implication that the next time they meet the same problem, their present thinking will also appear naive by comparison. Just as children are fascinated by the physical changes they see in themselves as they leaf through the family photo album, so, too, by returning repeatedly to the same problem, they can develop an appreciation for their own mental growth and recognize that, although day-to-day intellectual gains are rarely obvious, they do accumulate and lead eventually to entirely new forms of thought and perspective.

5. Improve Teacher–Student Relations

We have pictured students and teachers as adversaries in the competitive learning game, a no-win situation in which both sides are likely to lose. The authority of teachers to control student achievement is severely limited, their only power being the power to cajole, reprimand, and punish; whereas students can only disrupt or avoid learning, not change the basic causes of their frustration and fear. Neither teachers nor students are to blame, but rather together they are caught up in a contest that neither can win, and teachers are helpless to change things so long as the dominant classroom incentive structure remains failure-oriented.

According to this analysis, by promoting a condition of motivational equity, the rules of the game will change so that power is shared by both teachers and students. Naturally, many teachers are wary of sharing power. As comedian Bill Cosby observes, "You don't defend yourself by leaning into the punch!" And, by analogy, you do not compound an already difficult teaching situation by putting more power in potentially irresponsible hands. Indeed, one of the major fears of both beginning and veteran teachers is that they may lose control of their classroom. Today this is no idle worry. What teachers need – many will tell you – is more, not less, power.

However, teachers can be reassured by the results of several studies that have sensitized teachers to the ways in which they and their students antagonize one another. For example, Alschuler (1975) and his colleagues trained the staff and student body of a large urban junior high school to analyze the disruptive dynamics of the "discipline game" (as portrayed in Chapter 5). This exercise eventually led to a mutual spirit of experimentation in which, class by class, individual teachers and their students set about establishing new rules so that teachers could teach more and students had more freedom to learn on their own. Most often such restructuring involved setting time aside – what Alschuler called "mutual agreed learning time" – during which teachers had their students' undivided attention. Similar restructuring, with equally positive results – this time among high school dropouts and migrant workers – has been reported by Arthur Pearl (see Silberman, 1970, p. 346).

As a group these five guidelines represent the essence of the paradigm shift in thinking about school learning and motivation of which we spoke earlier in Chapter 1. But what might these changes look like in practice with all these guidelines joined and operating together in harness? An example is needed.

GLOBAL GAMBIT

Speak to the earth, and it shall teach thee.
Job 12:8

A hush falls over Mr. Rodriguez's ninth-grade social science class as the first international conference on global warming is convened at Jefferson High. This conference marks the concluding phase of a month-long instructional unit called Global Gambit. Six teams of students, each representing a different nation at risk, are poised, eager to make the case for their particular needs in a world of limited resources and dubious prospects. This electric atmosphere has prevailed ever since Mr. Rodriguez first presented some of the possible consequences of global warming – the so-called "greenhouse" effect: whole cities, like London, drowned in rising oceans; droughts severe enough in Los Angeles to trigger riots when it became known that an old woman had been secretly watering an ivy plant in her home; and the prospects for a bumper cotton crop in Siberia, which has become the new agricultural land of plenty.

The object of the conference is to negotiate a plan to deal with these and other potential dislocations. Two broad strategies suggest themselves. First, each country (team) can prepare its own local defenses against the warming trend without regard for the ac-

tions of other countries. Second, all the countries can band together to seek broader, regional or worldwide solutions that may fore-
stall or even eliminate the need for local responses. Whatever plans
are devised, they must take into account the varying needs of the
six participating countries. Several of the countries, like Holland,
are peculiarly vulnerable to any rise in ocean levels and tide
surges. But Holland is highly industrialized and can better afford
the costs of preparing to meet this threat than can other equally en-
dangered but poorer countries. Consider Indonesia, for example,
which possesses 15 percent of the world's coastlines with about 40
percent of its land vulnerable to a sea-level rise of as little as half a
meter. Some experts project the rise to be as high as three meters
by the end of the twenty-first century!

Mr. Rodriguez warned his students in advance that their negotiations will be complicated by several factors. First, as just noted, the
threat of global warming and the resources available to withstand it
vary from country to country. To reflect this reality, Mr. Rodriguez
provides each team with different amounts of credit at the World
Bank. The richest countries receive the most credit because of their
proven ability to repay debt. Each team is free to create its own safeguards but within the limits of its resources, and different solutions
have different price tags. For example, one likely consequence of
warming is that the level of freshwater lakes will fall due to increased rates of evaporation. For the joint American–Canadian
team, the cost of dredging the Great Lakes shipping channels five
feet deeper is two hundred credits; dredging ten feet deeper costs
three hundred credits.

If an underdeveloped country is not rich enough to create all the
safeguards it believes necessary for survival, then it must negotiate
to borrow credits from the wealthier teams. But the industrial nations are unlikely to be willing lenders. This is the second complication. Global Gambit has another cross-cutting objective – a game
within a game. The industrial nations are placed in competition to
determine who becomes the world's leading economic power. The
winner of this minigame is the country that amasses the greatest
wealth by the end of game play. Yet the wealthy nations cannot entirely ignore the plight of their poorer neighbors because these

countries are most vulnerable to any rapid change in climate. Even small dislocations in weather patterns can lead to disproportionate increases in hunger, trigger mass migration, and encourage political unrest, factors that can easily threaten world stability and end game play prematurely.

A third complication is that even in scientific circles, nothing is entirely certain. There is always room for controversy and the margin of error in making predictions is often great. Mr. Rodriguez's students soon learn that, although there is general agreement that increases in global temperature are closely associated with rises in global carbon dioxide levels, such correlations are not necessarily evidence for causation. Moreover, even if all the teams agree that carbon dioxide buildup *causes* warming, it can still be argued that such a buildup is not always bad and may, in fact, compensate for some of its own negative effects. For example, although reductions in usable farmland are projected, some laboratory experiments suggest that carbon dioxide acts as a sort of fertilizer that accelerates the growth and size of plants, so perhaps less farmland will be needed after all. However, these findings can be debated – if Mr. Rodriguez's students are clever enough to draw certain conclusions from the graphs and charts he will provide them. Is it only the leaves and stems of the plants that get bigger, or the grain and fruit as well?

By presenting his students with a series of such debates, Mr. Rodriguez expects them to recognize the range of uncertainty that surrounds their choices, and hopes they will come up with what, according to many experts, is the key question regarding global warming (Schneider, 1989): how fast and how far will climate conditions change relative to the world's ability to cope? It is out of this array of unevenly distributed resources, uncertainty, and mixed motives – some favoring competition and others cooperation – that Mr. Rodriguez's students must hammer out a prudent plan for dealing with the potential crisis.

But there was much to do before the conference could begin. For starters each team had to familiarize itself with the country it represents – the particular geography involved, the economic base, and population density, all in order to assess their country's potential vulnerability to global warming. Mr. Rodriguez provided each team with a list of primary sources where the necessary information could be found. He also drew up a test covering the assigned material. Each student had to pass the test at a minimally acceptable level before his or her team could proceed. This requirement posed no particular problem for any of the teams, not because the questions were easy, but because passing the test became a matter of cooperative teamwork. Team members paired up and monitored one another's study, and anyone falling below the minimum on their first test try was permitted a second chance after additional peer tutoring. Things were also made easier, especially for test-anxious students, by Mr. Rodriguez's decision to allow unlimited time to answer the questions. As a further inducement, everyone scoring above the minimum had their surplus points converted into additional credits at the World Bank for their team.

But the real payoff for passing the test was the opportunity to work on several additional assignments that represented the final gateway to the negotiating table. One task was designed to acquaint students with the various consequences of global warming, some of which are economic, others political, and some medical. In this latter case, the Moroccan team was dismayed to find that increased temperatures in central Africa might spread encephalitis-bearing flies out of their current living range to adjacent territories that are presently free of the disease. Because of the enormity of this global search for consequences, Mr. Rodriguez proposed that the teams assign each of its members to become expert on specific topics with one student responsible for, say, surveying the possible effects of warming on agricultural production in his or her country and another for exploring the potential psychological impact on its citizens. After all these "experts" had done their homework, each team reconvened and combined these various knowledge sources in much the same way that pieces of a jigsaw puzzle are put together.

Although most students enjoyed these assignments, this was not true of Ralph, the *failure-accepting* student whom we first met in Chapter 2. Ralph was a constant source of disruption – handing in assignments late if at all, losing team notes, and always talking out of turn. Clearly, he was out to sabotage Global Gambit. Things were not helped by the fact that Ralph was the last person in class to be picked for a team – actually not picked as much as simply assigned by default as a booby prize to the group unlucky enough to have no choices left. Ralph's reputation as a troublemaker had preceded him from Mrs. Sorensen's room even before he was transferred last week in the hope that a male teacher might have more luck in providing a much needed source of authority and discipline in Ralph's life.

In order to minimize Ralph's disruptiveness, yet also provide him with some sense of accomplishment and discipline, Mr. Rodriguez decided to negotiate a series of learning contracts with Ralph. During their first meeting, Mr. Rodriguez gave Ralph some pages from a science text and asked him to choose one of the several experiments that demonstrates how acid rain is created. "Ralph, if you set up the experiment and give a demonstration to the whole class next Wednesday, I will give your team twenty extra credits at the World Bank," offered Mr. Rodriguez, "and five additional points if you follow the steps in the text exactly. How much is being careful worth to you?" Ralph looked startled. It had been a long time since anyone had asked his opinion.

Postmortem

The conference has just ended. An overall global plan was ratified, but barely. As Mr. Rodriguez had expected, the negotiations were often acrimonious, sometimes confused, but always engaging. Predictably, the wealthier nations spent much of their time maneuvering among themselves, seeking competitive advantage while often ignoring the proposals and needs of the poorer countries. But in the end, eight regional projects were funded to aid specific countries in addition to three larger projects involving worldwide cooperation including an unprecedented reforestation project in which Madagascar would be turned into a giant forest preserve to capture carbon from the atmosphere. And no country went bankrupt. This success was achieved because the classwide plan was based on the assumption that the effects of global warming, even if they were to prove substantial, would occur slowly so that additional adjustments could be made at five-year intervals.

"But was our solution OK?" demanded several students. They had a right to know, they pleaded, after all this work. They were being both serious and playful in their question. They were secretly pleased with themselves and intoxicated by the knowledge that Mr. Rodriguez was also delighted. At this point Mr. Rodriguez provided a final surprise. Unbeknownst to his students, Global Gambit had also been played by several atmospheric scientists. The scientists' solutions were accompanied by a detailed explanation of their reasoning at each step, the facts each weighed most heavily in making decisions, various sources of controversy, and how these controversies were settled, if at all.

Mr. Rodriguez's students spent the next few days in a lively postmortem, huddled together in their respective teams, poring over the scientists' reports – whispering, grumbling, and variously exclaiming, "*our* team knew this graph was important, but Argentina refused to see it," or, "so that's why our idea about plankton won't work." The scientists, too, came in for some withering criticism, especially when their reasoning differed substantially from that of the students. "After all," as one student was overhead to remark haughtily, "experts are only people from out of town."

In the end, most students felt comfortable with the probabilistic nature of their decisions, but others were still not sure. "What *really* is the answer?" someone asked. Mr. Rodriguez was about to dismiss the question, but suddenly stopped. He had long wondered how best to pursue the topic of the uncertainty of human knowledge, and to debate the proposition that even in science truth is often socially defined. Now he realized how best to spend the last two weeks of the spring term.

Postscript

In what ways does the Global Gambit scenario satisfy our instructional guidelines? And, is it a reasonable example of what is meant by a paradigm shift in the way we need now to think about schooling? Before taking up the first question, the answer to the second question is "yes, more or less," with the usual caveat that no single example can fully capture the larger concept it is meant to illustrate.

Still, it seems natural to ask if this is all there is? Is there really anything new in this example? No, not fundamentally. Virtually everything about Global Gambit is standard teaching practice. The popular "jigsaw" method of cooperative learning (Aronson, Blaney, Stephan, Sikes, & Snapp, 1978) is much in evidence, as is, of course, the use of educational games and the emphasis on using primary source material such as charts and maps. All these techniques are well known to teachers, even venerable. For instance, arguments favoring the use of primary source documents as the best way to stimulate children's thinking surfaced as long ago as the 1890s (Barnes, 1894).

Nor is there anything particularly novel with regard to educational philosophy. Clearly, this example embraces the philosophy of *reflective inquiry*, which was first promoted by John Dewey (1916), later articulated by Gordon Hullfish and Phillip Smith (1961), and most recently defended by Richard Pratte (1988). Reflective inquiry assumes that, for a society to remain open, there must be a free flow of information and an informed citizenry capable of evaluating it critically. Likewise, Global Gambit makes common cause with a *decision-making* approach to education (Engle & Ochoa, 1988), which assumes that informed choice stands at the heart of good citizenship. In short, there is nothing particularly new here either.

But no promises were made about desired changes being new, only that they should be workable and relatively easy to implement so long as they also satisfy the requirements of a motivational perspective. Thus in an important sense the purpose of this book is to elevate the commonplace to a new order of significance – in short, to help teachers recognize the profound in the ordinary. If this can be done, then familiarity becomes a hopeful sign, not grounds for contempt or dismissal, and for several reasons. First, a sense of the familiar tells us that what is needed is not only plausible but possible. Second, it suggests that many teachers are already on the right track; that they have been warm all along, but may not have always known it or always known why. This is why there is nothing as practical as a good theory! Good theories tell us how warm we are and how to get warmer still (see Activity 1 in Chapter 1).

So just what is so profound about the Global Gambit scenario from a motivational perspective? Basically, the answer is the difference between being *task-oriented* and being *ego-involved*. Mr. Rodriguez's students were more concerned with answers than with who thought of them; more excited by the challenge of the problem than worried about the risks of failure; and caught up, at least briefly, in an intellectual drama that demanded more of them than they may have thought themselves capable. Under the circumstances, time was no longer the property of Hermes – something to be sold, bought, or saved. It is this capacity for self-absorption that has been identified as the hallmark of the creative person (Barron, 1965). This transformation occurred for several reasons, each related to the instructional guidelines.

Inherently Interesting Problems. Mr. Rodriguez's overall assignment was highly engaging, not only because of its ghoulish appeal to adolescents – the imagined (fantasy) destruction of everything they are rebelling against anyway – but also because of its curiosity value, which depended largely on uncertainty and controversy. Moreover, by entrusting youngsters with a real, authentic problem that alarms us all, Mr. Rodriguez unlocked the supreme source of motivation for all human beings – being respected enough for one's counsel that others seek out our advice on urgent matters.

Motivational Equity. Now, more specifically, what positive reasons for learning did Mr. Rodriguez build into Global Gambit, and how did he reward them?

Mastery Learning. First, Mr. Rodriguez arranged the rules of the game so that the act of acquiring information itself became the payoff. For one thing, his students learned that knowledge creates opportunities. Remember that every student had to demonstrate a common, minimal level of mastery before his or her team could proceed with the negotiations. In this case, the reward for learning was the opportunity to apply what one had learned in a stimulating context of uncertainty and controversy. For another thing, Mr.

157

Rodriguez's students learned that knowledge buys power. Recall the built-in incentive for learning more than just the minimum amount of information – earning extra credit at the World Bank for one's team. Here the payoff for knowledge was the opportunity to extend game play, and to help one's team.

Incidentally, the testing procedures used by Mr. Rodriguez satisfied our guidelines in several additional ways. For one thing, success was defined in absolute, merit-based terms. Students knew in advance how well they must do in order to pass, and everyone was given sufficient opportunity to reach these minimum standards through extra practice, corrective feedback, and, when necessary, remedial assistance. In the case of Global Gambit, remedial help was provided to slower learners by those team members who satisfied the mastery requirements on the first try, a feature of "team-assisted instruction" (Slavin, 1983).

Another example of the mastery learning paradigm is *contingency contracting*, which Mr. Rodriguez used with Ralph. Here a teacher negotiates work contracts with students that involve a statement of what is to be done, when the task is to be finished, and the kinds of payoffs that are contingent upon completion of the contract (Atwood, Williams, & Long, 1974).

Contingency contracting further illustrates the potential motivational benefits of our guidelines. First, contract learning is essentially noncompetitive. Second, if properly negotiated, contracts create a match between the student's current skill levels and his or her aspirations, thus avoiding either the frustration of working beyond one's ability, or the boredom of being unchallenged. Third, clear expectations make learning more task-oriented (Helmke, 1988) and, as a result, less threatening to anxious, failure-avoiding students who would otherwise expect the worst in the absence of feedback and judge their performance as unacceptable (Butler & Nisan, 1986). Fourth, payoffs under a mastery system serve an *informational*, not an *arousal*, function. For instance, grades or credit become meaningful because each heralds a specific accomplishment – a study unit turned in on time or a term paper adequately completed, or, in Ralph's case, the experiment conducted exactly according to instructions. Moreover, when grades signal a disappointing performance in the context of a mastery goal, they carry direct implications for how to improve. Finally, contingency contracting in particular, and mastery learning in general, have the potential for making the teacher an ally of the student, where the emphasis is on accomplishment rather than on avoiding teacher disapproval (Knight, 1974).

Cooperative Learning. Mr. Rodriguez also encouraged a second source of motivational equity: cooperation for the sake of the team and for continued game play (Slavin, 1983, 1984). Mr. Rodriguez rewarded cooperation among nations by giving credit whenever teams took time to learn about the needs of competing countries, or when a wealthier team loaned economic credit to a poorer neighbor. Rewards were also plentiful for cooperating among players within a country, as when students tutored one another. Thus, when each team member passed Mr. Rodriguez's mastery test, then all those with whom the individual was cooperating likewise achieved the common goal, that of moving onto the negotiation stage of Global Gambit. These same cooperative dynamics also operated in the "jigsaw" example where each team member contributed to the group welfare by supplying specialized (expert) information about the consequences of global warming. Here, too, in this context cooperation allowed for a strengthening of students' beliefs about the multidimensional nature of ability, and recognition that there are as many different approaches to a task as there are problem solvers (Activity 2 in Chapter 4).

When properly used, cooperative learning equates the opportunity for everyone to feel successful both as individuals and as members of a group so long as each person maximizes his or her effort and shares in the risks of failure (Harris & Covington, 1989). Ultimately, the individual's accomplishments take on meaning because they add to the welfare of the group and promote a sense of belonging (Cooper, Johnson, Johnson, & Wilderson, 1980).

Altering the Meaning of Success and Failure. When rewards are scarce, failure takes on an exaggerated presence owing to its implication for low ability. But in Global Gambit, this distortion stands to be corrected. In fact, the very meaning of failure was transformed

159

by the introduction of the scientists' feedback. No longer was a "miss (failure) . . . as good as a mile" – hopeless and irretrievable. Not only did both students and scientists share a common task, but, most important, their reasoning revealed more similarities than differences. And because near misses are subject to correction, mistakes are likely to qualify for what John Holt (1964) has referred to as "nonsuccesses," events that reflect the vast middle ground between outright perfection and abject failure. Here, too, we can appreciate the potential of game play for changing the meaning of help seeking from implying incompetency to testimony that sometimes problems are so demanding that all of us, even experts, need all the help we can get. In this connection, when children ask for assistance on tasks that interest them and on which they freely choose to work, help seeking is seen as a positive action. By contrast, when tasks are imposed by others, and especially if students are offered rewards for complying, then help seeking is taken as a sign of incompetency by onlookers (Nelson-LeGall, 1985; Newman, 1990; Newman & Goldin, 1990).

Global Gambit also demonstrates how the otherwise divisive issue of winners versus losers can serve a constructive purpose. A competitive element was deliberately introduced into Global Gambit not, however, to arouse interest (the teams were already heavily engaged) but rather to instruct. Competition is an important reality and its dynamics must be understood, not denied – understood in light of other legitimate realities such as the possibility of personal goals that, according to Terry Orlick (1982), have little to do with winning over others, goals such as recovering from mistakes, improving self-control, and mastering new skills; and in light of the fact that the presence of competitive dynamics can be used to promote positive values. "What better place is there to discuss the true meaning of values that are important to children and adults alike, such as winning, losing, success, failure, anxiety, rejection, fair play, acceptance . . .? What better place to help children become aware of their own feelings and the feelings of others?" (Orlich, 1982, p. 102).

Teacher as Ally. So far teachers and students have been portrayed as opponents in the learning game. This negative relationship was

160

transformed when Mr. Rodriguez became an ally of his students – a coach, mentor, and a resource – as they prepared themselves for the upcoming contest of nations. This change from adversary to ally can have important, positive ripple effects in classrooms. For one thing, Mr. Rodriguez was no longer the sole disciplinarian, nor was he the only person concerned with intellectual excellence. His use of cooperative learning automatically placed much of this responsibility on the students themselves, where it must ultimately reside anyway. Whenever the fate of the group is tied to the actions of each individual, then there are powerful reasons within the group to see that everyone learns and to discourage offtarget behavior such as loafing, "goofing off," or being tardy (see Activity 1 in Chapter 9).

For another thing, when teachers become advocates for students they, too, are allowed to make mistakes, to admit to them, and to apologize openly, yet still be forgiven or even admired by students because now teachers are allies. As Herbert Kohl (1967) points out, it is the teacher's struggle to be fair and honest, not always right or righteous, that moves and excites students. Kohl goes on to reflect that his ghetto pupils "did not want to be defiant, insulting, idle; nor were they any less afraid of chaos than I was. They wanted more than anything to feel they were facing it with me and not against me. These discoveries were my greatest strength when I began to explore new things to teach the children. They were as impatient to learn something exciting as I was to find something that would excite them" (p. 31).

The key to teacher goodwill, as illustrated in Global Gambit and reinforced by Kohl's remark, is to arrange circumstances so that teachers and students face obstacles together and in the process learn together. Teachers, like everyone else, are most alive when they are learning.

Global gambit is a fictitious example, but a useful fiction nonetheless. Above all, it represents a vision of what might be and, to some extent, what is already happening in many classrooms. A few examples will suffice. For instance, Carole Ames and her colleagues (Powell, Ames, & Maehr, 1990; Tracey, Ames, & Maehr, 1990) modified the rules of the learning game in some one hundred elementary school classrooms favoring noncompetitive successes and the sharing of authority among teachers and students. Results indicate that restructuring has changed the learning climate for the better in ways portrayed in Global Gambit, especially among "high-risk" students. (Also, see Anderman & Maehr, 1994.)

In his study of factors that perpetuate student anxiety, Andres Helmke (1988) found that anxiety is particularly disruptive of school achievement whenever a premium is placed on performance per se, that is, on either winning or losing, rather than on learning, or when teachers provide little in the way of help for poor students including periodic feedback, study review, and clear standards. Helmke's work provides some of the best empirical justification for the use of mastery learning approaches in the quest for motivational equity.

So far our research examples for creating motivational change have been confined to the individual classroom. But as Martin Maehr and Carol Midgley (1991) point out, "the classroom is not an island. It is part of a broader social system and it is difficult to develop and sustain changes in the classroom without dealing with the wider school environment. Moreover, teachers alone cannot carry the burden of significant school change; one must also engage school leadership if the deepest structure of teaching and learning is to change" (p. 399). Seldom do educational researchers speak directly to school leaders and to the school community at large. Fortunately, here, too, things are beginning to change. For instance, Maehr and his colleagues (Maehr, 1989, 1991; Maehr & Braskamp, 1986) have convincingly demonstrated that school climate, defined by the collective instructional goals of the entire teaching staff and administration, impacts the quality of classroom motivation as surely as does individual classroom policy, and that in turn school climate is also amenable to positive change.

CONCLUSION

There is more to Global Gambit than merely setting motives right, critical as that is. There are also broad hints about another critical objective of schooling: enriching our children's capacity to think, to reason free of rhetoric, and to create plans for desired futures rather than merely accept the future by default. This additional objective will come as no surprise to the reader, given the rationale presented so far. Indeed, our analysis now comes full circle back to the opening arguments in Chapter 1 regarding problem solving and future survival. This round trip represents a natural progression. First, we considered the question of *why* achieve and concluded that for learning to endure and enrich, the reasons or motives for learning must be positive. Then we took up the question of *how* – how to arrange the conditions of learning to enhance the will to learn. Now we come to the question of *what*, what lessons are worth knowing as students struggle to create their own futures. Two kinds of knowledge are critical: knowing *how to learn* and knowing *how to think*.

By this reckoning, *learning* and *thinking* are not the same thing, although it is often assumed that if people simply have enough information they will also think effectively. Obviously, this is not necessarily true. We cannot teach facts alone and expect understanding to occur automatically. As Emily Dickinson remarked, "He has the facts, but not the phosphorescence of thought." Learning and thinking are different because they involve different goals – in the first instance, to recall what is memorable and, in the second, to make meaningful what is remembered. These different goals also involve different mental operations. Learning places a premium on the skills of precise rehearsal and effective recall, whereas thinking demands flexibility, openness, and a spontaneous play of mind.

In the next chapter we will consider the possibility of teaching facts in ways that encourage understanding. We will also explore the prospects for teaching children strategies of thinking, and ask if such instruction also enhances the *willingness* to use one's mind in creative ways. Thinking strategies are necessary for solving what J. W. Getzels (1975) calls "discovered" problems as contrasted to "presented" problems. In presented problems the solution is already known to the presenter in advance (usually a teacher) and must be worked out by the learner. Typically, such problems are presented in a neatly packaged, highly structured form, with all the information provided for a solution – no more, no less. Most presented problems are in themselves quite trivial. Who really cares how old Ruthie is if her age is two-thirds that of Mary's age? The answer is useful only as evidence that students have learned the concept of fractions. Rarely in schools is presented knowledge put to work for solving discovered or "created" problems where the presenter (who may be the student) usually *does* care about answers, and not just about the process – sometimes passionately, even desperately, and precisely because there is no known or preset solution, or at least no single answer on which everyone (not even their teachers) can agree. This is the domain of the truly creative act – seeking ways to help one's younger brother kick the cocaine habit, painting a picture that forces the viewer to see the world in new ways, or creating a worldwide network of cooperation to deal with global warming. By their nature discovered problems typically must be solved not once, but repeatedly, and sometimes by different players. For instance, the answer that satisfies a husband as to why the family budget was overrun may not satisfy his wife. Nor are the insights achieved by one generation always agreeable to the next. Today's assessment of the threat of global warming will change as decades pass. But just how these later appraisals will differ, no one can say except that they will likely prove the point made by R. H. Tawney that "the certainties of one age are the problems of the next." It is all part of the drama associated with what James Carse (1986) calls "infinite games."

Infinite games are defined as those human endeavors in which the goal is to extend play (or inquiry) indefinitely. Science is an infinite game, as is civilization. And so is the playing out of the lives of young children who must repeatedly renegotiate relationships with others as they grow into adulthood.

What are the prospects for teaching young people the broad mental strategies for creating the proper moves and countermoves required by such infinite game play?

SUMMING UP

1. The will to learn is threatened whenever one's sense of worth becomes equated with the ability to achieve competitively. Students who anchor their sense of personal worth in ability are

164

placed at considerable risk because school, like the rest of life, cannot guarantee an unbroken string of successes.

2. Preferred solutions to the educational crisis involve rearranging incentives so that the reasons (or goals) for learning are shifted from competitive to intrinsic – that is, learning for its own sake, for self-mastery, and for the sake of others.

3. Honoring intrinsic goals promotes *motivational equity* – equity in the sense that the satisfaction that comes from the struggle to achieve these intrinsic goals is within the reach of all students, irrespective of background or ability. These sources of equity are denied students when excellence is defined competitively.

4. Five broad instructional guidelines promote motivational equity:
   a. Providing engaging assignments
   b. Rewarding positive reasons for learning
   c. Putting students in control
   d. Promoting positive beliefs about ability
   e. Improving student–teacher relations

ACTIVITIES

Activity 1: Grading and Motivational Equity

So far we have not directly addressed an important fact of school life: grades and grading. How might Mr. Rodriguez evaluate the performance of each Global Gambit team and translate his evaluations into a team grade, using approaches to grading that encourage positive reasons for learning? Start by reviewing those characteristics of grades that are most likely to foster motivational equity, as described at the beginning of this chapter. When you finish working out some answers, you may wish to consult Appendix I.

Activity 2: Testing and Motivational Equity

Suppose Mr. Rodriguez wanted to administer a test at the end of Global Gambit to determine how much his students learned about, say, world geography. He wonders how he might modify or replace the typical competitively scored essay test in ways that further the goals of motivational equity, that is, (1) minimizing test anxiety, (2) encouraging positive reasons for learning, and (3) focusing on what students know, rather than detecting what they don't know.

Your previous work on Activity 2 in Chapter 5 will provide a head start with this assignment. Still, there may be other, quite different approaches to Mr. Rodriguez's question. What might they be? Appendix J offers some possibilities, once you have come up with some thoughts of your own.

7

STRATEGIC THINKING
AND THE WILL TO LEARN

Long-range planning does not deal with future decisions, but
with the future of present decisions.
Peter Drucker

DRUCKER'S REMARK CAPTURES THE ESSENCE OF THE RELATIONSHIP
between discovered problems and the future. The future depends on, indeed, eventually *becomes* a history of the kinds of problems we choose either to ignore, to postpone, or to solve, and of the
wisdom of our solutions.

It is not that we are without some guidelines for making the
best present decisions. Common sense is one source and so are
the lessons of history. Another oracle, although largely neglected,
is the accumulation of folk wisdom known as Murphy's laws or
the Official Rules (Dickson, 1978). This neglect is all the more puzzling given the uncanny accuracy of these laws. Who can easily
dismiss the observation that "for every human problem there is a
neat, plain solution – and it is always wrong." Or ignore the warning, "if you think the problem is bad now, just wait until you've
solved it."

Murphy's laws have become a user's manual for dealing with an
unpredictable world of perversity, surprises, and contrary events.
Naturally, they cannot tell us precisely *what* will happen or exactly
when. Still, Murphy and his intrepid band of lawgivers have put us
on notice *in advance* for *why* sometimes things may turn out badly,
or at least differently than expected.

By taking Murphy's laws seriously, we are compelled to wonder,
if the simplest solution is so often wrong, then why are we not more
suspicious of simplicity to begin with? And what is it about our solutions that so often makes them worse than the original problem?

If the future is just a lot of mistakes waiting to happen – the same ones made by past generations and similar to those *we* are now busily committing before the future overtakes *us* – then the message seems clear. Schools must work for the repeal of Murphy's laws! This means schools must teach children *how* to think, not simply *what* to think.

This brings us to the first main topic of this chapter. We will explore the nature of the kinds of thinking engaged in by Mr. Rodriguez's students, discussed in the previous chapter, as they struggled to reach a global accord. More specifically, we will inquire about the kinds of intellectual skills and knowledge needed when, in the words of Max Wertheimer (1959), individuals "discover, envision, and go into deeper questions." We will also glimpse something of the frailty and limits of human problem solving, and ask if the capacity for productive thinking can be increased through school instruction.

The second main topic involves our larger motivational concerns. We will inquire if learning *how* to think increases one's *willingness* to think.

All these questions are predicated on knowing what *thinking* is.

WHAT IS THINKING?

> Currently, there is a great deal of interest in improving students' thinking abilities, but there is also a great deal of confusion about what thinking is.
> Barbara Presseisen

One textbook on problem solving (Phye & Andre, 1986) defines thinking as the mental operations involved in dealing with problems. Today most psychologists think of these mental operations in terms of different kinds of knowledge arranged in a top-down structure of the type portrayed in Figure 7.1.

The practical significance of this model is best conveyed by example. Mr. Rodriguez assigned his students several exercises in order to acquaint them with the basic mechanisms of global warming.

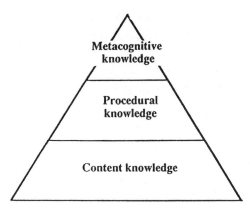

Figure 7.1. Knowledge hierarchy.

Source: Covington (1992).

One exercise required them to create a kind of "danger hierarchy" in which they ranked various practices such as deforestation and burning fossil fuels, from the least to the most damaging to the environment. Mr. Rodriguez explained that the creation of carbon dioxide gases by burning fossil fuels had always been thought to be the main cause of global warming. "But what is the latest evidence?" he wondered aloud. Are there greater dangers? And are there any wild-card players in this game, potential but as yet overlooked sources of danger? This was no simple assignment. In order to succeed, Mr. Rodriguez's students had to draw on all three sources of knowledge portrayed in Figure 7.1.

Content Knowledge

The basic requirement for all thinking is access to information: dozens, perhaps hundreds, even thousands of facts, figures, and other data arranged in charts, graphs, or text that in total represent what psychologists call "content" or "declarative" knowledge – knowing, for example, that each year Brazil burns or cuts down forests whose land area is the size of Pennsylvania or that methane comes from leaks in natural gas lines and is also produced by forest fires. Facts are the basic ingredient of all problem solving. They are not thinking, but thinking is not possible without them.

Procedural Knowledge

Next comes a repertoire of mental "procedures" needed to make sense of facts. Procedural knowledge represents the *how* of problem solving – knowing, for example, *how* things work, simple things like the rules of the Global Gambit game, or more complex things like *how* the credit banking system works. Typically, procedural knowledge relates closely to the content of the problem itself, so close in fact that sometimes procedural and content knowledge literally fuse. For example, in order to identify the most important causes of carbon dioxide buildup, Mr. Rodriguez's students must first understand that each potential source of warming – be it deforestation, burning fossil fuel, or methane gas leaks – is itself a part of a larger natural system, and only one system among many complex systems including the atmosphere, the biosphere, and the geosphere. Second, they must appreciate *how* changes in just one system, such as reduced carbon dioxide levels, can alter the growth rate of trees (biosphere), which in turn can have many effects on the atmosphere, some of which may cause additional warming and others of which may actually cause cooling.

Procedural knowledge can also transcend a given subject matter and apply broadly to most problems and disciplines. This is the realm of knowing *how* to think of ideas or *how* to look at old problems in new ways. Knowing *how* to evaluate ideas in light of new information is also part of procedural knowledge. For instance, *initially* Mr. Rodriguez's students might hypothesize that methane gas is a marginal danger to the environment because only a small volume is released into the atmosphere each year, *initially*, that is, until they reconsidered their judgment in light of a new fact: that each methane molecule contributes fifteen to thirty times more to global warming than does one carbon dioxide molecule. Perhaps methane gas is a greater danger than they had originally thought. To extend this example, rethinking the danger status of methane gas should prompt further concerns about the relative threat of deforestation. In light of these new data, it now appears that deforestation represents not just one danger, that of reducing the global capacity to absorb carbon dioxide, but a second danger as well – the creation of methane gas through burning.

Metacognitive Knowledge

Finally, at the pinnacle of the knowledge hierarchy comes an overall executive function, the integration of all prior sources of knowledge. Successful thinkers view problem solving in its entirety, not just as an assortment of isolated subroutines, disconnected facts, or disembodied skills. Nowhere is the statement "the whole is greater than the sum of its parts" more apt than when applied to problem solving. Good thinking is more than simply the sum total of all procedural and content knowledge. And there is the corollary that good thinking does not depend solely on the size of one's content and procedural knowledge base. It is what one does with one's knowledge that counts most – how information is selected, arranged, and prioritized. This is the realm of "metacognitions." The essence of metacognitive knowledge is embodied in Albert Camus's celebrated quip, "An intellectual is someone whose mind watches itself."

A key aspect of metacognitive knowledge involves knowing how to create plans of action and monitor them (Friedman, Scholnick, & Cocking, 1986). The parallel between *planful* thinking and a military campaign is near perfect. Successful generals arrange their troops (cognitions) in a marching order that is best suited for some overall purpose, whether it be to defeat the enemy or to withdraw gracefully to fight another day. These moves and countermoves are controlled by broad plans of action, which in the case of potentially less violent pursuits, such as plotting one's next move at the negotiating table or on the playing field, involve checking the results of that move and then revising one's strategies accordingly.

Broad planning strategies have wide application by analogy. For example, like chess masters who must "protect the center of the

171

board," politicians must protect their flanks, and television evange-
lists must control their revenue base among the elderly and gullible
by at least appearing to be respectable and pious. And even the
youngest of problem solvers have their survival strategies, a fact
appreciated by all parents who have been victimized by the "divide
(mom and dad) and conquer" ruse.

Sometimes these plans of action are best conceived of as a series
of abstract steps or mental operations that must be properly se-
quenced. From this angle effective problem solving involves deciding at a given point in one's work whether, for instance, it is more
fruitful to suspend judgment and give free rein to speculation in
search of entirely new ideas, or whether, on balance, it would be
best to proceed by evaluating the ideas one already has. This balancing act implies appreciating when one is on the right track or,
conversely, recognizing the danger of being overwhelmed by too
much information and, once having realized the danger, knowing
what to do about it.

At one point Mr. Rodriguez worried that his students might collapse beneath the combined weight of too many new, unfamiliar
concepts, introduced too quickly. The last straw was the notion that
climate change depends on a complex interaction among several
global ecosystems including the oceans, the continental land masses, and the vast ice fields of Antarctica and Greenland, not to mention plant and animal life. Mr. Rodriguez saved the day by asking
his students to think of everyday analogies or metaphors (a procedural skill) that would convert this complex concept into a simpler,
more recognizable form (Gick & Holyoak, 1983; Mayer, 1989). One
team decided to liken the dynamics of climate change to a mobile:
both weather and mobiles are in constant motion, with any change
in one element (e.g., the oceans) creating corresponding changes in
the total configuration.

Fortunately, there is evidence that individuals can be taught to
create and use analogies as a problem-solving tool. In one study
Ann Brown reported that following the administration of a special
reading comprehension program (Brown & Palincsar, 1989) children easily deduced why farmers use lady bugs to destroy aphids,

and then were able to apply this same reasoning several weeks later when it came to using manatees to rid inland waterways of weeds.

By helping his students transform the unfamiliar and overwhelming into the familiar and understandable, Mr. Rodriguez reduced cognitive overload. He also promoted better thinking. The ability to grasp the essential elements of a complex situation is the benchmark of effective thinking. As Nietzsche said, "He is a thinker. That means, he knows how to make things simpler than they are."

Prospects for Change

The educational significance of the top-down knowledge model (Figure 7.1) is reflected in a growing awareness that thinking, far from being a passive activity, is an active, constructive attempt by the learner to create meaning. Above all, this process involves the capacity to think about thinking and the purposeful arrangement, assembly, and orchestration of different kinds of knowledge to achieve a larger goal (Sadoski & Paivio, 1995).

By this accounting, thinking is a far more demanding and complex activity than typically envisioned by schools. Given all the complexities involved, and the many forms that problems can take, it is a wonder that humans think at all. At every level of the knowledge hierarchy there is evidence of massive deficits in thinking (e.g., Oka & Paris, 1987; Sowder, 1987). Recall those primary grade youngsters who blithely calculated the captain's age in terms of the number of sheep and goats on his ship, and were none the wiser (metacognitive failure), and the teenager's unintentionally witty stab at identifying Chernobyl (lack of content knowledge) as Cher's real name (Chapter 1).

We can place much of the blame for such "thoughtlessness" on three factors. First, youngsters are rarely led to see the larger utility of what they are learning in school. Surprisingly, many students do not realize that in order to write checks and balance a checkbook – in effect, to take charge of one's economic life – they must first know how to add and subtract; and, in order to vote, one must first be able to read the ballot and understand the issues. Moreover, even on those relatively few occasions when such functional relationships are discussed in school, it is rarer still that students are allowed to practice, say, voting or setting up their own household budgets – all in simulated form, of course, in order to appreciate firsthand what it means to be cut adrift without benefit of basic survival skills. As a result, students are typically unable to recognize that what they are studying in one subject-matter area relates to other areas (Bailin, 1987), nor do they appreciate the relationship between what they are learning now and what they hope to accomplish in the future (Stake & Easley, 1978).

Second, we have also implicated the fear of failure as a cause of "thoughtless" learning. When students are driven to outperform others, they retreat to low-level thinking strategies that favor rote memorizing (Nolen, 1987, 1988). Anxiety degrades intellectual functioning to the point that many students operate at an almost witless level of existence.

Now, we can add a third reason. Although the goal of teaching thinking is widely honored in school, very little time is actually devoted to it – at least thinking in the active sense we have defined it. All too often students believe that the reason for studying mathematics is to get the right answers, not to improve their quantitative-thinking skills; likewise, they believe the purpose of studying history is to memorize names, dates, and places; and the reason for writing compositions is because one must!

But even the goals of content mastery need not proceed in a mindless fashion. From a larger perspective learning facts is best conceived of as a process of assimilating new information to be fitted meaningfully into the child's conceptual world and, in turn, to stimulate the expansion of that world. As William James remarked: "The art of remembering is the art of thinking. . . . our conscious effort should not be so much to *impress* or *retain* (knowledge) as to connect it with something already there."

This observation brings us to the central question of this chapter: can the capacity to think about thinking and the ability to assemble and use different kinds of knowledge be taught to school children?

LEARNING HOW TO THINK

A child's mind is like a field for which an expert farmer has advised a change in the method of cultivation, with the result that in place of desert land, we now have a harvest.
Alfred Binet

The literature on teaching children to think is truly monumental (see, for instance, McKeachie, Pintrich, & Lin, 1985; Nickerson, Perkins, & Smith, 1985; Resnick, 1987; Sternberg, 1986; Tishman, Perkins, & Jay, 1995). Yet only a tiny fraction of this literature is appropriate to our concerns. For our purposes, the best evidence comes from only a handful of studies conducted in schools using instruction of sufficient scope to qualify as general mental skill training, and with enough evidence gathered on their effectiveness to permit reliable conclusions.

We focus mainly on the Productive Thinking Program (Covington, Crutchfield, Davies, & Olton, 1974) because of its emphasis on the training of metacognitive and planning mechanisms, and because of the large body of research evidence that has accumulated around this program over the years. Several other instructional programs will also be mentioned as they become relevant to our inquiries.

The Productive Thinking Program is a course in learning to think designed for upper elementary school children. The program consists of a series of self-instructional lessons, each centering on a complex detective-type mystery problem. As each problem unfolds step by step, students perform various problem-solving operations: writing down ideas, formulating the mystery in their own words, and suggesting what additional information is needed to solve it. At various points, students receive feedback in the form of possible suggestions or ideas that are appropriate at that particular

175

Table 7.1. *The thinking guides from the Productive Thinking Program*

1. Take time to reflect on a problem before you begin work. Decide exactly what the problem is that you are trying to solve.
2. Get all the facts of the problem clearly in mind.
3. Work on the problem in a planful way.
4. Keep an open mind. Don't jump to conclusions about the answer to a problem.
5. Think of many ideas for solving a problem. Don't stop with just a few.
6. Try to think of unusual ideas.
7. As a way of getting ideas, pick out all the important objects and persons in the problem and think carefully about each one.
8. Think of several general possibilities for a solution and then figure out many particular ideas for each possibility.
9. As you search for ideas, let your mind freely explore things around you. Almost anything can suggest ideas for a solution.
10. Always check each idea with the facts to decide how likely the idea is.
11. If you get stuck on a problem, keep thinking. Don't be discouraged or give up.
12. When you run out of ideas, try looking at the problem in a new and different way.
13. Go back and review all the facts of the problem to make sure you have not missed something important.
14. Start with an unlikely idea. Just suppose that it is possible, and then figure out how it could be.
15. Be on the lookout for odd or puzzling facts in a problem. Explaining them can lead you to new ideas for a solution.
16. When there are several different puzzling things in a problem, try to explain them with a single idea that will connect all together.

Source: Covington, Crutchfield, Davies, & Olton (1974).

point in the problem. Through such guided practice students are led to understand what counts as relevant and original ideas, how best to proceed in the face of uncertainty, and what strategies to employ whenever they encounter difficulties. This practice–feedback sequence is built around a set of sixteen thinking guides (see Table 7.1).

The managerial schema taught by the Productive Thinking Program is primitive but serviceable. Whenever students get stuck on a problem, they are directed to consult these thinking guides. In this way students are encouraged to review problems periodically, to consider whether the task has changed, to judge what has been accomplished so far, and then to decide what additional facts or next steps are needed to move closer to a solution.

Cognitive skill instruction is reinforced through the use of identification models. A storyline is developed around two school-age children (Jim and Lila, brother and sister). Students work on a problem in tandem with Jim and Lila – first students producing their own ideas, then Jim and Lila responding with theirs (feedback). The models are not meant to be perfect; they are depicted as making mistakes but also learning from them, and gradually improving, with the result that they become more self-confident. A sample sequence (see Figure 7.2) illustrates how such positive attitudes are systematically strengthened using a variation on attributional retraining (Chapter 3). This particular example involves enhancing beliefs about ability as a learnable set of strategies.

Enhancing Procedural Knowledge

The results of a number of studies using the Productive Thinking Program suggest that systematic instruction improves the procedural skills associated with problem solving. (For a review, see Covington, 1986.) For example, after instruction students generated more ideas and of higher quality compared with the idea production of a group of matched control students who had no mental skill training. Instructed students also demonstrated an improved ability to ask questions, especially when it came to strategic inquiries that helped them to identify the nature of the problem.

The number of actual problem solutions also increased after instruction. In one study (Olton & Crutchfield, 1969) students were challenged to think of ways to kill a malignant tumor deep inside the human body using X-rays but without harming the surrounding healthy tissue. Instructed students discovered solutions at a rate

Figure 7.2. Sampler from the Productive Thinking Program.

Source: Covington (1992).

178

twice that of control children. The fact that this particular problem was administered four months after training attests to the longevity of the instructional effects. Also of significance is the fact that these thinking gains occurred on a problem that was quite different in content from those used for practice.

Similar findings have been reported by researchers using the teacher-led Philosophy for Children Program (Lipman, 1985). This program emphasizes training on the more logical aspects of thinking, such as drawing syllogistic inferences. Some half-dozen studies conducted by Matthew Lipman and his colleagues provide strong evidence that systematic instruction leads to substantial increases in the capacity of children to provide reasons for puzzling events, to identify fallacies in reasoning, and to discover alternative interpretations of data (Lipman, Sharp, & Oscanyan, 1977). Also these positive outcomes were accompanied by improved teacher ratings of student academic readiness as well as corresponding gains in math and reading skills.

Likewise, Marilyn Adams and her colleagues (Adams, 1986, 1989; Hernstein, Nickerson, de Sanchez, & Swets, 1986) have reported positively on a course designed to teach Venezuelan school children various observation and classification skills as well as reasoning and decision-making strategies. This program is unique because it was developed under the auspices of the Venezuelan Ministry of Education as part of a countrywide effort to improve the intellectual functioning of all its citizens (Cordes, 1985).

Enhancing Metacognitive Knowledge

Now, what are the prospects for fostering the metacognitive, managerial aspects of problem solving? In one study employing the Productive Thinking Program (Olton et al., 1967), students were given an unfamiliar problem and asked to select the best planning steps from a list of alternative actions as the problem unfolded. Each set of decision-making options differed in appropriateness depending on previous events, but they always included a "best" decision; a "second best" decision (reasonable, but not as good as the first); a "contrary fact" decision (one that ignored an already established fact); an appealing but irrelevant decision; and finally, a decision that would bring the problem to a premature closure. Instructed students were better able than control students to track the most effective course of action throughout the entire problem-solving sequence and in the process were less attracted to "appealing but irrelevant" actions, and less likely to be seduced by "contrary" actions.

Other researchers have established the importance of metacognitive knowledge and also demonstrated that it can be taught. For example, in one study (Lodico, Ghatala, Levin, Pressley, & Bell, 1983) young adolescents learned two different recall strategies, one that was more effective for free-recall tasks (e.g., recalling the cranial nerves in any order) and the other better suited for remembering paired associations (e.g., recalling Spanish–English equivalents). In addition to this basic rehearsal training, half of the students learned about the importance of choosing between these two strategies depending on the nature of the task (metacognitive knowledge). The remaining students received no such instruction. Then these two groups were given both paired-association and free-recall tasks. Those students who had been provided with metacognitive knowledge more often used the most effective learning strategy of the two depending on the task and were better able to justify their choice.

Most school tasks involve elements of strategic planning. For example, writing essays consists largely of iterative cycles of planning, drafting, and revising, and, when necessary, redrafting the entire composition as the student strives to create a more satisfying product. Likewise, reading for comprehension usually involves a process of successive cycling as well (Anderson, 1995; Paris, Lipson, & Wixson, 1995): looking ahead to anticipate, looking back to check and test one's recall, summarizing what is important so far, and filtering new information through the lens of prior understanding. Also, at its most effective, study for a test is also an exercise in strategic planning. Knowledgeable students seek out information about the upcoming test to determine the kinds of demands it will place on them, by inquiring, variously: "What must I remember?" "Must I remember it again later?" "What kind of test?" "What aspects of the assignment will be most emphasized?" (Bransford, Nitsch, & Franks, 1977).

In one study of school assignments, middle school youngsters were asked to plan a hypothetical school report (Cox, Swain, & Hartsough, 1982). Prior to this assignment, one-half of the youngsters in this study were administered the Productive Thinking Program, while the other half served as controls. The instructed students posed more strategic questions about the sequencing and timing of work on the report than did the control children. Also, instructed students were more likely to judge the success of their plans in terms of intrinsic criteria such as how much they learned of value apart from any grade they received. These findings are particularly welcome in light of our earlier comments concerning Ferdinand Hoppe and the importance of self-defined success (Chapter 2).

The fact that students can be taught to plan better takes on considerable importance in light of speculation that links intelligence to the ability to plan (Sternberg, 1985). It has been proposed that intelligence, in actuality, represents the ability to think strategically, that is, the capacity to plan for and make the most of one's personal resources as situations change (Borkowski, Johnston, & Reid, 1985; Derry & Murphy, 1986).

These findings are likely what Alfred Binet, the father of the mental test movement, had in mind almost a century ago when he observed that "One increases that which constitutes the intelligence of the school child, namely the capacity to learn and improve with instruction" (1909, pp. 54–55). Binet would almost certainly have embraced the concept of "working intelligence" (Scribner, 1984). In school, working intelligence means being able to recognize when one does not understand a concept, knowing how to make a difficult assignment easier, and knowing what to do when previously successful learning strategies are no longer effective. All these actions can be trained, and it is in this sense that we say ability can be modified and improved. A more contemporary interpretation of Binet's position was offered by Terry McNabb (1987) when she also proposed that ability implies strategy, in that those students who

181

possess larger arsenals of thinking strategies are better able to solve problems. Thinking strategies as a concept, then, suggest a more fluid type of ability – more of a resource than a fixed capacity.

Motivational Consequences

McNabb's comments lead to the second main question of this chapter: does strategy instruction increase the *willingness* of students to think more deeply about problems? The prospects are encouraging for the fact that the notion of strategic planning bridges both cognitive and motivational domains in several ways. First, strategy knowledge increases beliefs that ability is an incremental process. As one child put it in my presence, "Ability is like a flower. It unfolds and grows as you work." We know that such incremental beliefs about ability are associated with an increased willingness to tackle more difficult problems, for longer periods, and with greater resolve and confidence (Dweck & Goetz, 1988). Second, a strategic view of thinking is also likely to alter the meaning of failure. If students can analyze problems, identify sources of difficulty, and create plans of action to overcome these obstacles, then alternative explanations for failure are possible other than low ability. This point is made graphically in Figure 7.2, in ways children can readily understand. In this particular instance, Jim tried hard but still failed because he made up his mind too quickly. Such a strategy interpretation implies that failure is reversible and, as a result, need not necessarily lead to the kinds of self-doubt and paralysis associated with learned helplessness. Recall that learned helplessness is that sense of despair that one can't succeed no matter how hard or how well one tries (Chapter 3).

A study by McNabb (1987) confirms this point. A series of mathematics problems was administered to two groups of upper elementary students. One group received strategy-related messages ("To solve problems like these, you have to use good methods"). The other group was given effort-related messages ("To solve problems like these, you will have to try harder"). Recall that simply exhorting students to greater effort may do little to improve performance. Although both groups received the same procedural training – how, for example, to diagram math problems – only the strategy group consistently employed these procedures and, as a result, performed better on a final achievement test. Moreover, when computational errors occurred, the strategy-method group was more likely to ascribe these lapses to modifiable causes such as inattention. Furthermore, strategy messages significantly increased the degree of enjoyment expressed by these students and their willingness to work on the math problems. Finally, those students who originally exhibited the lowest self-perceived competency in mathematics benefited the most from strategy-message training.

McNabb interpreted this latter finding as being consistent with self-worth theory in that strategy-linked messages provide insecure students with plausible nonability explanations for their performances, thereby freeing them to work harder.

Strategy training also appears to increase intellectual self-confidence. One index of self-confidence is the degree to which individuals exercise independence in judging the merits of ideas. Following administration of the Productive Thinking Program, Vernon Allen and J. Levine (1967) gave students false feedback allegedly representing the opinion of their peers regarding the correctness of various answers to a problem. Instructed students were less likely than control students to give up their own ideas simply because they differed from peer-group opinion. Moreover, these instructed students were selective in their judgments. Sometimes they changed their minds in favor of the group position when the group was clearly correct, and at other times they defended their own ideas when they believed they were right and the group was wrong. The fact that independence of judgment can be encouraged through strategy training is highly significant given the importance of self-regulated learning to school reform. Perhaps even greater importance can be attached to these findings in light of Binet's celebrated definition of intelligence, "Comprehension, planfulness, invention and *judgment* [emphasis added] – in these four words lies the essence of intelligence" (1909, p. 54).

The topic of self-confidence and its encouragement leads to a larger point concerning our motivational focus. Not only is having confidence in one's judgment critical to good thinking, but so, too, is what David Perkins and his colleagues (Perkins, Jay, & Tishman, 1993) refer to as "thinking dispositions." One such disposition involves being sensitive to situations that can benefit from the application of thinking strategies. Perkins's advice to teachers regarding ways to enhance such dispositions is illuminating (Tishman, Jay, & Perkins, 1993): "[You] want to find ways to help students to be alert to sprawling and aimless thinking, and sensitive to step-wise thinking opportunities. You might begin to cultivate such sensitivities by modelling them yourself: 'As I was working on such-and-such a project,' you might say aloud to the class, 'I realized my thinking was disorganized'" (p. 148).

Such informal modeling by teachers can be highly effective in encouraging the proper thinking dispositions. So, too, can formal problem-solving training, as reflected in research on the Productive Thinking Program. For example, in one study, both instructed and control students were given an open-ended assignment to write an essay on poverty. Both groups tended to produce the same number of *descriptions* of poverty (e.g., "These people don't have any money"). But whereas most control youngsters stopped short at this content level, instructed students, by a margin of over three to one, went on spontaneously to mention various *causes* of poverty (e.g., "They were replaced by machines") and to suggest *solutions* to the problems of poverty. These findings indicate that strategy instruction strengthens the readiness of students to use their minds in productive ways – "discovering, envisioning, and going into deeper questions" – to recall Wertheimer's phrase (1959). Such willingness and the thinking dispositions that support it should be a prime goal of education.

PLANNING FOR THE FUTURE

An optimist is someone who thinks the future is uncertain.
Anonymous

Now that we have explored the motivational benefits of the ability to think, and learned that thinking skills can, indeed, be trained, it is time to consider briefly two additional kinds of thinking essential for preparing students for the future: cooperative thinking and problem discovery.

Cooperation for Its Own Sake

Nowhere are the demands on strategic planning greater or success more imperative than in cases that require the cooperation of individuals within the family, among communities, and across nations. Today cooperation usually means sharing. As human and natural resources dwindle compared with rising global needs, greater sharing – of time, space, and even of one's own talents – will be the key to collective survival.

Fortunately, there is clear evidence that students can be taught to cooperate. Recall the study by Nelson and Kagan (Chapter 5), who demonstrated that under competitive rules, where rewards were insufficient for the number of players, children preferred to sabotage the game and lose any chance of winning themselves rather than let others win. These same investigators and their colleagues also showed that when children practiced cooperation first, they were more willing to work cooperatively under competitive conditions later on (Kagan & Madsen, 1971). These enlightened students simply divide the few prizes among the players at the end of the game. Also in some cases they decided jointly to alternate which of the players would receive the reward on a particular round as the game progressed.

But being cooperative is not always easy. One's good intentions to share can easily fall prey to greed, panic, and mistrust. This sad fact is the basis for one of the most disheartening problems of our time, the "tragedy of the commons" (Edney, 1980; Hardin, 1968). The "commons" is any communal resource, which referred originally to a grazing pasture shared by farmers from several nearby villages. If the carrying capacity of the pasture is, say ten cows, then as long as ten farmers graze only one cow each, the commons is not in danger of being overgrazed. The trouble begins when one farmer, more ambitious than the rest, concludes that by adding an additional cow he can double his milk production. The typical result is a stampede of farmers acting like cattle – all desperately seeking their "fair" share before it is too late. It is only later, usually after the commons lies depleted, that someone remembers the advice simple enough for children to follow: each player will receive more if everyone cooperates. The commons can be any shared but limited resource, including both renewable and nonrenewable items – air, water, or even the inadequate supply of rewards provided by Nelson and Kagan in their experiments on competition.

The obstacles to cooperation are ancient and many, part of a legacy of fear and suspicion that is not entirely irrational. Human history is a roll call of broken pledges and abused trust. But more stands in the way of cooperation than the tragedy of the commons. There are also certain human peculiarities that make the sowing of doubt and mutual suspicion virtually inevitable. One is the so-called fundamental attributional error. As humans we tend to explain the negative behavior of others in traitlike terms ("He cheated because he is dishonest"), while attributing the same behavior in ourselves to the situation ("I cheated because everyone else did"). Although understandable, and only too human, such biases bode ill for the kinds of delicate negotiations and planning required in emotionally charged situations where the stakes are high and the intentions of other participants already suspect.

Consider the problem of nuclear proliferation. According to these attributional dynamics, during the heyday of the cold war both the Soviet Union and the United States probably overestimated the hostility of the other side (Lindskold, 1978). Each interpreted any nuclear buildup by the other side as driven out of an inherent (traitlike) aggressive tendency, yet justifying increases in their own arsenal of weapons out of necessity, as only a natural (situational) response to those hostile intentions, and all without recognizing that this countermove would be seen as equally menacing by the other side. This "spiral" effect was compounded whenever a proposal made by one side to reduce nuclear arms – presumably for the sake of conciliation – was discounted by the other side as only a ploy to gain political advantage. Naturally, of course, sometimes adversaries are treacherous and ill-disposed, and to perceive them so may be critical to one's survival. Nonetheless, it is equally important to remain sensitive to these signs of potential change when confronting an increasingly agreeable competitor.

These same kinds of distortions and stresses are at work in any situation where emotions run high and resources are limited or contested, including courtroom battles between divorcing parents, costly commercial litigation, and acrimonious labor disputes. Given the growing necessity for cooperation, it seems clear that systematic instruction and practice in conflict management, planning, and the joint resolution of issues must form an indispensable part of the curriculum of the twenty-first century. Among other things, children must learn about attributional errors and other forms of mental and perceptual bias – how they can cloud one's judgment, when they are most likely to operate, and how to discount them. Moreover, students should experience for themselves and then master the stresses, uncertainty, and occasional failure of nerve that are an inevitable part of solving discovered problems – all, of course, in manageable amounts and limited to the instructional context. If properly orchestrated, hands-on experience with conflict management can promote the kinds of mature, stabilizing perspective that was so characteristic of Secretary of State George C. Marshall who, when asked why he could remain so calm in the face of the Berlin airlift crisis, replied "I have seen worse."

Problem Discovery

It was Albert Einstein who remarked that: "Raising new questions . . . [and] regarding old questions from a new angle requires creative imagination and marks real advances in science." By Einstein's reckoning, problem discovery is the highest expression of humankind's remarkable intellect. In its essential form, problem discovery reflects the challenge described by Getzels (1975): "pose an important problem and solve it!" The fundamental ingredients of this process are the continual readiness of individuals to find problems everywhere, to be puzzled by the obvious, and to see the extraordinary in the ordinary (Arlin, 1975; Wakefield, 1988). This description typifies the process of scientific discovery. The history of science is replete with examples of breakthrough discoveries that depended on being sensitive to the unexpected. This process involves serendipity, the art of finding something new of value when looking for something else (Shapiro, 1986). The classic example of serendipity is Alexander Fleming's discovery of penicillin. Instead of simply throwing out the bacteria killed by a strange green mold that spoiled his research and starting over again, Fleming paused to consider the meaning of this accident. Obviously, serendipity involves more than luck; it is not simply accidental. In Fleming's case, several other researchers had already seen bacteria destroyed in a similar fashion, but they did not recognize the full importance of what they saw; in effect, for them the familiar held no surprises. Fleming possessed the capacity to see the profound in the ordinary. Likewise, Wilhelm Roentgen saw the same fogged photographic plate as had other scientists before him, but while they considered it a nuisance, Roentgen asked, "Why is this plate fogged?" – a question that led to the discovery of the X-ray and eventually to atomic research.

The process of problem finding and the possibility of serendipitous discovery are largely omitted from schools. Yet these dynamics, too, are the stuff of which the future is made. It is the advent of new problems and new ways to deal with old problems that propels the observation that 90 percent of the jobs that will occupy America's labor force in the year 2020 do not yet exist. It is not typically the case, as some have argued, that humans solve their problems by outliving them, but rather in the process of solving them we create new needs and difficulties, and reshuffle our priorities.

Most school tasks are presented as exercises in rote learning. Yet the potential for problem finding in the curriculum is ever present. Problem finding comes into play whenever students must create their own assignments. This occurs in college as well as at the professional and postcollege levels whenever students are expected to carry out original research. It also occurs in high school whenever students invent worthwhile science fair projects, and in junior high when children must generate worthy term paper topics on their own.

188

THE TRANSFER OF KNOWLEDGE

We don't know what problems the future will have. . . . So the best way of preparation for the future is to learn to solve complex problems today.
Carl Rogers

The most important issue in preparing students for the future, besides setting right the reasons for learning, is the problem of transfer. As David Perkins and Gavriel Salomon (1987, 1988) explain it, transfer refers to a fringe benefit: in learning task A, an individual finds it easier to master task B. George learns to play tennis and discovers a talent for playing squash. Likewise, after learning to read musical notation for the piano, Bette finds that reading for the trumpet follows easily. Transfer of knowledge is the name of the game when it comes to preparing for the future. Because no one can possibly anticipate all future contingencies, it is vital that students be exposed to knowledge that has broad application. So far we have argued that the best preparation is to teach general problem-solving strategies and their metacognitive assembly. The merits of this generalist position seem self-evident. Although not always guaranteeing a solution, general strategies for mental management should at least help in solving problems, no matter what the future circumstance.

However, not all attempts to demonstrate the transfer value of general thinking strategies have been positive. For instance, researchers have been largely unsuccessful in demonstrating the benefits of teaching broad heuristics for mathematics problem solving. Students may understand these rules in the abstract but they do not always understand the principles of mathematics well enough to make use of them (Schoenfeld, 1985). Such failures of transfer led Allen Newell and Herbert Simon (1972) to conclude that focusing on broad mental principles is best characterized as a *general–weak* approach – *general* in that broad strategies are clearly applicable to all problems, but *weak* because their usefulness for solving a *specific* problem may be negligible.

This does not bode well for the arguments in favor of teaching

189

general problem-solving strategies. Moreover, contrary to our proposal, the prevailing evidence suggests that the key to becoming a
good problem solver in a specific area, say, accounting, involves a
very different strategy. It involves simply acquiring lots of specific
knowledge about the detailed ins and outs of the particular field.

In a classic study, William Chase and Herbert Simon (1973) used
chess players to demonstrate the importance of rich content knowledge in problem solving. These investigators found that master
chess players were no better than beginners at memorizing the lay-
out of pieces on a chess board if the patterns were purely random.
But recalling the past moves that emerged in the course of actual
game play was another matter. Here the grand masters excelled. In
fact, their memories were prodigious. They could remember all the
various moves of both players in the right order for hundreds of
previous games! This suggests that grand masters know something
very powerful but very specific about chess play, otherwise they
would have done better at recalling the random layouts. Grand
masters appear to think in terms of pattern or sequences of specific
moves with a repertoire of some 50,000 chess configurations, according to the conservative estimates of Chase and Simon. Knowledge of general strategies such as controlling the center of the board
appear to play little part in winning at chess once sufficient experience is accumulated.

On the other hand, unfortunately, for all of its undeniable importance, the accumulation of specific content knowledge also seems
decidedly limited when it comes to transfer. Once learned, subject-
matter knowledge in one domain, say, the ability to play chess well,
appears to have little positive impact on performance in other domains. Surprisingly, for example, learning to play chess does not insure that students will be better able to solve logic problems. Given
these findings, Newell and Simon (1972) characterized the accumulation of specific content knowledge as a *strong–specific* approach
when it comes to transfer – *strong* in the sense that subject-matter
knowledge is a powerful component of effective thought within a
given discipline such as biochemistry or astrophysics, but decidedly limited when it comes to solving a wider array of problems outside the discipline.

Here are the makings of a profound dilemma. If the evidence for the transfer of broad thinking strategies is spotty and, at the same time, specific knowledge is also of limited generality, can we *really* prepare students for a future of unknown possibilities where the specific content as well as the very nature of the problems themselves will likely be quite different if not unrecognizable today?

A Dilemma Resolved

Actually the picture is far less dismal than this, if only we are clever enough to look at the problem differently. The research of John Clement (1982) provides the proper perspective. Instead of asking expert chess players to solve chess problems, Clement gave grand masters unfamiliar, novel tasks for which their current experience was insufficient. Under these circumstances, grand masters as well as experts in any field revert to broad thinking strategies in an attempt to discover the underlying structure of the problem. They create analogies and metaphors to convert the unfamiliar to the familiar, just as Mr. Rodriguez's students were taught to do (Chapter 6). Experts also construct simple versions of the problem in an effort to detect the workings of the more complicated case. And, almost invariably, they try to identify the specific problem as belonging to a larger class of problems (Adelson, 1981). Additionally, experts establish a context for solving unfamiliar problems. For instance, before studying the specifics of a legal case, attorneys locate the particular decision in the larger context of who judged the case, the type of court that tried the case, and the kinds of parties involved.

In the face of unfamiliar territory, general thinking strategies come into their own. This problem-framing quality and the fact that future problems are by definition likely to be novel and unfamiliar justify the emphasis on training for broad problem-solving skills. Brown and Campione (1990) refer to youngsters who possess these general strategies as "intelligent novices." Intelligent novices may not yet have all the background knowledge needed for exploring a new field in depth, but know how to get it.

General and local (content) knowledge are allies, not rivals. Both fill important functions in the overall process of problem solving.

When tasks are unfamiliar, overly complicated, or fraught with emotional overtones, then general strategies are most valuable as a starting point. Yet, conversely, the ability of individuals to solve these initially novel problems with increasing sophistication, faster, and with greater assurance depends on the creation of a rich knowledge base of experience that is specific to the particular task. Once this specific knowledge base is in place, then general thinking strategies recede in importance, so that eventually, with enough experience and practice, even highly complex tasks like chess play may take on the superficial appearance of simplicity. That is why experts make hard things look so easy.

Teaching for Transfer

The most important implication of this chapter can be stated as a question: how can we best combine the teaching of local domain-specific knowledge and broad metacognitive knowledge in ways that maximize the chances for future transfer?

We have already provided one answer by example in the case of the Global Gambit scenario (Chapter 6) where high school students are portrayed as mastering the finer points of economic theory, meteorology, and conflict management (at a deep level of processing), all for the purpose of responding to the threat of the "greenhouse effect." In short, school learning should be arranged around the discovery and investigation of inherently interesting problems – not just the solving of mindless work sheet problems, ten to a page, a practice that trades effectiveness for efficiency.

Such a problem orientation heralds several important changes in the way we must think about school curricula, including the role of content knowledge. Content knowledge must be subordinated to the higher purposes of inquiry. Facts should be introduced sparingly, and only as needed. This can be accomplished in several different ways. First, as illustrated by Global Gambit, students can acquire factual detail in *anticipation* of problem solving. Here the demands of content acquisition readily conform to the mastery learning paradigm in which students are held responsible for various levels of understanding before they proceed. Second, facts can also be introduced *during* problem solving, even at the crucial moment of decision making, when, for example, students acting as emergency room physicians consult the patient's vital signs or his past history (facts) in a last-ditch effort to discover a lifesaving clue. What better way to convince students of the importance of having the proper information at the right moment? Third, content acquisition can also proceed *after* the fact by way of a postmortem review, as also occurred in the Global Gambit scenario. Students can search for, identify, and then learn those facts and principles which, had they been available earlier, might have saved the patient, secured the peace, or explained the mystery. Ultimately, the value of learning facts in these ways, as part of a meaningful endeavor, is that the traditional role of facts is transformed from things to think *about* to things to think *with.*

But then how should content knowledge be taught in a problem-focused curriculum, especially those subject-matter strands whose acquisition is largely a cumulative affair? Consider the logical scaffolding of mathematical knowledge that presumes the progressive step-by-step mastery of propositions, theorems, postulates, and proofs. Obviously, Mr. Rodriguez's students cannot properly interpret graphs on population growth or fully appreciate the meaning of the phrase "parts per million of oxygen" until they understand, respectively, the notion of rate of change among variables and the concept of percentage. Such understanding depends on starting at the beginning, years earlier, with basic number facts no matter what discovered problems these students may encounter along the way, and to begin anywhere else would invite disaster.

But being a novice does not mean merely memorizing facts or learning in a "thoughtless" way. The research of Gordon Cavana and William Leonard (1985) demonstrates that acquiring procedural and content knowledge merges comfortably with the goal of self-regulated learning. These researchers distinguish between the "proscriptive" aspects of thinking, what we have called procedural knowledge – knowing, for example, *how* to use a microscope or a titration buret – and the "discretionary" or managerial aspects of thinking, such as deciding which of several different methods to use in demonstrating the process of, say, mitosis. Most commercial science experiments are predominantly proscriptive in nature (basically what we have called presented problems), divided into a number of sequential steps that students must complete without variation in a virtual lockstep. As one example, the Biological Sciences Curriculum Study (1968) unit on water loss from plants consists of twelve interlocking tasks, each taking an average of five minutes to complete.

Cavana and Leonard altered these science curricula by allowing students to combine several steps into one, thereby transforming largely proscriptive exercises into partially discretionary tasks over which students could exercise more personal control, independent of both the teacher and textbook. In one experiment that involved changing the curriculum of entire biology departments in three urban high schools, students demonstrated an increasing ability to exercise discretion and for longer and longer periods of time (Leonard, Cavana, & Lowery, 1981). Many students who initially could not work without direct guidance for more than fifteen minutes at a time extended their discretionary capacity to periods of two to three hours by the end of the school year. Moreover, these same students demonstrated a significantly greater understanding of the laboratory concepts involved and produced higher-quality written reports than did students using the unaltered commercial versions of the same exercises.

Research of this kind suggests that effective educational reform lies not in tampering with the inherent organizational structure of subject-matter knowledge, but of arranging content in thought-evoking ways and also in making certain that children realize that what they are learning now about mathematics, science, or grammar has both immediate and future utility. This means that discovered problems (Chapter 6) must be coordinated closely with the growth and development of the child's procedural knowledge base so that the act of problem solving itself fulfills the promise of content relevance and also spurs further learning in the belief that this new knowledge, too, will eventually prove useful for some as yet undisclosed purpose or problem.

CONCLUSION
Dangers of Dilettantism

For all its potential benefits, problem-oriented schooling raises several legitimate concerns. First, is it possible that by arranging learning around problem-solving episodes rather than around chapters in a textbook that subject-matter coverage of, say, chemistry or biology will become spotty and uneven? Certainly this is a potential danger. We must be careful not to create the kind of dilettantism reflected in the world's first (and greatest) consulting detective. Sherlock Holmes simply followed his interests from one mystery (discovered problem) to another, capriciously and often on a whim. As a consequence his ignorance was as remarkable as his knowledge. Holmes was scathing in his rebuke of any content knowledge that was neither appropriate nor relevant to his immediate concerns, "What the deuce is it to me? . . . You [Watson] say that we go around the sun. If we went around the moon it would not make a penny's worth of difference to me or my work" (Doyle, 1967, p. 154). Holmes could afford this self-absorbed perspective because his peculiar talents suited his chosen profession so well. But today such a cavalier attitude bodes ill for future survival, at least among lesser mortals. Obviously, teachers must sample discovered problems carefully to ensure a wider subject-matter exposure than if students were totally free to choose only those tasks that hold immediate appeal as Sherlock Holmes was lucky enough to do.

However, having once acknowledged the need for caution, does a problem-oriented focus hold any greater dangers than those associated with the current hodgepodge approach to content coverage? As things stand, student understanding of most topics is confused, plagued by an overemphasis on the trivial to the neglect of the profound, and characterized by wide-ranging misconceptions and misinformation. According to Andrew Porter (1989) this occurs in part because of the widespread practice of "teaching for exposure." He reports that at the elementary level most key mathematics concepts receive only the briefest coverage. For example, Porter found that during the entire school year teachers in one sample devoted less than thirty minutes each to 70 percent of the mathematics topics scheduled for introduction including multidigit multiplication, number facts, and subtraction with borrowing. Although the reasons for this "once over lightly" approach to content coverage may seem plausible enough – briefly introducing work to be treated in later grades or reintroducing work from the previous years for review – the results are potentially disastrous. Quite apart from guaranteeing superficial, disjointed preparation, which is bad enough, students may also conclude what is even worse, that knowing very little about a lot of things is better than a deep understanding of a few central concepts. Indeed, there is growing support for the proposition that from an educational perspective it is better to know a few things well than many things superficially, an observation that reminds us of the advice of Alfred North Whitehead when he anticipated years ago (1929) that we must "teach for only a few main ideas . . . which should then be thrown into every combination possible" (p. 14).

Also at fault is the fact that school instruction is not well designed to help students make sense out of complex events. One might suppose that history, a topic that presupposes a rich variegated network of cause-and-effect relationships, would be organized around narrative themes involving people's reactions to events and the consequences of their reactions. Not so, according to the research of Isabel Beck and Margaret McKeown (1988), who analyzed the treatment of the topic of prerevolutionary America in several elementary school history books. Apart from the usual ambiguous statements, confusing references, and simple errors of fact, all deplorable enough, the larger problem was that these texts failed to provide information that would allow students to see connections between events or to understand why events overtake people. For instance, in no case was there a discussion of why previously loyal British colonists would become revolutionaries within one generation. In effect, little was offered that would help students begin to build a sophisticated understanding of American history, so that, when the factual details are long forgotten – it seems the colonists were especially fond of porridge – students will still be able to draw cogent relationships and attach the proper meaning to historical events.

The Cult of Efficiency

A second concern about problem-focused schooling involves assigning the highest priority to teaching students how to think. By realigning priorities, we challenge the cult of efficiency. Americans are known for their ability to get the job done, quickly and on time. And when productivity suffers we become uneasy. It is not surprising, then, that a mentality of efficiency pervades our schools, aided in part by a factory model of education that, although sufficient for promoting the interchangeable assembly-line skills needed during rapid industrial growth in the nineteenth and early twentieth centuries, has proved hopelessly outdated today. Nonetheless, the vision of schools as factories or as workplaces still lingers (for a critique, see Marshall, 1988).

Compared with acquiring content knowledge, at times thinking appears to be an enormously inefficient proposition. Solving problems takes time, lots of it – time to reflect, define, speculate, and then – true to the convoluted nature of thinking – additional time to *redefine* the problem, to discard false leads, and sometimes to start over. Group problem solving is the most cumbersome of all – time out to negotiate with others for their cooperation, time taken to overcome stalemates by searching for the next-most-acceptable alternative for all parties, and even extra time to create controversy deliberately in order to challenge overly simplistic solutions. The importance of this latter function cannot be overstated. For instance, testimony to the presidential commission on the explosion shortly after the launch of the American space shuttle *Challenger* in 1986 indicated that no one on the launch team wished to voice his concerns about its safety for fear of appearing troublesome or not being a "team player."

On the face of it, then, teaching thinking appears to confront schools with a cruel trade-off between promoting either broad content coverage or depth of processing. But actually, in the final analysis, this dilemma may be more apparent than real. For one thing, putting a lot of thought into a problem up front by preplanning has been shown to pay dividends in the long run, with better solutions and even greater efficiency in tackling other, similar dilemmas. In effect, teaching for thinking promotes transfer. For another thing, by improving the ability of students to think strategically, they also increase their capacity to learn and to retain more of what they learn. What could be more efficient?

SUMMING UP

1. Schools must teach children *how* to think, not merely *what* to think.

2. Far from being passive, thinking is an active, constructive attempt by the learner to create meaning.

3. "Thoughtless" education occurs when students do not see the larger utility of what they are learning, when the fear of failure degrades intellectual functioning, and when schools neglect systematic instruction in how to think.

4. Teaching students *how* to think increases their *willingness* to think because they are now more likely to see ability as an *incremental* process, and because learning *how* to think alters the meaning of failure. Failure now becomes something that can be overcome by analyzing problems better and setting more realistic goals.

5. The skills of problem discovery, like those of problem solving, are an important part of personal and economic survival, and fortunately, they, too, can be enhanced through systematic instruction.

6. Increasingly, problems of the future will involve the cooperation of individuals, communities, and nations and learning how to share. There is also clear evidence that youngsters can be taught how to overcome obstacles to cooperation.

7. The most important element in preparing students for the future is to teach them how to *transfer* knowledge, that is, how to apply their thinking skills to new, unfamiliar, or unexpected situations.

198

ACTIVITIES

Activity 1: Metacognition and Study Skills

Metacognitive knowledge is central to effective study, especially when it comes to self-monitoring (Pressley, 1995). For example, good students know when they understand something well enough to pass a test, and when they do not.

Think of ways that teachers might modify the testing procedures described in Appendix H (Chapter 5) so students can practice self-monitoring skills as they study. Appendix K provides some additional ideas once you have thought of your own.

Activity 2: Promoting Problem Finding

We have made a case for problem finding as a tool for future building. Problem finding means many things. For one thing, it means being sensitive to the puzzling features of a situation and sometimes discovering when there is insufficient information to understand it ("problem identification"). Problem finding also means literally creating problems where none were presumed to exist before ("problem creation"). For example, public health officials ask questions about potentially dangerous conditions that otherwise would go undetected, and social workers note human needs that would otherwise go unmet. Problem finding also involves question asking, especially raising questions about the wisdom of a particular plan of action. Recall the warning, "If you think the problem is bad now, just wait until you've solved it!" ("problem anticipation").

How might teachers introduce each of these three different aspects of problem finding into the regular curriculum? Appendix L presents some possibilities that may complement your own ideas.

8

AN IMMODEST
PROPOSAL

Had I been present at the act of creation I would have had some
helpful suggestions.
Anonymous

I T IS NOW TIME TO DRAW ALL OUR RECOMMENDATIONS TOGETHER
into a single, unified proposal for educational change. But first, a
recap. We argued from the outset in favor of John Dewey's observation (1938/1963) that "the most important attitude that can be
formed [in schools] is that of the desire to go on learning" (p. 48).
Our analysis of achievement motivation led to a set of instructional
guidelines intended to foster the will to learn, which depends largely on establishing a motivational equity.

Then, we added a distinctively cognitive element to these motivational concerns, something also anticipated by Dewey
(1938/1963) when he remarked that "all which the school can or
need do for pupils, so far as their minds are concerned, is to develop their capacity to think" (p. 152). In contemporary terms, this
means strengthening the capacity of students to reflect on their
thinking, to create their own mental strategies, and to encourage a
view of learning as an ongoing, open-ended process in which meaning is created by the learner, not simply dispensed by authority.

The point of contact between these two educational objectives –
one cognitive, the other motivational – is the concept of strategic
thinking. A strategy orientation mobilizes the will to learn because
it encourages a belief among students that intellectual capacity ex-
pands through the wise management of one's mental resources.
Also, by focusing on mental strategies, not on ability per se, students become task-oriented, and, as a result, more positive, em-
powering explanations for failure become possible.

Finally, to complete our analyses, we maintained a future-oriented perspective. In Chapter 1 we proposed three essential ingredients for future building: first, the need for students to develop a set of marketable skills – be they reflected, occupationally, as a welder, a social worker, or an architect, but reflected, in any event, in doing the job well; second, a sense of commitment, a willingness to become engaged; and, third, a preparation for change and acceptance, with grace, of the inevitability of change. How, then, can we restructure the prevailing educational experiences of children to accommodate this entire future-oriented legacy and, at the same time, address both motivational and cognitive concerns? That is the fundamental question posed in this chapter.

SERIOUS GAMES

Play used to be regarded as a harmless release of surplus energy, but it has come to be regarded as useful to the process of learning.

Jeremy Campbell

My proposal can be summarized in a nutshell: schools should teach students how to play games, serious games – to use Clark Abt's (1987) colorful oxymoron – under instructional conditions that (1) favor motivational equality, (2) promote strategic thinking, and (3) reinforce the positive lessons to be learned from failure. Serious games are essentially synonymous with what we have called discovered problems whose solutions and consequences cannot always be known in advance. Most discovered problems can be viewed as games. Any political, economic, or social issue, whether it involves a nation, a neighborhood, or an individual, is a contest of sorts typically played by adversaries with specific objectives in mind and with various resources available to players, including knowledge, skill, and power. Even luck and chance play a part. And, perhaps most notably, adversaries are not always other players. In the case of many, if not most, discovered problems, players must cooperate to achieve common cause against obstacles not of their own making. Sometimes these long odds are due to a lack of information, and sometimes because there is simply not enough time. At other times the main player may be nature itself, which yields up its secrets only reluctantly.

The word "game" has a rich surplus meaning that goes far beyond the barest dictionary definition, which suggests mere amusement, or frivolous diversion. On the more serious side, games can also mean any test of skill, courage, or an ideal of endurance, as in the "game of life." Games also refer to objects of pursuit, especially business and vocational pursuits, as in the "sales game." Also, we play for high stakes, risk danger, sometimes gamble recklessly, and in the process we hope to overcome obstacles and uncertainties, all for the sake of winning the "big game."

And, by "play" it should now be clear that I do not mean undisciplined activity. Rather, I mean perceiving that an activity is interesting or worthwhile enough in its own right to commit all of one's resources, unreservedly, even joyously. Other more colloquial meanings of the word play also broaden its meaning for true learning: to use one's resources in the most effective manner, as in "playing one's cards right"; and mobilizing one's skills to best advantage, as in "making a play for"; or enjoying the "subtle play of the mind." By the same token, not everything about "work" is contrastingly bad. Not when we recall that work implies purposeful activity as in the "collected works of Walt Whitman," or the importance of "good works," or the quality of "workmanship." Unfortunately, it is these uplifting interpretations of work that too easily become the casualties of schooling as presently structured.

It is this combination of the joyous and creative coexisting with the serious side of play – the analytic, the empirical, and the deliberate – that most recommends gaming and role playing as ideal vehicles for encouraging both the will to learn and the capacity to think. Abt (1987) puts it well when he suggests that "in dreams begin responsibilities . . . and in games begin realities" (p. 5). These realities benefit particularly from the fact that serious games provide a union between thought and action. They offer an unparalleled opportunity to explore significant intellectual, personal, and social problems – the *thought* side of the equation – and to accumulate experience by *doing*, on the action side, all through the process of role playing that prepares youngsters for the real roles they will play in later life.

Abt puts it well when he observes that "It is not difficult to imagine a school of the future as a 'laboratory school' – a school making massive use of educational simulation games, laboratory exercises, and creative projects – a school in which almost everything to be learned is to be manipulated, physically or mentally" (Abt, 1987, pp. 120–121).

More specifically, what kinds of games do we have in mind besides Global Gambit (Chapter 6)? And exactly in what ways do they satisfy our instructional guidelines, especially the motivational benefits? Here are some examples.

Exponential Growth: A Mathematics Game

Not everyone was satisfied with Sally's approach. She tried again, raising her voice for emphasis: "Assume the original pair is labeled (0); and that the first offsprings of these parents are labeled (0) (1) . . ." Sally and her classmates are struggling with a precollege mathematics problem dealing with growth functions. Their task is to figure out ways to verify that a single pair of rats (male and female) and their progeny would multiply into a colony of 1,808 rats by the end of one year given various parameters including an average gestation period of twenty-one days and an average litter size of six with half being female (de Lange, 1987, p. 46).

Here mathematics is being learned basically as an empirical discipline, one consisting of data and discovery much like biology, physics, and chemistry. What is being discovered are the rules of the mathematics game rather than the rote application of presented rules. In this context learning becomes a community enterprise in which truth, according to Alan Schoenfeld (1989), becomes "that for which the majority of the community believes it has compelling arguments. In mathematics truth is socially negotiated, as it is in science" (p. 9). Sally's team is engaged in this truth-seeking process whenever anyone argues for his or her own notation system. And the teacher's task is not necessarily to certify which is correct, but rather to draw students into more sophisticated ways of stating problems in mathematical terms, which in the rat colony example means bringing students to the threshold of matrix algebra.

Indeed, from a motivational perspective, this example works because of its potential for altering the student–teacher relationship. The adversary is no longer adult authority, but rather the challenge of an interesting task. The role of the teacher is largely that of a resource and coach as well as an ally of students, rather than the teacher being a disciplinarian or mere lecturer.

This example also illustrates the most formidable challenge facing teachers as managers of the discovery process: recognizing when the child's intuitive appreciation of a situation outstrips his or her formal knowledge, and then knowing how to help consolidate these informal insights into more advanced systems of formal thought so that the stage is set for the next intuitive leap forward. Immanuel Kant said it all when he observed: "Thus all human cognition begins with intuitions, proceeds from hence to conceptions and ends with ideas."

This progression as applied to mathematics teaching is much in vogue today. The Netherlands has built a nationwide high school mathematics curriculum around such a problem-focused approach (the rat colony problem is but one example from this curriculum). Because of its success, the program has been extended downward to the elementary levels (de Lange, 1987).

Although ultimately, by our definition, such exercises are presented problems, they also share an important element of discovery because it is the process, not the answer correctly calculated, that remains the focus. The means by which Leibniz created the calculus shares more in common with the struggle of the schoolchild to discover and understand it than was once suspected. In effect, the capacity for productive thinking can be found in every individual, and among all groups, not merely among a chosen few.

The Health Futures Game

A group of junior high students is huddled around a game board, absorbed in the task of negotiating friendships (Covington, 1981).

In the early rounds of the game (representing the teenage years), the goal is to gain "popularity" points. One of the simplest ways to be popular is to provide one's peers with a ready supply of cigarettes and to smoke whenever others light up. Actually, the real purpose of this game goes deeper than teaching youngsters about the best, and worst, ways to negotiate friendships. It is also designed to illustrate that a tactic which may be effective for one purpose now can become ineffective (or, in this case, even destructive) later on as situations change. Having chosen to smoke in the earlier rounds of the game puts players at a decided handicap in future rounds where the objective, in the adult years, is to establish financial independence and provide for one's family. This task is made more uncertain by increasing health risks in later life, ineligibility for life insurance, and unexpected medical expenses due to having been a smoker in earlier years.

It is now widely accepted that before physical health messages can be truly effective in altering risky behavior, the perceived linkage between one's actions (e.g., smoking) and their consequences (e.g., decreased lung capacity) must be made personally vivid. Also the relationship between one's intentions and actual outcomes must also be clarified. In our society accountability for one's actions depends as much on intentions as on the gravity of the actions themselves. Hence, for instance, if one person harms another, but without intending to do so, then his culpability is diminished. Applying this same logic to health risks, many adolescents truly believe that if they do not *intend* to smoke (but did so because of social pressure), then they will suffer fewer negative health consequences compared with those instances in which they choose freely to smoke (Covington & Omelich, 1988). Such primitive thinking represents a major obstacle to health promotion. Demonstrating the fallacies of magical reasoning is best pursued by providing youngsters with a life-cycle perspective that relates short-term decisions to long-term consequences. In this particular simulation, cause-and-effect dynamics can be discovered and the implications more readily appreciated by the young adolescent without adult preaching, and in a situation that is inherently interesting and encourages the development of an extended future time frame.

Chief among the motivational benefits of this serious game is the authenticity of the assignment. The struggle of young teenagers to establish a sense of belonging and friendships outside the family poses an unparalleled opportunity for teaching. What better way to demonstrate the instrumental value of knowledge, combined with practical experience? Knowledge buys power, in this case the knowledge needed to further one's self-interest by negotiating social relationships effectively.

Forbidding Planet: The Space Colony Game

A group of high school students is given the task of designing a space colony that will occupy a drone planet in a nearby galaxy for the purpose of harvesting minerals for commercial use. As a first step, team members must discover those laws of physics, chemistry, and biology that prevail in this distant world – laws that may not conform to more familiar earthly patterns. What, for example, would conditions be like if life was based on methane, not carbon, building blocks? What would be the consequences and risks to humans? Or what if these explorer-students were confronted with a world of only two dimensions, a situation that faced the inhabitants of Edwin Abbott's classic science fiction fantasy, *Flatland*. Certainly the numerical base for mathematics would be different, likely requiring a binary base, which incidentally provides a convenient introduction to the fundamentals of computer language.

In this simulation, our explorer-students have available a limited set of experiments as the means to discover these prevailing laws and conditions. Team members take on the roles of individual subject-matter experts – chemists, engineers, and even biostatisticians – each of whom learns to conduct a single experiment, record the results, and then interpret them. Naturally, certain levels of technological sophistication must be attained before these experiments can be run, because so much rides on their accuracy. Under the circumstances it is the students, not the teacher, who will likely monitor the quality of individual contributions. Once all the experiments are completed team members meet to share their individual

206

findings and search for a larger pattern of meaning, reminiscent of the rules of the cooperative jigsaw paradigm.

Motivationally speaking, this assignment takes advantage of the energizing qualities of fantasy as well as demonstrating the benefits of cooperation in sharing a common task, if not a common fate. Indeed, if mistakes are made and false conclusions drawn about the nature of the planet, then the wrong kinds of equipment will be chosen for the voyage and the mission runs the risk of being aborted. This particular feature of the game illustrates yet another motivational principle that encourages positive reasons for learning: it is the players themselves who create the rules by which their efforts are judged a success, a failure, or a nonsuccess. More specifically, before setting out on the voyage, team members decide how long the colony must survive in order to be declared a successful venture, and also the quality of life that must prevail for the colonists to establish a viable community.

Viral Invasion: The BioAlert Game

Several fifth-grade students stand by watching anxiously as one of their friends struggles to save himself from a massive viral invasion, all thanks to a computer simulation. With the cunning of video-game junkies, students organize and arrange their antibodies to mow down wave after wave of invaders. Although good motor coordination is a decided advantage, ultimately the patient will be saved only by understanding the intricate relationships found among the body's various immune systems and, in particular, specialized knowledge about the use of antibiotics. Prior to game play students master the necessary information and concepts. For example, they learn that antibiotics, for all their benefits, are potentially dangerous and may actually increase the risk to the patient if they are administered in improper combinations, under the wrong circumstances, or in inappropriate dosages. For these young students, the rewards of learning include surviving the viral attack and the opportunity to learn more about the human body so they can challenge an even more virulent breed of invaders in the next round of the BioAlert game.

Once again, we see how easily rewards can be incorporated as an integral part of the learning activity itself, rather than being imposed from the outside. In the BioAlert game the reward for defeating one virus is the opportunity to learn more in order to play better next time. Also, from a motivational perspective, this game illustrates how task involvement can be aroused and sustained when youngsters are permitted to exert control over the challenge they face. There is that delicious moment when players realize that this time they may have given the virus too much of a head start. But if they try their hardest and learn just enough, they still might snatch victory from the jaws of defeat. Here there is room for the playful exploration of what it means to take risks, and how it feels to fail after having given it one's best shot – hopefully not feeling shattered, as would be true if failure were defined competitively around ability status, but rather feeling the satisfaction that comes from having tried one's hardest. In this context effort is not a threat.

This situation is analogous to the game of tag. As will be recalled, tag permits each player to adjust the level of challenge to his or her own physical abilities by choosing whom to chase and by modifying the distance to stay away from whomever is "it." In the BioAlert game children can select their own odds for success and failure, which creates drama and excitement by sometimes leaving the chances of success uncertain but not hopelessly out of reach.

Psychic Income: The Career Placement Game

Mrs. Rollins's eighth-grade students remained skeptical. Could it really be that most adults find their jobs more satisfying than leisure activities, such as watching television or going to movies (Juster, 1985)? But if true, conceded the students, then something very strange indeed must happen between junior high school and the future because everyone knows television is more fun than work! And then there was the other bombshell: those same loopy adults report that happiness on the job depends on more than how much money they make.

This young, disbelieving audience is about to be transported into the adult world of work where things will become clearer thanks to the Psychic Income game (after Abt, 1987). In this simulation students become employees and employers in a small electronics manufacturing firm. The firm is structured hierarchically with most job openings at the production level (hourly wages); fewer jobs in middle management (annual salary), and fewer still at the top management level (annual salary plus bonus). The task for the players is to assign themselves to the available job openings while maximizing satisfaction for all. One approach is to make every job equally attractive despite the differential pay rates.

Players begin by listing various sources of on-the-job satisfaction besides money, what economists call "psychic income" (Strober, 1987) – security, independence, power, status, and opportunity for leisure. *Power* is measured by the number of people one supervises; *independence*, conversely, by the number of supervisors above one's level; and, *leisure* by the number of free, nonworking hours available per week. Players establish their own personal priorities and then begin negotiating among themselves for their own ideal mix of pay, leisure time, and status. One player may value monetary rewards so much that he is willing to give up all the leisure credits allotted him if he can but find someone willing to trade time for money. Another player finds the idea of rotating among different lower-paying production jobs (lateral movement) attractive because the resulting diversity of experience will make him or her more marketable in the event of a layoff.

Once again, motivationally speaking, this example works because the task is authentic. It deals with real, pressing issues of great personal importance to students at a point in their lives when they experience the dawning realization that eventually they must enter the work force.

Today many youngsters make career and vocational choices inadvertently without an accurate understanding of how these decisions will affect their lives. Some children drift from one part-time job to another in essentially a random fashion, often accepting the first offer of permanent employment, even though they may have applied for many jobs of widely varying characteristics (Osterman, 1989). Other young people aspire for something better but lack the preparation to implement their dreams. For instance, black females sometimes express career aspirations that are comparable with or even higher than those of white females (Gibbs, 1985; Smith, 1982), but they often lack sufficient information to make realistic plans to achieve these goals.

An important part of career education involves providing youngsters with systematic opportunities to gauge their own strengths and weaknesses, to discover preferred working styles, and to consider life goals. When students must determine their own "winning" formula in the Psychic Income game, they are considering just what they want from a job – and, for many, this may be the first time they have consciously thought about their life aims. Hopefully, such self-reflection will encourage the beginning of a rational choice of occupation, especially coming to terms with the fact that the most prestigious, well-paying jobs in our society are in relatively short supply compared with the number of young people who aspire to them (see Chapter 9).

PLAYING SCHOOL

> Education will also become creative – a game under the control
> of the person being educated. Everyone will have a chance to
> discover exactly what he or she enjoys.
> Lee Kravitz

Now that we have considered serious games from a motivational perspective, how might they encourage strategic thinking and help prepare students for the future, all in one? First, consider the prospects for encouraging a future orientation.

A Future Orientation

Serious games provide an ideal vehicle for dealing with those issues that most experts believe will increasingly characterize the future. First, the future is problematic, and becoming more so, because the greatest dangers are not necessarily the most obvious ones. Second, more and more future problems will be without precedent in human history. Third, it is increasingly clear that these problems cannot be solved in isolation, one from another.

Low-Profile Risks. Robert Ornstein and Paul Ehrlich (1989) remind us that humans are notoriously prone to react quickly and often ineffectually to the dramatic but infrequent threat – being held hostage by terrorists, falling victim to a mass murderer, or being struck by lightning – and slow to respond, if at all, to the more insidious, low-profile threats that adversely affect everyone, such as the rising tide of human population, the accelerating extinction of animal and plant life, and the slow but sure poisoning of our environment.

An example from the field of public health illustrates the difficulties of teaching for an awareness of low-profile risks. The consequences of using heroin and skateboarding are immediate, potentially fatal, and capable of graphic portrayal. But other risks, such as poor diet and chronic cigarette smoking, are more subtle. They involve low probabilities of occurrence over extended periods of time. For instance, relatively few smokers will die of cancer. Moreover, the harmful effects of smoking are often long delayed. Thinking seriously about such low-probability, time-delayed risks depends on a growing understanding of the probabilistic nature of future events.

Specific examples of such future-oriented reasoning include being able to entertain the idea that the benefits of taking preventive actions now – say, going on a low-sodium diet – may be delayed in their appearance sometimes for years, and then may only become manifest, if at all, through an *absence* of symptoms like heart disease. Then there is the possibility that taking risks now may never have an adverse impact on one's health unless other seemingly unrelated risks are also taken at a later time. For instance, the lung damage done by heavy smoking in adolescence may not manifest itself as emphysema until years later when the individual (by now a longtime ex-smoker) moves to a polluted metropolitan area.

Such understanding is exceedingly difficult to convey, if not nearly impossible, because of a compressed view of future time and the concrete, absolute nature of the thinking of young people. However, by incorporating these lessons in realistic scenarios, like the Health Futures game, and by starting in the earliest years, hopefully we can promote a true appreciation of the low-profile risk.

Problems without Precedent. Future problem solving will be increasingly characterized by either too little or too much information. The former case includes situations so novel to human experience that there are few precedents for decision making so that the future consequences of our present actions can only be dimly foreseen today – decisions about the commercial exploitation of outer space or the ethical consequences of humankind's capacity to change its very nature through biochemical technology. Fortunately, however, as will be recalled in Chapter 7, these are the very kinds of problems that are most responsive to broad problem-framing strategies, skills that can be readily practiced in the naturally occurring context of serious games.

Too much information is just as serious a threat to effective problem solving as too little. Today the information glut is so severe that even experts working in highly arcane, narrowly defined specialties cannot keep up with all that is potentially important. The statistics are staggering. Worldwide, seven thousand books are published each day (Wurman, 1989). There is also the daily blizzard of memos, abstracts, and reports, most of it generated and stored by computer, and much of it only marginally relevant to any particular problem. This means that tomorrow's adults must be prepared to handle large masses of information, certainly not to remember it all, but at least be able to make decisions about what is relevant and what can be ignored. Such preparation takes practice. For example, it would seem reasonable that students spend as much time learning whether problems can be solved in the form stated and, if not, how to reformulate them, as they now devote to practicing specific procedural rules, such as adding double columns or subtracting with borrowing. Subject-matter experts in all fields differ from novices in the amount of time they spend in the problem-formulation stage (Johnson, 1990). Novices tend to look immediately for a solution, whereas experts begin by analyzing the available information. Only after the dimensions of the problem are well understood do experts begin the search for answers. If children were taught these lessons early on, far fewer of them would try to calculate the ship captain's age in terms of the size and content of his cargo, and be none the wiser (Chapter 1).

Interconnected Issues. The future of present decisions will depend increasingly on how well we handle deeply interconnected issues. For example, pesticides do, in fact, control plant-eating pests. But overspraying, by just a small margin, can have a more devastating effect on insect enemies of plant eaters than on the plant eaters themselves. Thus a hoped-for solution to the problem of the global food shortage can in the end be counterproductive by creating an unexpected dislocation in a larger chain of interrelated events. Global Gambit illustrates the kinds of thinking demanded by this perspective. It demonstrates that neither the players nor society at large can succeed solely by doubling up on brain power, that is, by simply creating more specialists. Such a narrow frontal assault on problems exposes too many knowledge gaps. Rather we must prepare our students to array their expert knowledge in an overlapping fashion more akin to the pattern of fish scales so that common, continuous fields of knowledge are created (Campbell, 1986). The lessons taught in Global Gambit required students to arrange their individual knowledge in a collective jigsaw fashion (Aronson, Blaney, Stephan, Sikes, & Snapp, 1978). Teaching these "jigsaw" dynamics is also illustrated by the Space Colony game in which students must assign overall meaning to a series of scientific experiments conducted by individual team members.

Students must shift their view of themselves as separate entities, each seeking to satisfy only his or her particular goals, to a broader, collective conception of group well-being and to appreciate anew the deep interconnectedness of events and issues. Serious gaming seems an ideal vehicle for this purpose.

Enhancing Metacognitions

We have surveyed the quality of planning that typifies many students and found it marginal at best (Chapter 7). On the brighter

213

side, we now know that these deficiencies can be offset by systematic instruction. Also, encouraging the proper reasons for learning will help. No one can think effectively when fear is the instigator. Now, a third source of help presents itself: serious games.

Playing serious games automatically reinforces a strategic, planful mindset for several reasons. First, strategic questions about what one should know, how well, for how long, and for what purpose are all answerable in terms of the demands of the game. For example, in some popular board games remembering what information was discovered in previous moves, as in the game of Clue, is vital if players hope to win. For this reason, taking notes is highly advisable. In other games, such as Monopoly, recalling what happened in previous rounds is less important than establishing a strategic plan for economic takeover early on. In effect, the game itself dictates the kinds of working knowledge and strategies needed for a solution. Moreover, successful game play becomes feedback, confirmation that enough information was acquired and the proper meaning extracted to get the job done. Second, serious game play transforms the purpose of knowledge. No longer does learning imply the rote recall of isolated facts for no particular purpose other than getting the right answer. For instance, many geography textbooks routinely dispatch the topic of Siberia (if it is covered at all) in a few sentences concerning its remoteness and frigid climate. However, for those students about to negotiate a nuclear disarmament treaty with the former Soviet Union, Siberia takes on enormous geopolitical importance. And given the stakes involved, the desire to learn more about Siberia increases and in ways that promote game play. In this case, to recall a point made earlier, facts become things to think *with*, not just things to think *about*.

The Benefits of Failure

We have concluded (Chapter 2) that it is the meaning individuals attach to failure, and not its mere occurrence, that controls the quality of achievement motivation. Serious games are especially well suited for conveying the invaluable lessons of failure. As Max Beerbohm remarked, "There is much to be said for failure. It is more in-

214

teresting than success." Failure is interesting partly for the fact that successful thinkers actually make more mistakes than those who give up easily and thereby preserve their unblemished record of mediocrity, and also for the fact that mistakes can usually be set right by trying again.

Many cases illustrate the value of persistence, including Edison's trial-and-error attempts to find a suitable filament for the first electric light. Legend has it that Edison made over a thousand mistakes before succeeding, an impressive but unenviable record that caused him to observe that "invention is 99 percent perspiration and 1 percent inspiration." According to Richard Wurman (1989, p. 194), Jonas Salk, discoverer of the polio vaccine, spent 98 percent of his time documenting the things that did not work until he found the thing that did. Likewise, Charlie Chaplin often insisted on several hundred retakes of a single movie scene before he was satisfied with the results.

Edison may have relied too much on blind variation, and perhaps Chaplin persisted to a fault. Nonetheless, the value of not giving up easily is plain to see.

It should also prove instructive for students to replay famous failures in history so that they, in their turn, will be better prepared to avoid the mistakes of their predecessors. For instance, after students witness the kinds of leadership that led to the disastrous Bay of Pigs invasion of Cuba, they could replay events again, this time hopefully avoiding the divisive consequences of "groupthink," a condition in which groups value harmony above dissent (Janis, 1982). In the same vein, one might challenge students to discover the flaws in reasoning that led authorities to build a nearly disastrous rapid transit system in the San Francisco Bay area. In hindsight the mistakes seem obvious (Hall, 1980).

Given our concern for the future, it would also seem wise for students to make a study of the failure of humans to anticipate the future. The record of prediction is basically dismal; it is not even a history of near misses. In fact, even when the projected target dates are only one or two decades hence, most expert guesses still prove wide of the mark, often ludicrously so. One of the most stunning examples of technological predictions gone wrong is TRW's "Probe."

215

This 1960 study claimed to anticipate the products of the 1980s. Virtually all the predictions were either flatly wrong or the predicted time frame for their occurrence wildly optimistic. For example, it was estimated that the first manned lunar base would be established by 1977 and that by 1980 commercial passenger rockets would transport people to the moon and back around the clock. These wrong guesses were largely the result of psychological errors, including the tendency to be overly impressed by the wonders of technology, or what has been called the "gee whiz effect." Other mistakes in forecasting are driven by wishful thinking. Consider the often predicted cure for cancer. Then there is egocentrism, the presumption that consumers will see the same value in a new product as does the inventor. Obviously, these kinds of errors have implications for individual decision making and should be well understood by students lest they, too, make the same kinds of mistakes in arranging their personal and collective lives that have led to enormous miscalculations in political and social policy in this century.

Serious Games and the Disadvantaged

Educational reform must also address the special problems associated with disenfranchised youth, immigrants, and children of color. For many of these youngsters, school is essentially a foreign country, foreign in that the goals traditionally associated with schooling are narrowly defined around unfamiliar middle-class values, including achievement for the sake of competitive excellence or merely for attaining a high test score. Moreover, the *means* to these predominately middle-class goals are foreign to many minority students, who prefer the cooperation that comes from tight-knit neighborhood and family traditions. If black ghetto youngsters and their families often survive by a kind of collective sharing, as documented by Carol Stack (1974), then it is only natural that these same children would feel most comfortable learning by cooperative means (Richmond & Weiner, 1973; Shade, 1987; Slavin & Oickle, 1981). Yet if minorities want to play school, they must play by essentially competitive rules.

We concluded earlier (Chapter 2) that these sources of estrangement can be overcome in part by encouraging more varied achievement goals than those associated with high test scores and by honoring alternate ways of achieving, largely through noncompetitive approaches. Serious games can help promote these changes in several ways.

First, we have already noted how playing serious games can transform the teacher–student relationship for the better. Such changes would seem especially welcome for disenfranchised youngsters who often see adult authority as an intrusion into their lives (Ladner, 1978; Silverstein & Krate, 1975). But when the rules decree that the goal of school is to solve problems, not to usurp power or defend against powerful others, then the role of the teacher as a potential adversary can give way to the teacher as helper, explainer, and possibly even a player. Evidence reported by Abt (1987, p. 70) suggests that even the most rebellious student, fearing exclusion by peers, is more likely to accept and play by those rules mutually agreed upon by the group than by the rules of discipline imposed by a teacher.

Second, because game play is a familiar, concrete activity, it makes an ideal vehicle for the introduction and mental manipulation of complex concepts like history, justice, and civilization in ways that might not otherwise be possible if they were presented solely as abstractions. Indeed, some researchers suggest that black and Hispanic children are favored by learning environments that focus on whole concepts and real situations rather than on fragmented skills (Cohen & DeAvila, 1983; Gilbert & Gay, 1985; Ramirez & Castaneda, 1974). While this may well be true, our evidence points to a greater truth. It is not simply minority students who profit most from the manipulation of ideas physically and intellectually. All children do best under these conditions.

Additionally, children of widely differing intellectual capacity and social background can participate in the same game with equal enthusiasm, yet learn quite different lessons. John Blaxall, one of the developers of a simulation designed to demonstrate the economic forces at work in the industrial revolution of the 1880s, observed that quite apart from the original intentions of the designers, slow learners came to understand for the first time about the idea of charging interest on money, while more advanced students learned about the effects that fluctuating demand has on prices (see Abt, 1987, p. 75).

Third, the problem is not that disadvantaged youth lack the ability to learn or that they are disinterested. Rather what is being taught is too often perceived as irrelevant to their lives. Yet when it really counts, minority and poor children, like all youngsters, are capable of extraordinary achievements. The research of Geoffrey Saxe (1988) illustrates just how extraordinary. Saxe studied poor children in the urban barrios of Brazil who survive by selling candy. These young entrepreneurs (many never attended school and some were as young as five years old) created a serviceable, intuitively based system of arithmetic rules and notations that allowed them to carry out the complex calculations involved in buying candy wholesale and then setting the daily retail price which had to take into account the Brazilian inflation rate which often exceeds 250 percent per year! Improvisation is the name of the game. For example, the youngest children who are as yet unable to identify the numerical value of currency – not knowing the difference between, say, a 1,000-cruzeiro or a 10,000-cruzeiro bill – make do nonetheless by substituting the color of the bill as the way to distinguish value. In the circumstance, learning also became a social event. Older children (sometimes brothers and sisters or older candy sellers) taught the younger children how to count and calculate, and sometimes wholesale store clerks helped sellers with their purchases by reading the prices of the candy boxes. Saxe's research is but one example of the newly emerging field of ethnomathematics (D'Ambrosio, 1987; Millroy, 1991), which investigates different modes of mathematical knowledge that arise outside formal schooling and across different cultures.

One can envision a classroom counterpart of Saxe's real-life situation in which students – not just minorities, but all children – acquire and manipulate the basic number facts through exchange, bartering, and trade, all in a larger social and economic context in which learning serves an immediate tangible purpose and children are encouraged to help one another. Perhaps, too, older children and even parents can be drawn into this process of game play.

We do not propose that teaching mathematics, or any topic, remains solely an intuitive exercise. Intuitive knowledge as Kant rightly points out is a starting point; but intuition alone is not enough. Although Saxe's candy sellers who did not attend school made do for a time, in the long run they were unable to build on their intuitive understanding of mathematics in the same ways that school attenders were able to do. I do suggest, however, that teachers can help students make explicit their tacit, working knowledge on any topic by using the child's intuitive understanding as a gateway and stimulant to abstract knowledge and by modeling formal concepts and strategies, all for the purpose of encouraging students to continue learning on their own. Nor do I suggest that disadvantaged students can learn only by concrete example. Actually, the evidence indicates that *all* children are likely to profit from authentic, hands-on experience as the first step toward abstract knowledge (Oakes, 1987).

Finally, whatever approach is taken toward minority education, we must be careful that the school experience does not imply or require that children of color assimilate into the white middle-class culture. In the words of John Ogbu (1978): "Some inner-city black children need to know, for example, that one person can be a good mathematician and be black; another person could be a good mathematician and Chinese. Yet both may have become good mathematicians because they learned similar rules of behavior and skills that make people anywhere good mathematicians, without requiring them to give up their cultural, ethnic or racial identities" (p. 66).

Obviously, in the last analysis, the massive problems associated with educating the disadvantaged – just to mention the horrendous dropout rate as one example – will not be easily solved, or quickly, and certainly not simply by restructuring schools around the lessons learned from solving meaningful problems. Other changes must also be initiated simultaneously, many of which lie outside the influence of schools. These changes include reducing the barriers to minority employment and relieving the crushing burden of poverty that stalks America's urban ghettos and barrios. It is one thing to arrange learning so that disadvantaged youth will come to appreciate that how much and how well they learn now will influence their lifetime income on the job (Bishop, 1989). But if in the end there is no tangible payoff for trying hard in the form of enough jobs that offer a living wage and provide a reasonable source of dignity, then only disillusionment and resentment will result.

SCHOOLS AND JOBS

The end of the rainbow, you know, is not training and a diploma. The end of the rainbow is placement in a job and work.
Russell Tershy

Our vision of educational reform is broadly compatible with the requirements of the workplace as revealed by the findings of the National Academy of Sciences Panel on Secondary School Education for the Changing Workplace (1984). Employers were asked to describe the kinds of employees they will need in the years ahead. Overwhelmingly, the answer was individuals who are able to take responsibility and are willing to learn throughout a lifetime. The panel went on to describe the necessary skills that characterize such individuals: "Able to identify problems . . . adjust to unanticipated situations . . . work out new ways of handling reoccurring problems . . . determine what is needed to accomplish work assignments" (pp. 20–21).

Clearly, what is being called for is preparation for a working life of constant learning, problem solving, team work, and effective communicating rather than a continuation of the outmoded practice of preparing students for what Robert Reich (1989) calls "cog" jobs – being trained to follow directions for relatively simple, routine tasks that can be repeated over and over – while sending only a small minority of students on an advanced track to become decision makers at the top of the heap. Reich argues that productivity in America can no longer be viewed as a matter of producing a greater volume of goods, like cars or refrigerators, at a low cost per unit.

220

Today there are simply too many other countries able to mass-produce things better and cheaper. According to Reich, America must now rely on producing fewer goods, but of higher quality and tailored to the needs of specific customers in a timely fashion. By this reasoning, the manufacturing of television sets must be replaced by the production of television shows for specialized audiences worldwide. Likewise, mass-producing refrigerators must give way to the job of filling these refrigerators with specialized kinds of food.

In order to maintain a competitive edge, American industry must continually improve its ability to respond quickly to changing tastes. This vision implies not only a rapid turnover in jobs, but also requires flexibility in shifting work roles within a company so that, for instance, a worker may become a production engineer on one project and part of the sales force on another. Likewise, production workers are increasingly expected to maintain and make repairs on equipment themselves, thereby reducing the need for expensive specialized mechanics (Bailey, 1990). All this requires that the work force be capable of upgrading skills continuously and of acquiring new skills as well as the ability to think about information, not simply to remember it.

These demands are consistent with David Stern's notion of "enterprise training" (Stern, Hoachlander, Choy, & Benson, 1986), that is, helping students become job-ready through systematic instruction in individual and group problem-solving techniques and by learning to communicate effectively. Stern's recommendations are also compatible, uncannily so, with *our* evolving arguments that have approached the problem of student unpreparedness largely from a motivational perspective. The point of clearest overlap is an agreement that all students should practice creating potentially useful and personally meaningful ideas and products. By this reckoning, the world of work becomes another subject-matter topic equal in status to, say, physics or chemistry – actually, in fact, a premier opportunity for the practical application of physical and biological principles (Andrew & Grubb, 1995; Stern, Raby, & Dayton, 1992).

The lessons to be learned can start surprisingly early as Myra

Strober (1990) found to her amusement when she began to cut in half a dollar bill borrowed from a fourth-grader whose room she was visiting. "The children began wailing 'Oh no!' So I asked them, 'Why is this piece of paper special? How is it different from any other piece of green paper?'" Strober repeated the same maneuver on a credit card, "and again they cried out as only fourth-graders can, 'Oh no!' From there we discussed what money means – and what kind of trust one needs in a society to have money as a medium of exchange. We discussed why these kids would be willing to take money for chores and not insist on having food or a sweater, or whatever else they were going to buy with the money. And we looked at the dollar bill – we looked at the pyramid on it and the god's eye, and talked about what these symbols mean" (p. 5). Predictably, Strober's demonstration opened a floodgate of questions driven by a healthy curiosity about real events. So, too, did the actions of one third-grade teacher who decided to share the details of her paycheck in class as a way to explore the concept of benefits and deductions, and why her take-home pay was so little!

This spirit of inquiry can be rekindled when, several years hence, these same youngsters begin to wonder what their parents do "when they go to work," and again later still when they begin to contemplate those mysterious factories and offices that they themselves will soon be entering. Serious games serve not only to keep these curiosities alive, but they can also help provide a fundamental grasp of business law and accounting as well as the principles of industrial psychology and labor relations. Consider, for instance, the Production Line game through which youngsters can experience firsthand the dynamics of mass production and division of labor in the workplace (as described in Jamieson, Miller, & Watts, 1988). Students are organized into teams whose task it is to assemble a finished product out of component parts – perhaps building toy cars or fabricating paper notebooks out of raw materials. Students quickly realized that they can increase their efficiency (and the payoff) by assigning themselves to subtasks within the larger process. Eventually this division of labor may become complicated enough that the group will choose supervisors from within their ranks to coordinate the production process. In more sophisticated versions of this game, students can experience key facets of the real work environment, including the wearing of industrial clothes, clocking in, and taking work breaks. During such breaks students might receive printouts describing the financial condition of the company, its cash flow, earnings, and daily production schedules. When the financial well-being of the company – and, in effect, the opportunity for continued game play – depends on the proper interpretation of such data, we can count on students to be motivated to learn.

Obviously, too, business decisions can be practiced in lifelike situations, a prospect well illustrated by the Teddytronics game in which young entrepreneurs manufacture teddy bears (as reported in Jamieson et al., 1988). In the process of studying the topic of yearly quotas, players learn to distinguish between fixed and variable costs. The seasonable (variable) nature of the teddy bear market introduces unexpected complications that may make these lessons quite graphic, even painful unto bankruptcy. For instance, students must figure out how to negotiate favorable interest rates with a banker (teacher) and minimize rent increases in periods of low demand in order to stay in business.

The use of business and career games can also help repair many of the problems besetting education in general and vocational education in particular.

First, it has already been remarked that many students rarely see any relationship between what they are learning now and what they must or might accomplish in the future. Serious vocational games can make vivid the future utility of what is being learned now.

Second, by casting vocational education in the form of serious games, the quality of learning can be controlled directly by schools. Students need not be thrown willy-nilly into the marketplace of jobs in order to gain experience, which often turns out to be a brutalizing and demeaning experience (Bailey, 1993). Ian Jamieson and colleagues (1988) describe a number of school-linked work experiences including refurbishing old houses, tutoring young children,

running recycling centers, and setting up food-growing coopera-
tives. Stern (1984) calls these experiences "good work" because the
evidence he presents suggests that they better prepare youngsters
for future careers than does their random placement in odd jobs
and part-time employment.

Third, and finally, we have concluded that although competition
is a poor reason for learning, it is an undeniable force in society that
cannot be ignored. Serious games provide an ideal springboard for
creating a broader context within which to consider competitive dynamics: for clarifying the differences between cooperation and
competition, for demonstrating how they blend as mixed motives
in the marketplace, and for identifying what kinds of activities are
best reserved for cooperation. In the Teddytronics game, competition favors the consumer when teams compete among themselves
in order to offer the most attractive product at the lowest cost. But
when players within a team vie among themselves for competitive
advantage, everyone is the loser. In this case, game play largely follows gambling principles driven by the need for a team to recoup
its losses quickly before players are fired or demoted. These decisions depend little on the reality of cash flow, production demands,
or market variations. The usual result is a rapid expansion of teddy
bear output followed by a drastic reduction in the labor force when
hundreds of teddy bears remain unsold during periods of low demand (Jamieson et al., 1988).

There is broad agreement that schools should prepare students
for the world of work as it now exists. This is part of John Dewey's
legacy. So, too, is the conviction that schools should encourage a
vision of what work might become at its best – part of Stern's
(1984) "good work." Good work means an environment free of
physical danger, fair wages, and the chance for individuals to do
those things they do best. The quality of life in the workplace, like
that in schools, also depends on the rules by which people relate.
And these rules, too, can be changed for the better, a possibility to
be explored beginning in the earliest years of school by the very individuals who will eventually inherit the workplaces of the future.

This perspective suggests that dealing with issues of work, employment, and economics is in the final analysis as much a moral enterprise as a scientific or sociological activity. As Strober (1987) puts it, "I want students who study economics to come away not simply with an ability to analyze but with an ability to care, to feel deeply the excitement and pathos of trying to meet human wants with scarce resources" (p. 136). Achieving this objective requires that students gain a unifying perspective of how each of us, and the problems we confront, fit into the physical, social, and biological worlds. Note then that our earlier Global Gambit example is as much an economics game whose purpose is, in Strober's words, "to meet human wants with scarce resources," as it is an exercise in ecology. Such a perspective does not render learning about morals obsolete, but rather creates a world in which the nature of moral choice is unprecedented.

The vision of serious gaming requires that schools shift from being places characterized by deep divisions between vocational and academic subject matter to places that integrate disciplines and draw together college-bound and employment-bound students to the mutual benefit of all. Equally pronounced today are differences in teaching style and pedagogical method, namely, the didactic, teacher-focused approach favored by academic instructors versus student-initiated, project-oriented approaches associated with vocational classes. Here, too, the possibilities for creative borrowing are unlimited, especially when teachers begin collaborating to establish interdisciplinary programs.

A number of models for integrating academic and vocational education have been identified (Grubb, 1990). One possibility is to replace conventional vocational and academic programs at the school site with departments arranged around occupational groupings such as technology, health and business, or communications. This arrangement would provide academic instructors with a vocational theme to incorporate into their own teaching. As Grubb points out, the more ambitious of these proposals go far beyond attempts simply to integrate academic and vocational strands and can be regarded as efforts to overcome some of the more serious failings of schools, including the isolation of teachers both from their students and from one another.

PROSPECTS AND CONCLUSION

To reiterate, our proposal for change can be stated quite simply: educational reform should proceed by teaching students (and teachers) to play serious games with rules that promote positive, ennobling reasons for learning – reasons accessible to all students – and which will sustain game play into the future. In many respects this proposal is quite modest compared with the enormity of the problems facing American education today. It has become axiomatic that big problems require big solutions. Yet, as promised, these recommendations require no major dislocation in educating our youth. Educators and teachers remain in control and ultimately would still be subject to the wishes of the community. Neither is a massive infusion of additional monies necessarily called for, since limits on spending are not the most serious roadblock to change (Hanushek, 1989), although at a minimum clearly something must be done to repair the physical blight and decay of schools, upgrade antiquated equipment, replace books, and bring teachers' salaries more in line with the indispensable services they provide.

Moreover, there is little that is novel in the proposal to organize schools around discovery projects, lifelike simulations, and role playing. Actually, what John Stevenson (1921) called the "project method" of teaching was already well established in American educational circles long before the turn of the present century. In those early years the emphasis was on teaching the principles of science through their application to farm management and home economics. If there is anything new in our proposal, it is the suggestion that discovered problems should form the core of the entire school experience, not merely provide another source of enrichment or, worse yet, simple amusement. Simply to suggest the occasional use of serious games would at best improve things only marginally, if at all. Rather the intention is to transform educational policy. No small part of this transformation involves focusing attention squarely on our motivational objectives and on the future. All this suggests that our proposal is capable of relatively rapid implementation. The ingredients of change are all around us.

Yet despite the appearance of modesty, we have described this

226

proposal as immodest. There are several reasons for this. First, the proposal is clearly controversial, if for no other reason than the fact that the emphasis on thinking threatens the status quo. As Dewey correctly observes, "Let us admit the case of the conservative: If we once start thinking, no one can guarantee where we shall come out; except that many ends, objects and institutions are doomed." We can already hear the complaints of some parents as anticipated by Ornstein and Ehrlich (1989): "Children can learn about how their minds work in college . . . my child doesn't need to waste his time learning about farming; I want him to become a lawyer . . . concentrate on the basics . . . youngsters need to learn *our* values not those of other people . . . [our] kids don't even know what the Bill of Rights is or who was president during the Civil War. Teachers will chime in too: I can teach Roman History, but I don't know Lucy from Neanderthal . . . Probability? I have enough trouble explaining Geometry! . . . Anthropology should wait until college" (p. 201).

Second, the proposal is immodest because it challenges deeply held beliefs about the nature of teaching and learning. Chief among these beliefs is the proposition that teachers can control the quality of student effort through an appeal to tangible rewards and to the threat of punishment, and its corollary: that the more valued (scarce) the reward, the more eagerly students will compete. We have shown these beliefs to be largely illusory, but still they are intuitively appealing and difficult to give up. The Protestant work ethic and the entrepreneurial system of extrinsic rewards that sustains it are deeply ingrained in the American experience.

Third, and finally, it is worth noting that our proposal requires more than merely shifting instructional priorities. It also means flying directly in the face of current trends that stress teacher accountability, which these days is increasingly defined by how well students do on standardized achievement tests. Teachers themselves are perceived as competent to the extent that their students excel, with excellence defined in an ever narrowing arc. Whenever teachers believe that their role is to ensure high test scores rather than to help students learn, they pressure themselves and in the process use controlling, autocratic teaching techniques. Here control means emphasizing extrinsic rewards (particularly when they are dispensed competitively), allowing students little choice for how they go about learning, and threatening to withdraw emotional support as a means of punishment.

Such a regimen forces teachers to deemphasize topics not covered on standardized tests (Darling-Hammond & Wise, 1985; Shepard, 1989). Moreover, not only is the *content* of instruction altered by such narrow preoccupations but, more important, the *depth* of instruction is affected negatively as well. With standardization and greater accountability in school performance comes superficial coverage, and the possibility that we may be simply teaching children a series of "tricks" that enable them to perform well on standardized tests yet leave them deficient in basic understanding. What the advocates of intensification have forgotten is that *standardization* and *standards* are not the same thing.

Today it is only the brave, dedicated teacher who deemphasizes immediate performance goals for the sake of teaching to more lasting objectives, which include encouraging the will to learn and the productive use of the mind, especially when these goals are not easily measured.

Fortunately, it is now feasible to assess these elusive objectives, thanks to the advent of new measurement techniques referred to collectively as "authentic" or "performance-based" assessment (e.g., Brown et al., 1989; Lave, 1988; Wiggins, 1989). John Fredericksen and Allan Collins (1989) explain these techniques, using the example of "verbal aptitude," a construct that might be defined as "the ability to formulate and express arguments in verbal form." Traditionally this construct is assessed using tests of vocabulary knowledge or verbal analogies. By contrast, in the case of authentic tests the cognitive skills associated with verbal aptitude are evaluated as they are expressed in the performance of some extended, meaningful problem, such as requiring students to develop arguments favoring their side of the law in a small-claims-court action.

A number of authentic assessment tasks are currently undergoing development and large-scale tryouts under the auspices of the Common Core of Learning Assessment project (COMPACT Dialogue, 1989) sponsored by the state of Connecticut. For instance, high school students are required to use principles of physics and mathematics to determine whether speeding contributed to the death of a pedestrian in *A Case of Manslaughter*. In another problem students are given evidence that the earth is flat and are then asked to figure out ways to prove their belief that the earth is really round. In the area of social science, students are given a number of artifacts from various civilizations in different time periods and required to make inferences about these long-extinct cultures.

At its most profound, authentic testing becomes an integral part of the instructional process itself (de Lange, 1987). Above all, authentic testing stands as a means of diagnosis and feedback. For example, authentic testing has the potential for providing students with various absolute landmarks of success and near success in the form of sample answers that might be labeled "beginner," "intermediate," and "expert." Students should have unrestricted access to sample answers of varying quality so that it becomes clear just how a particular performance is being judged and how students can improve. Hopefully, authentic testing will encourage students to become their own critics and autobiographers, and to begin to notice what is distinctive about their own work, what has changed for them over time, and what is still missing and needs to be accomplished (Levin, 1990). This is precisely the reason that Mr. Rodriguez provided his students with expert feedback at the conclusion of the Global Gambit scenario.

The idea of performance-based assessment also helps place the issue of transfer of learning in its proper perspective. If complex behaviors – say, developing authoritative arguments and presenting them persuasively – are judged important enough to target in schools, then the skills that support effective communicating should be both trained and assessed directly and transparently. In effect, teaching to the test is no vice if the test itself reflects highly valued, complex human qualities that have broad application. If students can learn to express themselves clearly and forcefully, perhaps as judged by their performance in a simulated legal action, then it is likely that they can also act as effective advocates for themselves in other related, real-life situations as well. Conversely, however, simply passing a word-recognition vocabulary test is no guarantee that these words can or will be used properly or to good advantage in *any* situation.

This is not to suggest that vocabulary is unimportant. Nor do I mean to downplay the importance of mastering, say, the steps involved in creating geometric proofs. The mechanics of every subject-matter field is essential to good thinking. What concerns me, however, is that those kinds of learning that are most *easily* measured, like vocabulary acquisition, are not necessarily the most *important*. We laugh at the bizarre logic of the drunk who upon losing his car keys one night decides to search for them on another street where the light is better. Yet, when it comes to educational matters, the public often insists on training students on questions whose answers are the easiest to assess and interpret; but these are not necessarily the right questions. Where education is concerned, easy is rarely best. By focusing attention on the memorizing of mathematical proofs, students can doubtless be coached into passing standardized tests with flying colors, but they will not necessarily learn how to reason mathematically. The point is put bluntly by Elfrieda Hiebert and Robert Calfee (1989): "Citizens in the 21st century will not be judged by their ability to bubble in answers on test forms: Their success both personally and professionally will depend on their capacity to analyze, predict, and adapt – in short, to think for a living" (p. 54).

SUMMING UP

1. Schools should teach students how to play games – serious games – under rules that promote motivational equity, encourage strategic thinking, and reinforce the positive lessons to be learned from failure.

2. Serious games provide an ideal vehicle for preparing students to deal with the future. The future is problematic because the greatest dangers are not necessarily the most obvious ones, because more and more future problems are without precedence in human history, and because these problems cannot typically be solved in isolation, one from another.

3. Serious games also enhance strategic thinking because they transform the purposes of knowledge. No longer does learning imply rote recall of isolated facts for no other reason than passing a test.

4. Serious games are especially effective for dealing with individual differences among learners, because game play is a familiar, concrete method for introducing complex abstractions like history, justice, and civilization to all students.

5. Serious games are well suited for demonstrating the functional value of knowledge, especially for helping students make decisions about jobs and about their place in the world of work.

ACTIVITIES

Activity 1: Arranging Payoffs for Learning

Recall how Mr. Rodriguez arranged payoffs in the Global Gambit game to encourage various positive reasons for learning (Chapter 6). Choose two of the five serious games described in the beginning of this chapter. Then answer the following questions. First, what positive reasons (motives) would you reinforce using the games of your choice? Second, what kinds of payoffs would you use? Third, if you use tangible payoffs – grades, points, or praise – what precautions would you take to avoid undercutting the will to learn for its own sake?

Note that any given motive, like curiosity, mastery, or cooperation, is probably better served by some of these games than by others. Also, the most effective payoffs may differ depending on the age level of the students involved.

Activity 2: Cooperation versus Competition?

It often seems that cooperation and competition – like oil and water – do not mix; certainly, as motives they are different. Yet actually, in real life, competition and cooperation are often linked. For example, no matter how competitive a society becomes, some degree of cooperation is essential. At the very least there is the tacit agreement (cooperation) among its citizens (players) that everyone will play by competitive rules!

How can teachers demonstrate the vital balance between cooperation and competition, and reward students for honoring a cooperative spirit, even in the face of otherwise competitive rules? Create a game or activity that will demonstrate the intimate connection between cooperation and competition. Mr. Rodriguez provided one example in Global Gambit. Be sure to review his strategy. Additional ideas are found in Appendix M.

9

OBSTACLES TO CHANGE:
THE MYTHS OF
COMPETITION

Competition prepares one for life. But what kind of life?
Marie Hart

TODAY WHEN PARENTS ARE ASKED ABOUT EDUCATIONAL GOALS, they typically give high ratings to promoting self-esteem and the will to learn, right along with competency in reading, writing, and mathematics (Reasoner, 1986). This is surprising for the fact that only a few decades ago reading and mathematics dominated these polls, with esteem and motivational goals trailing badly. Perhaps even more remarkable is the fact that these shifts in priority hold across a broad socioeconomic spectrum. Both working-class parents as well as those in the professions endorse self-worth values. It seems that the lay public has come to intuit what we have demonstrated empirically, that feelings of self-worth stand at the center of the achievement process, and also that competency and feelings of worthiness go hand-in-hand.

These ratings are also remarkable for what they reveal about public misunderstandings of the instructional process. Other expectations are also at work, too, behind the scenes – factors that threaten the delicate balance between competency and confidence. First, as we know, there is the widely shared belief in our society that schooling should be efficient. Second, many parents and teachers believe that arranging incentives around competition is the best way to ensure efficiency as well as creativity (Collins, 1975; Elleson, 1983; Grenis, 1975). This latter belief is so pervasive that, as will be recalled, George Leonard (1968) charged that competition is being taught in schools as an end in itself. If Leonard is correct, then a ma-

233

jor, if misguided, value perpetuated by our schools never appears on any public relations statement of the educational mission: competitiveness for its own sake!

What may not be so obvious to the lay public is that the values associated with efficiency and competitiveness in schools are essentially incompatible with the promotion of student self-esteem. We have argued from the outset that it is through improved performance that self-confidence grows, and increased self-assurance in turn triggers further achievement (e.g., Skaalvik & Hagtvet, 1990). However, it is not always the case that confidence and competency are mutually reinforcing. As we have shown repeatedly, despite records of great distinction, some students never feel personally secure. This situation describes the overstriver who accomplishes much, not necessarily out of curiosity or caring, but out of a compulsive need to demonstrate perfection. Indeed, much of our attention has been devoted to understanding why esteem and competency do not always increase together.

How, then, can the goals of self-acceptance and competency prosper despite the presence of competition in schools and a growing public clamor for efficiency? Regarding the cult of efficiency, our answer (Chapter 7) was that the goal of efficient learning need not be abandoned as much as subordinated to the larger concerns of effective thinking. Efficient learning and effective thought are not the same; but neither are they incompatible. By increasing the capacity to think, students learn faster and retain more of what is important.

Dealing with competition is more complex because the issue is not simply one of degree of compatibility. Competition in any amount – even in moderation, whatever that means – creates noticeable declines in academic performance (Boggiano & Pittman, 1992; Rubin, 1980). This suggests that competition should be minimized, whenever possible, not just moderated. Yet can we risk jeopardizing the very factor that some observers (e.g., Ford, 1974; Levin, 1983) argue has brought America to preeminence in the world? This question requires that we reevaluate the wisdom of abandoning the competitive mode of learning in schools. At first blush, this suggestion appears deeply contrary to the entire weight of our earlier arguments. Is there *any* legitimate reason to teach children that other students are impediments to their own success? One would think not. Nonetheless, there still remain powerful reasons thought by many to justify competition as a central enabling force in our schools. These claims must be dealt with, and dismissed, before we can take seriously the possibilities for educational change proposed in previous chapters.

THE MYTHS OF COMPETITION

We say that if you win, you're dedicated, hardworking, altruistic. If you lose, you're none of the above.
Thomas Tutko

A major obstacle to true educational reform involves the uniquely American commitment to competition, and its corollary, that competition is the best way to ensure at least a minimum level of competency among all our students. This beguiling but mistaken belief is enormously powerful because of its intuitive appeal to reason. After all, if a competitive edge has sustained America's unprecedented economic prosperity through most of the twentieth century, will not the same formula work in our schools? The answer, as we now know, is probably not. But the reasons why are not always immediately obvious. Moreover, even after having demonstrated the falsity of the argument that competitive adversity builds character, as was done in Chapter 5, and pointing out the flaws in the belief that competition motivates students to do their best, there still remain two other powerful arguments favoring competition as a way of life, arguments that have little to do with the process of learning itself. The first of these arguments relates to the undeniable fact that there must be some orderly way to distribute individuals proportionately across the available jobs in our society, some of which are more attractive than others. Competitive grading in schools has long been the primary mechanism for assigning talent according to the demands and availability of jobs (Campbell, 1974). In effect, the better a student's grades, the more likely he or she is to be selected for further schooling, and it is higher education that forms the gateway to

235

the most prestigious occupations. If competition is deemphasized in schools by what mechanisms will individuals be apportioned to jobs? A related question concerns the second, remaining argument favoring competition: by minimizing competition in schools, do we not do an injustice to students who will grow up ill prepared to survive in the world of adulthood?

What about these two arguments? Are they fatal to any suggestions for reform that depend on deemphasizing the role of competition in learning? Let us consider each in turn, starting with the argument that children must learn to compete in order to survive as adults.

Competition and Survival

Will not the future survival of our children be jeopardized if the competitive aspects of the learning game are deemphasized? This question implies that teaching competition prepares children for success later on in an impersonal job market and, conversely, that to elevate cooperation or individual excellence as the higher good is to prepare them for a world that does not exist. Faced with this argument, many teachers may feel coerced into accepting the competitive status quo, despite their noble sentiments to the contrary. After all, resistance to competition is viewed in many quarters as faintly un-American anyhow. And the arguments that competition is an unavoidable fact of life or even basic to human nature are numerous and beguiling. (For a critique of the "human nature" myth, see Kohn, 1986.)

If we accept the argument that schools serve to move children progressively from the support-centered family group in their early years to an uncaring world of adulthood, then it might seem that requiring children to compete is basically a beneficial exercise. No small part of this benefit is thought to be getting used to losing. Aside from the perfectly valid point that schools should teach students how to deal with failure, this argument falls short on several counts.

For one thing, far from preparing children for the rigors of the future, learning to compete with others actually undercuts their ability to succeed in *any* kind of world, competitive or otherwise. For another thing, the world of work as it now exists is far less competitive than is often assumed.

Early Adversity. If competition is as devastating to productivity and self-esteem as it appears, then the real issue is not one of preparing students for a cutthroat world via competition, but rather facing the bleak prospect of delivering them into adulthood without the skills to cope effectively on any terms. Despairing of one's ability to face an unknown, quixotic future is not the kind of preparation we would choose for our children, nor is growing up with high ambitions driven out of compulsive attempts to resolve doubts about one's worth. Yet these are the eventual legacies of competitive incentives. As to the argument that children ought to compete in order to get used to losing, this notion is based on the largely discredited assumption that depriving children is the best way to prepare them for the rude shocks of life (Kohn, 1986). Even philosopher Richard Eggerman (1982), who argues in favor of competition as a "mixed good," concedes that "children may be peculiarly liable to dangers of comparisons of relative worth in a way that adults are not, just as it is reasonable to suppose that children should not be exposed to pornography, violence, and so forth" (p. 48). Although some experience with failure is important for maturity, the context within which it occurs and its meaning are pivotal (Chapter 3). As we know, when failure is judged by competitive norms, it signals falling short as a person. This exceedingly noxious message carries with it feelings of self-loathing and humiliation. On the other hand, when students fall short of their *own* expectations, failure can encourage the very virtues often mentioned as the fruits of competition: self-discipline, tenacity, and resiliency (Kennedy & Willcutt, 1964).

The point is that even if survival in adulthood depends on being competitive to the degree that some claim, then teaching these lessons in childhood destroys the will to compete long before most youngsters enter the battle for economic survival. Herein lies the essential paradox facing those who advocate competition in schools: preparing for a competitive world by creating winners and losers in

237

school destroys the capacity to compete in that world. And, what is more, I am unwilling to concede the basic assumption on which this wrongheaded argument rests – that competition is the fundamental reality of adulthood.

Outperforming Others. The tenacity of the myth of early adversity derives largely from a false reading of the true nature of the world of work, and of the personal qualities best suited for survival. This brings us to the second flaw in the argument that links competition and survival. Basically, proponents of competition have overstated the extent to which the economic well-being of individuals depends on outperforming others. What, in fact, is the role of competition in keeping a job, and of getting ahead?

Keeping a Job. It is an undeniable fact that the American economic system is grounded in competition. However, what is less often appreciated, but of equal significance, is the fact that the mechanisms of supply, demand, and competition that operate on a broad, economic macroscale depend in the final analysis on the collective efforts of millions of individuals who are themselves unlikely to be in direct competition with one another. Competition in the sense of a pure zero-sum game operates largely between corporations, within business sectors, and between countries, but far less frequently among the individuals who make up these larger aggregates.

Arthur Combs (1957) makes the case for cooperation as the ultimate enabling force in American society:

> We are impressed by the competitive features of our society and like to think of ourselves as essentially a competitive people. Yet we are thoroughly and completely dependent upon the good will and cooperation of millions of our fellow men. From the engineer who keeps the electric turbines running through the night to the garbage men who keep our cities liveable, each of us must rely on others to carry out the tasks we cannot perform ourselves. . . . Although it is true that we occasionally compete with others, competition is not the rule of life but the exception. Competition makes the news, while cooperation supplies the progress. (p. 265)

238

Of course, it is true that when a business fails or is substantially restructured in order to remain competitive, individual workers will be affected. But it is difficult to see how learning to be competitive from an early age will prepare employees for the trauma associated with unemployment and dislocation. Advocates for competition can only hold out the forlorn hope that by learning to outwit one's peers, it will be *"someone else* and not me" who is the victim of future economic upheaval. Obviously, schools cannot give such guarantees. Nor should they. The mission of schools is not to provide a training ground for future rivalries. Nor can schools insure against future job loss. Even if they were to try, enhancing competitiveness is the wrong way to proceed because in most cases holding a job does not depend on outperforming others. It has been estimated that most American workers, some 80 percent of them, are compensated on the basis of group effort or simply by being competent enough (Deutsch, 1979). Less than 20 percent of the work force is paid according to individual productivity, that is, paid strictly on a merit basis – the more one produces, the more one earns. This latter arrangement includes piece-rate workers in garment factories and sales people on commission. But most important is the fact that only a small fraction of these relatively few merit workers – probably less than 1 percent of the total work force overall – owes its livelihood to being able to outperform potential competitors. These data suggest that for the overwhelming majority of jobs merely being competent is enough; most workers need be neither overqualified nor demonstrably better at what they do than anyone else, but only capable of performing satisfactorily.

Certainly, there are exceptions to this general observation. But these exceptions are exceedingly few, as just noted. It is only because of their exceptionality that they capture the public imagination, and in doing so are often thought to be representative of the larger world of work. The corporate executive whose year-end bonus depends on being more ruthless than his rivals is an image that readily comes to mind. Another is the professional athlete whose starting position on the team depends not simply on being good enough, but on being better than any upcoming rookie, year after year. And then there is the professional musician whose position as "first chair" violinist in the orchestra is perpetually in jeopardy from the challenges of any other member of the string section. These examples conjure up arguments about the inevitability of competition on the grounds that it is all simply a matter of economic necessity. The social reform literature of the early 1900s is replete with images of unscrupulous business tycoons and other cutthroat predators who act on the principle of survival of the fittest. Although these portrayals were doubtless true then, and are still true today, they misrepresent the vast majority of jobs and occupations.

Direct economic competition among individuals is likely to occur only when the total number of goods or services offered for sale or hire exceeds the demand. The unemployed music teacher who moves to a new community only to find that a cadre of well-established teachers has already cornered the market on young, aspiring pianists is but one example of this supply–demand imbalance. So too is the cyclical overabundance of unemployed aerospace engineers caused by reduced federal spending on defense. But the economic hardships caused by these imbalances will not be corrected by teaching young children to be ruthless. This would simply further encourage a mentality of winning and losing. Rather schools must help youngsters gauge the wisdom of their career choices in advance against projected needs for their services in the future, and of having alternative skills available should their best guesses go awry or if their chosen life-style no longer appeals to them.

Finally, it is important to realize that very few individuals lose their jobs merely because someone else is marginally better qualified. In part this is because it is simply not economical for most businesses to pursue a policy of pure competition in which jobs remain continuously open to challenge by other workers, much in the same way that the starting quarterback's job is always up for grabs. The cost of pursuing such a policy in the workplace would quickly become prohibitive in terms of falling productivity caused by plummeting morale. Then there would also be the costs associated with upgrading or relocating displaced workers, not to mention the possible illegality of such practices. "Revolving door" competition is largely unworkable in the business world, yet we tolerate it in our schools whenever children are required to compete for a shrinking supply of rewards that depend on doing better than others. Of all the groups in our society, it is children who are the most subject to continuous, unremitting public scrutiny and evaluation, and all too often in a competitive atmosphere – a combination of factors rarely experienced in adulthood; and when it does occur, as in the case of professional athletes, at least the financial rewards are usually proportional to the stress involved.

These observations place the arguments for early adversity in the proper perspective. Presently many children are not only being prepared for the rigors of adult life but, because its competitive nature is exaggerated, they are being *overprepared* for competition! Rarely will the economic well-being of young adults depend on outwitting and outmaneuvering others in the caustic fashion we have come to associate with the zero-sum game in schools. In the final analysis, apart from sheer incompetency or simply not caring, the major causes of job loss are impersonal, cyclical economic forces over which individuals have little direct control. The best way for individuals to prepare for the vicissitudes of automation, foreign competition, overspecialization, and seasonal fluctuation in jobs is to increase their range of marketable skills, which means continuing education (Hull, Friedman, & Rodgers, 1982). But people are most likely to continue learning only if learning is not threatening.

Getting Ahead. So far we have spoken only of keeping jobs. But what about being promoted once the individual enters the job market? If we leave aside seniority – which is the major reason for promotion in most jobs (Berg, 1970) – upward mobility on the job otherwise depends on becoming increasingly valuable as an employee. And becoming more valuable typically involves further schooling and the development of additional skills or technical expertise. As long as one's competencies keep pace with potential opportunities, promotions will likely depend on those personal qualities associated with noncompetitive striving, such as cooperativeness and a willingness to continue learning.

I do not mean to imply that competency plays no part in the promotion process. Sometimes promotions do depend on being more

241

competent than others. This is especially true in hierarchically structured occupations where there are fewer and fewer job openings as one moves up the career ladder. Consider the military. Officers on the promotion list at any step in rank typically outnumber the openings available at the next higher rank. As a result, many qualified officers are denied promotion on a given round, and must await advancement at a later time. In this way, all officers will rise through the ranks until eventually each is promoted no further, even though he or she may be perfectly capable of discharging the duties associated with a higher rank. Much the same can be said about management positions in many business organizations.

Hierarchical job structures are an economic fact of life. They cannot be ignored; but neither should they serve as a model for how students are taught. Parents can certainly expect schools to aid in the development of their children's talents but in the clear knowledge that even an outstanding record of school achievement is no guarantee of limitless promotions or of unrestricted financial rewards later on. No matter how well prepared students may become, barriers to further progress will eventually be encountered, whether they be limits of talent, unfavorable economic realities, poor timing, or just plain bad luck.

But surely, will not those individuals who are more aggressive and ambitious (in the spirit of Hermes) enjoy greater occupational success? Not necessarily. Janet Spence and Robert Helmreich (1983) studied the relationship between the successes of adults in several career fields and personal dispositions such as competitiveness, a willingness to work hard, and a mastery orientation (e.g., "If I am not good at something, I would rather keep struggling to master it than move on to something I may already be good at"). In one sample involving scientists, success was defined as the number of times each participant's research was cited by colleagues; for a sample of businessmen, success was calculated in terms of yearly income; and, for a sample of college students, grade point average was the measure of success. The results for these disparate groups were remarkably similar and striking. In all three cases, the more individuals preferred hard work and the mastering of new skills, the more successful they were. For task-oriented individuals personal competitiveness was an unnecessary ingredient for achieving at the highest levels. In fact, being competitive actually interfered with the productivity of these high-achieving individuals. The image of the successful businessperson as highly competitive and the presumption that competition is necessary for a successful career are called into question by these data. What really counts in the march toward career prominence is being task engaged, interested in one's work, and always striving to become more skillful.

Why then should schools indoctrinate students into a competitive life-style when the world of work is simply not as competitive as some believe – when a reliance on competitiveness may actually impede one's progress? The evidence shows that personal qualities engendered by cooperation, sharing, and achieving by independence are better predictors of future productivity and more likely to attract the attention of potential employers (Chapter 8).

Competition as Head Start

Now what about the other general argument that competition is necessary to distribute students among the available jobs in society, some of which – the fewest in number – are highly prestigious? Although competitiveness may play a negligible, even contrary, role in succeeding on the job, what about landing the job to begin with, and what kind of job? It is a truism that most individuals aspire to more rather than less prestigious jobs, and it is the high-paying, challenging jobs that are in shortest supply. Schools have become the central selection agent by which individuals are allocated proportionally to the available jobs. This is done largely by ranking students in terms of grades. Indeed, adult occupational status depends closely on the kinds of grades received by individuals in school. This linkage between grades and continued access to education holds schools hostage in the battle for future economic security and prestige, a contest that absorbs millions of American parents and turns their teenagers into compulsive, test-anxious, grade grubbers.

Obviously, too, the process of competitive selection occurs not just once at the transition between high school and college, but numerous other times as well. This is why some parents are so desperate to enroll their toddlers in just the right nursery school as a kind of head-start insurance. Moreover, the impact of this competitive gauntlet is felt not only by those who stand to gain the most by such maneuvering – the children of upwardly mobile, affluent parents – but also by those who have relatively less access to the top, largely minorities and youngsters from low-income families. These, children, too, are ensnared in the same grade-grabbing game, perhaps not as active participants, but they become savaged nonetheless. If disadvantaged youngsters should choose to stop playing the competitive game or simply drop out, as many do, they will likely feel themselves failures rather than recognizing the game as a failure. Ultimately everyone pays for a contest that is actively engaged in for profit by only a relative few.

Given the potential cost in human terms, powerful forces indeed must be perpetuating this selection function of schools. The main benefactors are business, government, and industry. Business relies heavily on schools to sort individuals into various occupational tracks based on ability and intellectual potential so that, eventually, only a relatively few persons remain to compete for the most prestigious jobs in the professional ranks, while lesser-endowed or less well prepared individuals are left to compete for less-demanding jobs. Thus much of the task of job sorting is done in advance of the time individuals actually apply for work. It is this selection function that has most enraged critics, who charge that the domination of school learning by competition is driven primarily by economic factors rather than pedagogical concerns. For instance, David Campbell (1974) observes that the whole frantic, irrational scramble to beat others is essential for the kind of institutions that our schools are – namely "bargain-basement personnel screening agencies for business and government" (pp. 145–146).

There is no denying that competitive sorting serves an important economic function: the allocation of individuals to jobs. Indeed, it can be argued that the system works with considerable efficiency because (1) once outstanding talent is identified (through competition), then (2) further competitive rewards sustain the enormous effort needed for these relatively few gifted individuals to acquire advanced degrees. Consider these two claims briefly.

244

Competition and Effort. First, take the latter proposition that competitiveness arouses the kind of intense, dedicated effort needed to prepare for entry into prestigious occupations. If a link can be established between personal competitiveness, on the one hand, and persistence in school, on the other, then the case would be strengthened for encouraging competition on the grounds that only the strongest and best prepared candidates will eventually prevail. But the available evidence on this point (presented in Chapters 1 and 5) is quite the opposite. When youngsters perceive school largely as a way to further their economic interests or to enhance their prestige at the expense of others, they are *less*, rather than *more* likely to continue their education (Nicholls, Patashnick, & Nolen, 1985). It is reasonable to suppose that those youngsters who are dominated by considerations of status suffer the most from the competitive climate of schools and, as a result, are inclined to drop out sooner, perhaps driven to escape the noxious implications of failure, given the rules by which they have chosen to play. By contrast, for others the excitement of discovery and learning likely buffer the harsh competitive lessons of school.

Identifying Talent. As to the other interlocking argument, there can be little doubt that competition is a highly efficient way to segregate individuals by talent. This is true for both athletic and academic gifts. But we can still inquire if competitive sorting by ability is the *only* or even the *best* way to assign young people to jobs. As it turns out, competing for jobs is costly and, for many if not most individuals, unnecessary. As to cost, we have already documented the decline in academic productivity caused by ability ranking and its devastating influence on the will to learn (Chapter 5). As for being largely unnecessary, consider the fact that currently most jobs in America demand no great intellectual talent, but only basic competencies within the grasp of most people. In fact, many entry-level jobs – some estimates range as high as 90 percent – can be performed successfully with only a high school diploma, irrespective of the student's grade point average, and less than six months on-the-job training or technical instruction (Deutsch, 1979).

245

It appears that many policy makers may have overestimated the level of skills necessary for successful performance at entry-level for most jobs. It may be a sad commentary on the times, but thanks to the dubious blessings of automation and the advent of work-related computer systems, the need for computational and organizational skills in many parts of the workplace may actually be declining (see Braverman, 1974; Gottfredson, 1986; Gottfredson & Sharf, 1988; Spenner, 1985). Of course, this is no reason to deemphasize the teaching of the basics. Being able to read, write, and compute is important for more than job survival. These are the gateway skills to creativity and innovation – all the more reason why the basics should be acquired in ways that are not subject to the corrosive effects of competition. The virtues of sensitivity, understanding, and creativity transcend any temporary benefits of competition as a goad to learning. No one wants to apply conditions of scarcity to these human qualities.

The important point is that the teaching and certification of broad competencies, at relatively modest levels, are all that schools should or need do to prepare the vast majority of students for successful entry into the work force. This preparation is best achieved through noncompetitive means.

Granting this, however, isn't competitive sorting still necessary for assigning people to jobs that require extraordinary talent? Obviously, no one wants to trust the design of skyscrapers to architects of limited gifts, or undergo surgery at the hands of a physician of doubtful qualifications. Architecture, law, and medicine as well as teaching and public service deserve the best and the brightest. Actually, even in these special cases information about one's ability adds little to the accuracy of the selection process when future occupational success is the criterion. Some talent is needed, of course, but often less than is generally thought. For instance, it is estimated that 40 percent of the general adult population in America possesses the intellectual capacity to become physicians (Collins, 1979). But since less than one-half of 1 percent ever become physicians, selection factors other than ability are also at work, such as availability of financial support, interest, and willingness to persist. But what makes for outstanding, not just competent, physicians? If the research of Spence and Helmreich is any indication, extraordinary success (by any definition) depends on more than a combative spirit (and perhaps even on its relative absence). It also depends on cooperativeness and on a willingness to continue learning.

In any event, it cannot be assumed that those highly gifted youngsters who survive the high-stakes scramble for grades are always the best suited for professional and public service. Students who jostle their way to the top by reason of a near perfect academic record are often driven by motives that may work against career success once they finish their formal schooling and enter the job market. Our self-worth analysis of the overstriver provides a glimpse of this possibility. Recall that it is overstrivers whose excellent academic records are built on a deep-seated fear that they must achieve perfection to be worthy.

Little wonder, then, that neither high school nor college grade point average predicts the quality of performance on the job, or one's satisfaction as a worker (see Berg, 1970; Spenner, 1985). It is not the grades themselves so much as the underlying reasons for achieving them that count most in sustained occupational success. Obviously, we cannot tolerate incompetency in high places; but neither can we afford to promote the fear and self-doubt that, once having driven individuals to positions of power, then compromise their ability to use that power wisely. Cheating is but one form of such abuse, whether it be industrial espionage, deceptive advertising practices, or a failure to disclose potential defects in commercial products. Such deception would seem inevitable if Combs (1957) is correct in arguing that competition does not necessarily trigger a search for better products, but rather a scramble to sell competing products at any cost.

Given all these observations, one wonders once again why schools do not deemphasize the competitive nature of classroom learning. Such a move is long overdue and would appear highly beneficial. As things stand, the preemptive use of competitive incentives undercuts academic productivity, jeopardizes self-confidence, and – no less troublesome – encourages timidity and opportunism; moreover, competition dislocates talent and teaches students to strive for self-limiting, selfish goals.

247

Yet, for all these arguments, there is still one overarching reality that works against change. Parents fear that if their children do not enter the star-spangled scramble for grades, others will, and as a result their youngsters may lose forever the chance at prestigious occupations and economic security. Basically competition in schools is perpetuated by the fear of being left out. The inevitable stampede for limited rewards mocks the best efforts of teachers. And these fears are real enough. They are confirmed by the undeniable fact that the occupational status of individuals as well as their eventual income level depend heavily on the number of years spent in school (Bishop, 1989; Mincer, 1989).

As long as these anxieties persist, change is unlikely. What, then, are the possibilities for more open access to higher education and jobs through noncompetitive avenues? Can things be altered so that young people (and their parents) have less reason to feel left behind? There is no shortage of reform proposals, all of which address the basic question posed originally by Morton Deutsch (1979): "Suppose . . . everyone was equally qualified to do the more interesting, challenging and rewarding jobs available in the community. And also suppose that only a small fraction of the jobs were desirable. How would one allocate these scarce, good jobs?" (p. 394).

Would people bid for the better jobs? Would they be assigned them by seniority? Some reformers argue that educational credentials should be banned entirely as the basis for job selection and that all workers be allowed to share both attractive and not so attractive jobs. According to one theorist (Collins, 1979), "the great majority of all jobs can be learned through practice by almost any literate person . . . how hard people work and with what dexterity and cleverness, depends on how much other people can require of them to do" (p. 54). As a practical example of this reasoning, workers might rotate through jobs, or job ladders might be created so that, over time, individuals could move up from less rewarding to more rewarding tasks. For instance, a person might work up to the full status of a physician through a series of steps, beginning with hospital orderly.

Although these various proposals reflect considerable ingenuity, they are not particularly appropriate for our purposes because they are unlikely to be taken seriously, at least any time soon. We seek a more modest example of change, one that is both reasonable in scope and practically feasible; one that depends on altering educational policy, not society itself; and, finally, one that is broadly compatible with the arguments of the self-worth position, namely, that positive reasons for learning are jeopardized when the individual's sense of worth becomes equated with the ability to achieve competitively.

IF NOT COMPETITION, THEN WHAT?

It is a trifle unsettling, I grant, to contemplate the idea of going to college merely for an education, rather than for a degree. But after one lives with the notion for a while, its strangeness some-what recedes.

Robert Wolff

Can schools themselves do anything to moderate the competitive scramble? Are there any words of reassurance that can be offered students (and their parents) here and now if they do not get top grades? First, consider the matter of reassurances.

Although it is true that the single best predictor of lifetime in-come is the number of years completed in school, it is also the case that this relationship does not necessarily depend on where one's schooling was obtained (Berg, Bibb, Finegan, & Swafford, 1981). Having gone to Yale or Harvard may be more impressive than hav-ing started one's college career at a local community college. But the prestige of the postsecondary institution attended is essentially un-related to one's eventual standard of living. Nor is institutional prestige a good predictor of later on-the-job satisfaction; neither does it predict well one's effectiveness on the job as rated by super-visors. In effect, Ivy League graduates on average become no richer (holding their parents' wealth constant, of course), nor become more famous, nor are they likely to feel any more successful in their work than do graduates from schools of lesser reputation. These statistics may dismay some parents, but they also give powerful re-assurances. If a student is denied access to the most prestigious col-leges, it is not the end of the world.

From this perspective it is important that America continue to ensure open access to postsecondary education with the main gatekeepers being only the desire to learn and evidence that one is willing to work hard. Today the community college system in America provides one such source of upward mobility in a society heavily stratified by wealth and power. Typically, anyone can attend community colleges (and often at bargain basement fees) as long as they hold a high school diploma or continuation certificate. There are even provisions for completing a high school degree on many campuses. Here the standards for admission are just high enough to command some commitment to learning yet are not so prohibitive as to discourage further schooling.

The majority of community college entrants plan to get a bachelor's degree or higher (Astin, Hemond, & Richardson, 1982). In 1980 56 percent of all postsecondary minority students nationwide were enrolled in community colleges (Grant & Eiden, 1982), a figure that included one-half of all black college students and two-thirds of all Hispanics (Astin, 1982). Moreover, most minority students who eventually receive a bachelor's degree – up to 50 percent of them by one estimate (D. Reagan, personal communication, November 1990) – began their postsecondary schooling at a community college. Such developments tend to loosen the chokehold of high school grade point average on access to further schooling, which has often precluded all but the most able or the most fortunate from better jobs, because a poor start in school or detours along the way need no longer represent insurmountable barriers.

A second kind of reassurance – a reminder, actually – is that a successful occupational career depends not only on the number of years one spends in school, but also on the reasons for learning. Recall that students who perceive schools as an opportunity to better themselves are more likely to persist longer, whereas those who see schools as a way to bolster a sense of worth by outscoring others are likely to quit sooner (e.g., Nicholls et al., 1985). Given the importance of motivational factors in the decision to continue in school, parents often fear the wrong thing. Far from being worried if their children do not enter the frenzied rat race for grades, they should start worrying when their children do. All too often the result is not excellence but self-doubt, anger, and a decline in true task involvement. Competition focuses attention on the wrong issues. What matters ultimately is not performance but learning; not short-term gains but the reasons for achieving. If the reasons are right, achievement will likely flourish without the goad of competition. Otherwise, children may do just enough to win the prize and little more.

CONCLUSION

What can schools do to moderate the competitive scramble for grades? This scramble is activated largely by the fact that too many individuals are chasing too few positions at the top of the occupational ladder, such that 80 percent of our young people aspire to 20 percent of the available jobs (Covington, 1992; Paterson, 1956). This mismatch is driven in part by positive factors – by youthful exuberance and the natural desire of individuals to excel. Unfortunately, it is also propelled by wishful thinking and ignorance, and sometimes by parental pressure even when the children's interests and talents may lie elsewhere. Schools should encourage realistic dreaming, dispel ignorance, and at the same time promote a healthy perspective for dealing with the massive disappointments reflected in the statistic just cited.

In Chapter 8 we argued for the creation of a work force that could respond flexibly to the changing needs of the workplace, which today stresses independence of judgment and a willingness to cooperate. Now additionally we argue for providing students with sufficient information and self-understanding to make informed judgments about which kinds of jobs would be most meaningful to them personally. Among other things, this involves helping students assess the risks, challenges, and satisfactions associated with different careers and encouraging an understanding that occupational satisfaction depends largely on matching job demands with one's interests, personal styles of thinking, and tolerance for risks (Andrew & Grubb, 1995; Spenner, 1985). Consider competitiveness as a personal style. Some individuals are clearly more risk seeking and combative than others. And the same can be said for jobs: some

251

are riskier and less secure, especially those we have characterized as hierarchically organized. As part of career education, one can envision students living and working for a time in competitively structured climates, where individuals compete for fewer and fewer placements at each rung of the promotion ladder – all vicariously, of course, through realistic simulations and role-playing exercises, as well as sampling other alternative occupational structures, where, for instance, rewards may be best pursued by moving laterally rather than vertically within an organization. Students can also benefit from games like Psychic Income (Chapter 8) in which the players seek out their own preferred mix of status, pay, and amount of leisure time as different compensatory sources of reward (Bailey, 1993).

Hopefully, such instruction would also help redress a potential irony inherent in the policy of open access to higher education (Thurow, 1975). If students can drop out of school and subsequently reenter the educational mainstream without prejudice and continue learning despite false starts and detours, then will not the job scramble simply intensify given more rather than fewer qualified candidates? Not necessarily, if increased competency also implies greater self-realism and an improved capacity for making informed occupational choices. I do not suggest that children be encouraged to accept second best for themselves. Nor is it likely that schools can entirely cure the overmatch between aspirations and opportunity cited earlier – people will always aspire to something better, as they should. What I do suggest, however, is that students can learn that there are often many unforeseen employment opportunities, potential windfalls waiting to be discovered, and always the prospect for substituting one goal for another. For instance, a student may choose to become a paramedic rather than a physician, or a paralegal, not an attorney – consoled in the knowledge that the attractiveness of a given occupation is not simply a matter of more or less money or only a matter of status, but rather depends on a mixture of compensatory factors. Physicians may have a higher annual income, but paramedics have better hours and are less subject to malpractice suits.

Approaching occupational choice not as a matter of job sorting but of informed self-selection makes students active participants in the process of their own future building so that, if one particular move proves unsatisfactory, they can always design a new route without feeling they have fallen short as a person. This dynamic has all the characteristics of partially contingent paths (Chapter 2), a concept used to describe Atkinson's success-oriented individuals.

Elevating competency and good judgment over competition is no easy proposition. Nor have I meant to imply that there are no risks in trying. Actually, the perils are considerable. Perhaps the greatest risks are those inherent in defining competency. On the one hand, we must encourage students to do more than the minimum. This much is obvious, but the dangers are more subtle than one might imagine. For instance, David Ainsworth (1977) points out that the psychological implications of the language of achievement itself may well discourage excellence – that is, "if a student is competent, then surely that is enough" (p. 329). Obviously, it is not enough if by competency we mean simply tolerating the lowest common denominator of performance. Competency in school must never be equated with mediocrity. If this happens the result will be bored and indifferent students. On the other hand, demanding too much of students in the absence of the skills needed to pursue excellence can be equally devastating. Fortunately, as we know, there is a middle ground between too much and too little, where one's aspirations hover at or near the upper bounds of present competencies. It is in this zone of challenge, so to speak, that excellence is promoted. For all the difficulties involved in maintaining this balance on a day-by-day basis, at least we know it can be done. Competitiveness offers no such prospects. There is no middle ground here, no such thing as "just enough" competition.

In the struggle to change priorities teachers can be reassured on several counts. First, those who desire change are not limited to a handful of academic troublemakers or professional curmudgeons. Many parents, too, are convinced of the need to foster competency, not competition, if we can judge from the research of Carole Ames and Jennifer Archer (1987b). These investigators found at least as many mothers of elementary school children who preferred that schools promote "mastery" goals – striving for the sake of self-

253

improvement through effort – as mothers who believed in "performance" goals, that is, striving to do better than someone else by reason of ability.

Second, and of equal significance, Ames and Archer (1987a) also discovered that promoting mastery goals does not require the complete elimination of competition. They observed various kinds of classrooms – those in which a mastery orientation predominated, those that were largely performance oriented, and combinations of both performance and mastery orientations. As long as mastery goals were in evidence, the presence of competition did not diminish those behaviors we have come to associate with intrinsic task engagement. Students focused on effort explanations, used sophisticated planning strategies, and preferred problems where "you can learn a lot of new things but will also have some difficulty and make many mistakes." And, most important of all, student enthusiasm for such challenges did not depend on their self-perceived ability level.

These findings are critical because if the pursuit of excellence required the virtual absence of competition, then the chances for reform would be bleak, indeed. In reality, competitiveness can never be entirely banished from schools. Witness the many students as well as some parents who have an uncanny knack for turning everything, even joyous games, into competitive contests. The question of how much or how little an emphasis on mastery is needed to offset the inevitable press of competition was not part of the original Ames and Archer research, but obviously it is an important next point of inquiry. Yet whatever the eventual answer, there is cause for optimism. Perhaps far fewer and less radical changes are needed to tip the classroom balance in favor of spontaneity, involvement, and creativity than was ever thought.

SUMMING UP

1. Far from preparing children for the rigors of the future, teaching them to compete actually undercuts their ability to succeed in *any* kind of world, competitive or otherwise.
2. The world of work is far less competitive than often assumed.

Rarely does one's economic well-being depend on outwitting and outmaneuvering others.

3. It is being cooperative and competent, not combative, that is the key to economic survival. Once individuals become competent, it is those personal qualities associated with cooperation, sharing, and independence that best predict future productivity. In fact, personal competitiveness can actually undercut future occupational success.

4. Students who jostle their way to the top by reason of a perfect or near perfect academic record are often driven by motives that work against career success later on.

5. Although the single best predictor of lifetime income is the number of years completed in school, this relationship does not depend on where one's schooling was obtained. Thus, if a student is denied access to the most prestigious colleges, it is not the end of the world.

ACTIVITIES

Activity 1: Making Cooperation Cooperative

We have championed cooperation as a major element in the equation for educational reform. The promise of cooperation comes from its potential for encouraging constructive reasons for learning that are within the reach of all students. If the team wins, all savor victory – another important source of equity, that is, a shared payoff. In theory, each student will give his or her best effort because being rewarded individually depends on each team member trying as hard as possible.

Yet, despite these advantages, working in groups is not always positive. Groups are sometimes prone to conflict and frustration. For example, some students may not always do their fair share of work, yet may still receive the same rewards as others who did extra work to make up for these "free riders."

What might teachers do to minimize the chance of having free riders who do not do their fair share of work? Appendix N suggests several possibilities that might compliment your ideas.

Activity 2: Cooperation over Competition

We have rejected the competitive, ability-based games that schools often play, and argued for their replacement by learning activities – often cooperative in nature – that are based on considerations of equity. But a competitive mentality is so entrenched at all levels of our society that, at first, it may seem strange, if not exceedingly difficult, to think of ways to convert a competitive activity into a cooperative one. But with a little practice, any initial awkwardness recedes. Start with some nonschool examples.

King of the mountain, musical chairs, two-legged races on stilts, and being "it" in a game of tag are several highly competitive games, but games that can be transformed into cooperative exercises with only a few simple changes in the rules. How might this be done? Some clever possibilities are presented in Appendix O, all of which and more can be found in Orlick (1982).

EPILOGUE

This may not be the beginning of the end, but it is the end of the
beginning.
  Winston Churchill

NOW THAT OUR BLUEPRINT FOR CHANGE IS IN PLACE, WE COME TO
a potential new beginning. The proposal can be stated quite
simply: educational reform should proceed by teaching students
(and teachers) how to play serious games as a way to promote
strategic thinking and a sense of real-world and personal relevance,
using incentive systems that encourage positive reasons for learning – reasons accessible to all students and which will sustain game
play and learning into the indefinite future. This proposal enjoys
the benefits of being closely guided by theory and well grounded in
research. Moreover, it appears workable and is difficult to dismiss
as merely utopian. The practical elements are already in place, existing if not thriving in individual classrooms across America, despite the presence of powerful contrary forces. Many teachers already encourage the proper motives for learning by holding fast
when possible to absolute standards of excellence, by encouraging
students rather than praising them, and by dispensing incentives in
ways that permit unlimited rewards, open to all, which, despite
their frequency, remain undiminished in their motivational value.
These recommendations come, then, not as strangers but rather as
typically overlooked, often underappreciated ways of thinking
about schooling.

  Indeed, there is nothing new here when we consider each component singly. Rather the novelty (and value) of this approach turns
on the fact that when familiar, even commonplace, ideas are re-
arranged or combined in new ways, they can excite new perspectives.

  But what of the potential benefits of these remedies? Are they

257

worth all the effort? Can the value of such change be measured in terms of increased school achievement scores, reduced dropout rates, and revenue savings to the states, or perhaps reflected as improvements in America's economic standing worldwide? Obviously, such tangible benefits are difficult to estimate, and it may be downright dangerous to try. Many reform movements have ended in disaster following exaggerated claims for success.

Ultimately, the benefits of this proposal cannot be calculated in dollars and cents, but rather in terms of a broad hoped-for vision, one that is perhaps best reflected through the reactions of those young Cuban children described in the closing paragraph of Chapter 1. Recall that when these young revolutionaries of the 1960s were asked to describe the study of history, they hotly proclaimed themselves to be history in the making. Without realizing it they had become players in an "infinite game." James Carse (1986) defines infinite games as those in which the goal is to extend play indefinitely and where there is no victory or defeat in the usual sense, but only the changing of rules to suit the evolving needs of players. By comparison, Carse characterizes "finite games" as inherently self-limiting. The goal of finite games is to end play as soon as possible in order to determine winners and losers. By now this win–lose mentality is quite familiar to us and calls to mind the competitive features of the learning game. In competitive games, the past (history) has little standing. It is only the outcome of the current contest that counts. By contrast, those who play infinite games look forward toward ongoing play in which the past requires repeated examination. The rise and development of cultures is an infinite game on a vast scale; so too is history itself. More modest, but highly personal examples include marriage, parenthood, and the development of a career – any sequence of meaningful events that place players in transition and passage.

Strategic thinking clearly fits the category of infinite games for which the end is merely arbitrary, and to continue play means to be constantly discovering and growing, with the possibility of occasional surprises that may lead to a radical transformation of the game itself. Indeed, we have argued that cultivating a capacity for surprise (serendipity) is one of the best preparations for personal future building.

History as an infinite game is reflected in the BioAlert exercise (Chapter 8). When stripped of all its packaging, this game stands as an allegory for adaptation and change on an infinite scale. All biological systems, including the broader concept of nature, are open and dynamic, a point that can be vividly conveyed to students when they encounter dangerous viruses that play by different, unfamiliar rules – rules that fortunately can be deciphered, controlled, and then eventually altered by human ingenuity. And so it is with the game of human relations. Here, too, there is change and infinite variability with no end (and sometimes no relief) in sight. The rules that define the relationship between parent and child change as both grow older; so do the rules that govern the relationships between newlyweds and elderly couples. These examples convey best the meaning of change and its inevitability, and underscore the need to accept change, even welcome it as part of nature's order.

Infinite games are important to our story for other reasons as well. First, according to Carse, the concept of "power," which is associated with winning in finite game play, is transformed in infinite play to mean "strength" – strength of will, strength of persuasion and of endurance. Anyone can be strong, a quality open to all, and another source of equity. But only a few can be powerful, and only one the *most* powerful. Second, as Carse explains it, finite games are defined by boundaries, while infinite games are limited only by horizons, and there is nothing in the horizon itself that limits vision. To move toward one horizon is simply to create another.

Movement, growth, and passage – these are the qualities that define the future, a place of infinite moves. Infinite players, like our young Cuban students, cannot say how much of their studies they have completed, but only that much remains to be learned. Nor do they wish to determine when their education is over, but only what will become of what they know. Infinite players see themselves and their culture in transition, a most healthy educational perspective; and it is economically sound as well. Only by being open to future possibilities can we create new jobs and revitalize old market sectors sufficient to the needs of a free society. From this viewpoint, then, the most important obligation of American education as we enter the twenty-first century is to provide the means by which our children can continue to create that which they can never finish.

APPENDIXES

APPENDIX A

Someone is washing, folding, and storing laundry! All good theories, including this one, explain otherwise puzzling events and draw them together into a meaningful whole. Seen from this perspective, there is nothing more practical than a good theory. For instance, as you will soon see, the self-worth theory of achievement motivation will help explain the following classroom puzzles:

1. Why is it that when teachers reward student effort by giving credit for studying hard, many youngsters remain unmotivated?

2. Why, when students do study, some of them hide their efforts or are reluctant to admit that they study at all?

3. Why is it that for some students, getting high grades does not necessarily lead to a sense of pride and personal satisfaction?

4. Why is it that for some students who have always done well in school, it takes only one failure to jeopardize their sense of worth and confidence?

These and other similar puzzles must be solved before effective school reform can be fully realized. Theories, such as the self-worth theory and the attribution theory, provide the blueprints for these solutions.

APPENDIX B

The change Alschuler introduced was simplicity itself. He merely asked his students to indicate in advance what percentage of test problems they would strive to answer correctly on each weekly

261

math quiz. Students were paid for the accuracy of their judgments – the coin of the realm being Monopoly money. Realistic aspirations were critical because students would lose money if they either overestimated or underestimated their eventual performance. Thus, success depended more on an accurate match between students' aspirations and their current knowledge than on their absolute level of performance (a la Hoppe). And, because the implied goal was to maximize their earnings, students were expected to make their estimates near the upper reaches of their present ability, thereby setting in motion an upward cycling of achievement – just as Hoppe's ring-toss subjects did over half a century earlier. This is exactly what happened. On average, math achievement scores increased three grade levels for this group during the school year! Students who had done nothing in mathematics before now began completing homework assignments on time and taking their books home.

More rigorous laboratory research has since confirmed Alschuler's compelling anecdotal findings regarding the importance of student goal setting. As one example, James Sofia (1978) found that when students analyzed learning tasks for sources of difficulty and indicated the levels of performance to which they aspired, they did better on achievement tests. These goal setters also felt most satisfied with the results of those tests for which they studied the hardest, irrespective of the grade they received.

APPENDIX C

Merit-based standards will form an important part of our overall proposal for school reform. For this reason it is important to recognize in advance just how much society depends on merit-based standards that measure and recognize excellence, virtually everywhere in our lives – that is, except in schools. Schools have such a long history of turning learning into a contest that these competitive practices have discouraged the use of the merit-based standards and in the process have obscured the fact that students do best when they strive to attain standards of excellence that do not necessarily depend on how many other people also succeed.

A partial list of the many diverse competencies in our society that are measured in terms of absolute criteria to which anyone can apply themselves are found below:

New York City taxi driver's licensure test

Coast Guard Seaman and Navigation test

Ballroom dancing instructor's test

Police detective examination

Registered nurse certification

U.S. citizenship examination

Trucker's tests

Culinary academy tests

Air traffic controller's examination

Baseball umpire's examination

State bar examination

Teacher's competency test

Wine taster's certificate

Test of judo competency (e.g., brown belt, black belt)

Pilot's license

State trooper examination

Engineer's competency test

Pharmacy licensure test

Real-estate licensure

In later chapters we will consider how school learning can be viewed as a process of individuals striving to attain various levels of competencies – competencies measured not in terms of the performances of would-be competitors, but against the obstacles inherent in the process of mastering appropriate skills.

APPENDIX D

Rather than assigning spelling words to students on a random basis, as is typically the case in school, Richard de Charms (1972) gave each student a choice of three kinds of words to spell: easy, moderately difficult, and difficult. Students were kept from automatically choosing easy words because spelling them gave their team only one point, whereas spelling the moderately difficult word meant two points, and three points were given for hard words. Easy words were those that the student had spelled correctly on a test several days before; moderately difficult words were those he or she had previously misspelled but had studied in the meantime; and hard words were taken from the next spelling assignment, which no student had yet seen.

By this arrangement students quickly learned that success depended on a careful evaluation of one's own skills – in this case, spelling skills – and that if they disregarded these realities, no matter how bright they might be, they penalized themselves by failing. Moreover, they learned that a realistic goal is the most challenging kind, and incidentally the one that yields the greatest payoff.

APPENDIX E

1. Why is that high grades do not necessarily lead to a sense of pride and satisfaction?

There is no reason to expect that high grades will lead automatically to feelings of pride. Pride depends less on high grades than on the reasons students learn in the first place. For some students pride *does*, in fact, follow from doing well because for them a good grade is evidence of self-improvement or of overcoming a personal challenge. However, for other students, like overstrivers, just the opposite is true. Here, a high grade point average is often interpreted in negative terms, as the successful avoiding of failure. In this case relief, not pride, is the dominant reaction.

2. Why is it that the self-confidence of some otherwise apparently successful students can be devastated after only one failure?

Self-worth theory argues that success, even many successes, may not enhance a sense of confidence. This occurs when the reasons for learning are negative, as when, for example, overstrivers struggle to succeed – not necessarily for the sake of learning but to avoid failure. In these cases, success masks, but does not resolve, lingering doubts about their ability. A single failure simply acts to confirm what these students have feared all along, that they are less capable than perfection demands.

3. Why should failure-prone students sometimes actually perform better when the odds are hopelessly against their succeeding or when they have excuses for why their effort might not pay off?

Simply put, these students now have the "freedom" to fail, and can work up to their capacities openly because failure no longer necessarily implies low ability. Such "risk-free" failure also provides secondary benefits. We all admire the individual who struggles stoically for a worthy cause against overwhelming odds, no matter the outcome.

APPENDIX F

One well-known list of multiple abilities comes from Howard Gardner (1993), who divides general intelligence into seven components:

1. Linguistic ability: the ability to express one's thoughts through writing and speaking.
2. Logical-mathematical ability: the capacity to think in abstract, quantitative terms, and to think logically.
3. Spatial ability: the ability to process thoughts in visual or spatial terms.
4. Bodily-kinesthetics ability: the ability to express oneself through gesture and physical movement.

5. Musical ability: the capacity to manipulate musical forms, and sensitivity to rhythm and pitch.

6. Interpersonal ability: the ability to recognize various motives, needs, and feelings in others, and to act on this knowledge for the good of individuals or groups.

7. Intrapersonal ability: an appreciation of one's own moods, feelings, and styles of thinking, and the ability to make sound judgments about one's motives and intentions.

Following is a brief list of sample activities that might allow students to express their ideas and understanding using these different ability modalities. How much of an overlap is there with your list?

1. Create a mask.

2. Role-play a character or event.

3. Imagine the future or invent the past.

4. Set up a mock trial.

5. Create a game to illustrate a concept in science.

6. Draw a political cartoon.

7. Create a photo essay on the topic of poverty.

8. Build a three-dimensional architectural model.

9. Create a journal of someone's travel through history.

10. Create rhymes or dances.

11. Write poetry to express emotions or historical events.

12. Create metaphors, analogies, or similes.

13. Compose a song to capture the mood of a time, place, or event.

Encouraging the expression of multiple abilities not only allows students a choice in the ways they demonstrate their knowledge – *choice* being a highly motivating ingredient for learning – but it also permits students to draw on their own strengths and preferred styles of thought, thereby reinforcing the positive side of learning.

As we will soon see, students are more enthusiastic about learning when they can demonstrate what they know, rather than being tested for what they don't know, and in ways consistent with their natural style of expression, whether it be predominantly verbal, spatial, or even interpersonal. Thus encouraging multiple abilities becomes part of the larger effort to establish motivational equity – everyone striving for positive reasons open to all via their preferred style of expression.

For the reader interested in learning more about the multiple abilities approach and its place in the wider education mission, the following references are recommended.

Armstrong, T. (1994). *Multiple intelligences in the classroom.* Alexandria, VA: Association for Supervision and Curriculum Development.

Gardner, H. (1993). *Multiple intelligences: The theory and practice.* New York: Basic Books.

APPENDIX G

1. Might some of your competitive players try to guarantee high scores by standing very close to the target? In school this reaction takes the form of low-goal setting, a behavior that may ensure some modest success but which sacrifices creativity and creates boredom in the bargain.

2. Might some players pursue other erratic strategies, such as standing so far away from the target that the odds of succeeding are small? This strategy is often found in school whenever risking failure is an unacceptable threat to students. As we know from Chapter 4, the logic of this apparently illogical action is that, "If no one else can do any better than me [standing that far from the target], then failure can be attributed to the difficulty of the task, not to any shortcomings of mine!"

3. Might some players lose interest in the game ("just going through the motions") or refuse to play? When students believe

themselves to be losers in the school learning game, they, too, often withdraw or drop out mentally.

4. Might some players argue among themselves about issues of fairness or cheating, and whether someone is breaking the rules? Anger and resentment are the likely result of competing for a limited number of rewards, not only in this experiment but in school as well.

5. Might players blame others or themselves unduly for any disappointing performances? This, too, is a common legacy of schools when a competitive mentality prevails.

APPENDIX H

Several testing strategies that Ms. Jefferson might consider take their inspiration from the research of Richard de Charms (Activity 2 in Chapter 3), in which, it will be recalled, students were allowed to select the level of challenge that best suited them on a spelling test.

1. Ms. Jefferson could give her students a set of questions about geography whose answers range from easy to hard. Answering harder questions would be worth more points than answering easy questions, but the likelihood of answering the latter questions is greater! Students could select any of, say, twenty such questions to answer. Each student's grade would depend on how many total points he or she amassed over the twenty items.

Thomas Rocklin and Angela O'Donnell (1986) found that such "individual self-testing" reflects a truer estimate of what students have learned than when all students are required to answer the same questions. Also, students learn with greater enthusiasm when their grades depend more on what they choose to be tested on, compared with when grades are calculated in negative terms, that is, based on attempts by others to find out what they do *not* know. The idea is to give students opportunities to feel confident in their own ways and on their own terms.

2. A different approach to individualized testing lets students choose how much each of several assignments would be weighted toward their overall grade. For instance, if allowed to divide one hundred points among ten different tests, one student might assign a majority of points to the test covering the material that intrigues her the most. Another student might choose to weight more those assignments he feels most secure about.

3. The benefits of student choice can be expanded beyond test taking to include test preparation. Giora Keinan and Moshe Zeidner (1987) showed that merely providing students with a choice of which practice problems to work on, rather than being assigned the practice items, reduced feelings of anxiety during study and also eventually led to higher test scores. By gaining some measure of personal control over events, these students were better able to concentrate on the task at hand.

APPENDIX I

First, let's recap our earlier analysis of how grades and grading can become a positive motivational force. For one thing, in order to encourage the proper reasons for learning, teachers need to make clear to students in advance specifically how and what behaviors will be given credit. For another thing, credit should be awarded on a merit basis, that is, grades should reflect how much each student (player) measures up to the challenge of the task, and not on how much better or poorer a student does relative to other students. Finally, grades should act as feedback for how students can improve in the future.

Each of these motivating features of grading was incorporated into the structure of Global Gambit. First, teams accumulated grade credits in the form of points given by Mr. Rodriguez for specific actions that were made clear before play began – rewards given, variously, for being curious, being cooperative, and mastering content. Second, there were no limits on the number of teams or the number of times these actions could be taken; hence, rewards were plentiful and open to any team that met the challenge.

But how might these accumulated credits be converted into actual grades? Before game play Mr. Rodriguez provided a schedule indicating the total points needed for a given grade, so many points for an A, so many points for a B, and so on. In effect, Mr. Rodriguez's teams could work for any grade they chose, the only restriction being that the higher the grade to which they aspired, the more they had to do and the better they had to perform.

This kind of grading system, sometimes referred to as a grade-choice arrangement (Covington, 1992), allows teachers to maintain their standards of excellence by determining how much students must do, and how well they must do it, yet at the same time permits youngsters a wide latitude in *how*, *when*, and, to some extent, *what* they must do to achieve a given grade.

APPENDIX J

As you know (Chapter 6), equity goals are best promoted to the extent students control their own evaluation, whether that means allowing them to choose the level of challenge they face, or deciding how much each of several assignments will count toward their final grade.

A different kind of student control derives from other, quite different principles including the multiple-ability perspective (Activity 2 in Chapter 4). For example, Mr. Rodriguez might allow his students to demonstrate their understanding of geography in any one of several different modes of expression such as drawing a map of the world and locating participating countries (visual/spatial ability). Alternatively, they might make a chart with numbers (spatial/quantitative), conduct interviews with foreign visitors (interpersonal), or develop a travelogue radio script (musical/verbal).

Yet another approach to assessing student knowledge is the use of portfolios modeled after the kinds of résumés collected by artists and writers (Levin, 1990). In order to demonstrate their understanding of geography, Mr. Rodriguez's students might collate worldwide weather reports, or create fictional accounts from the diaries of world travelers. Applied more broadly as an evaluation tool, beyond this particular example, portfolios can reflect a whole range of student experiences and accomplishments, and they can be arranged chronologically or by subject-matter areas. For instance, science portfolios might contain a journal used to record observations collected during science experiments, student-generated graphs and tables, as well as field drawings from nature.

APPENDIX K

One way to encourage students to study in active, planful ways is to provide them a pool of practice test items on index cards with several possible answers listed on the reverse side, varying in quality from unacceptable to satisfactory and superior. Students select a random sample of these items, say, ten cards, at the end of each study session in order to test themselves.

Such feedback allows students to discover gaps in their knowledge, and to gauge how well they will likely do on the actual test. This study/self-testing procedure reinforces a mastery motive, and discourages learned helplessness by strengthening the belief that the more one studies *effectively*, the better one is likely to do.

APPENDIX L

1. The art of "problem anticipation" can be encouraged by presenting students with plans for solving a specific problem (e.g., shortening worldwide lines of commerce by building the Panama Canal). Students are given credit for detecting consequences of carrying out the plan – things about the solution that might create new problems. Well-documented planning disasters provide an excellent opportunity to anticipate problems, a number of which are provided by P. Hall (1980).

2. The topic of "problem identification" can be illustrated when teachers withhold critical pieces of information for solving a prob-

lem, with the challenge that students identify what additional facts or data are needed. This exercise is particularly suitable for arithmetic word problems. Here students are encouraged to analyze the kinds of steps needed to solve problems, which will help to avoid the spectacle of those hapless youngsters who blithely calculated the captain's age by manipulating the number of sheep and goats on board his ship (Chapter 1).

A variation on this exercise involves presenting problems with an *excess* of information that is irrelevant or nonessential to the solution. Students are given credit for identifying surplus information, which, if gone unrecognized as such, might create confusion and divert attention from relevant material.

This suggestion brings to mind those kinds of questions often encountered on achievement tests that assess one's ability to detect irrelevant information and divert attention from the real steps needed to solve the problem:

Which value(s) in the problem below is(are) necessary to solve it?

A factory in Elmtown has 40 work spaces and 60 workers. If the supervisor-to-worker ratio is 1:20, how many supervisors are there?
   A. 20 only
   B. 40 and 60 only
   C. 1, 20, 60 only
   D. 1, 40, 60 only
   E. 1, 20, 40, and 60

3. The theme of "problem creation" can be pursued by directing students to create arithmetic word problems for other students to solve using numerical information based on historic events (e.g., building the Panama Canal: "If steam shovels remove 2,000 cubic feet of earth a day, how long will it take them to remove 100,000 cubic feet?"). By inventing or discovering problems, not just solving problems presented by others, students gain a sense of greater personal participation in the process of learning.

APPENDIX M

The tacit objective of Global Gambit was to create a plan to avoid the worldwide consequences of global warming. This objective required considerable cooperation, for which each of the teams was rewarded. Recall that Mr. Rodriguez awarded points whenever teams took time to learn about the needs of competing countries, or whenever one team helped another, by lending credit at a reasonable interest rate. A second objective of Global Gambit – a game within a game – was a contest (competitive) to become the world's leading economic power, winner take all, by amassing the greatest number of points by the end of game play. Thus, Mr. Rodriguez provided two alternating sources for rewards, one competitive and the other cooperative, an arrangement that required a balancing of strategies – being competitive, but not too competitive, because out of self-interest alone wealthier nations needed to help poorer nations. If poorer countries defaulted, then they could end game play prematurely so that no one would win.

This situation represents what social scientists call a "mixed-motive paradigm" (Axelrod, 1976; Jervis, 1976). Payoffs in this game favor competition as much as cooperation, and the negotiations involved are reminiscent of other classic dilemmas that are only likely to intensify in the future, including the tragedy of the commons, which, as we know, arises whenever the collective consumption of a scarce shared resource exceeds the supply (Chapter 7). The dynamics represented in Global Gambit apply generally to any mixed-motive paradigm, including conflict resolution at a personal level – between parents and children, husbands and wives – and the societal level as well, among ethnic groups, between the sexes, and in business and industry.

APPENDIX N

There are several things teachers can do to discourage free riders, some of which are probably already included among your ideas:

1. Keep groups small, say, no more than three or four students; the fewer the number of group members, the harder it is for any individual to shirk.

2. Ask each group to create a plan for dividing up work responsibilities among its members early on; it is harder to shirk when assignments are clear and agreed upon in advance.

3. Have groups establish checkpoints along the way, with all members required to make progress reports; it is harder to be a shirker if one is not allowed to fall behind.

4. Announce in advance that when group projects are completed, each member will be asked to submit an anonymous, confidential assessment of the degree of participation of all other group members – who shirked work and who did extra work. If several members indicate that an individual did less than his or her fair share, that person receives a lower grade than the rest of the group.

5. Allow groups to dismiss a member, by majority vote, who is not carrying a fair share of work. Students who are dropped must persuade the group to reconsider, or find acceptance in another group.

APPENDIX O

King of the Mountain. In this competitive game only one person can be king (the sole occupant at the top of the mountain). In the cooperative version, the rules are reversed so that the object now is to get as many people as possible balanced on the small space at the top, without anyone falling off.

Musical Chairs. Instead of competing for diminishing space on fewer and fewer chairs, players now see how many individuals can safely balance on a single chair. A variation for classroom use involves seeing how few desks are needed for a whole class to be off the floor.

Two-Legged Race on Stilts. Two-legged races on stilts can be instantly converted into a cooperative venture by creating three-legged stilts in which a pair of individuals share a common stilt. Learning to defy gravity as a cooperative activity now replaces winning over others as the objective.

Being "It" in a Game of Tag. The challenge for creating a sense of equity in this game is to keep any one person from being "it" for too long. One strategy is to have many individuals who are "it" so that lots of activity reduces the spotlight on any one individual. Another approach is to handicap the faster runners by requiring them to hop, not run, or not to use a safe base.

By these examples, we do not mean to suggest that there is an easy translation between the objectives of cooperative play and the more complex objectives of schooling. Nor do we advocate converting schools into a vast play yard filled with physical games of cooperative dexterity. The point of these examples is to demonstrate how really small the changes in the rules need be to tip the balance from competitive striving in favor of more positive reasons for becoming engaged. These examples also illustrate how emotionally profound the results of such modest changes can be. Readers need only recall their own childhood experiences of cooperation in which they felt secure enough to risk failure and felt free from the threat of being rejected or excluded. For most of us, these feelings stand in stark contrast to those equally memorable, yet often less pleasant reactions when "winner takes all" was the rule.

REFERENCES

Abbott, E. (1983). *Flatland: A romance of many dimensions.* Totowa, NJ: Barnes & Noble.

Abdul-Jabbar, K., & Knobles, P. (1983). *Giant steps: The autobiography of Kareem Abdul-Jabbar.* New York: Bantam.

Abramson, L. Y., & Sackeim, H. A. (1977). A paradox in depression: Uncontrollability and self-blame. *Psychological Bulletin, 84,* 838–851.

Abramson, L. Y., Seligman, M. E. P., & Teasdale, J. D. (1978). Learned helplessness in humans: Critique and reformulation. *Journal of Abnormal Psychology, 87,* 49–74.

Abt, C. C. (1987). *Serious games.* New York: Lanham.

Adams, M. J. (Ed.) (1986). *Odyssey: A curriculum for thinking* (Vols. 1–6). Watertown, MA: Charlesbridge.

Adams, M. J. (1989). Thinking skills curricula: Their promise and progress. *Educational Psychologist, 24,* 25–77.

Adelson, B. (1981). Problem solving and the development of abstract categories in programming languages. *Memory and Cognition, 9,* 422–423.

Adkins, D. C., Payne, F. D., & Ballif, B. L. (1972). Motivation factor scores and response set scores for ten ethnic-cultural groups of preschool children. *American Educational Research Journal, 9,* 557–572.

Ainsworth, D. (1977). Examining the basis for competency-based education. *Journal of Higher Education, 43,* 321–332.

Alexander, K. A., & McDill, E. L. (1976). Selection and allocation within schools: Some causes and consequences of curriculum placement. *American Sociological Review, 41,* 969–980.

Allen, V. L., & Levine, J. M. (1967). *Creativity and conformity.* Technical Report No. 33. Madison: University of Wisconsin Research and Development Center for Cognitive Learning.

Allington, R. (1980). Teacher interruption behaviors during primary grade oral reading. *Journal of Educational Psychology, 72,* 371–377.

Alschuler, A. S. (1969). The effects of classroom structure on achievement motivation and academic performance. *Educational Technology, 9,* 19–24.

Alschuler, A. S. (1973). *Developing achievement motivation in adolescents.* Englewood Cliffs, NJ: Educational Technology Publications.

Alschuler, A. S. (1975, March). *Radical psychological education.* Keynote address at the Convention of the Virginia Personnel and Guidance Association, Williamsburg, VA.

Amabile, T. M. (1979). Effects of external evaluations on artistic creativity. *Journal of Personality and Social Psychology, 37,* 221–233.

Amabile, T. M. (1982). Children's artistic creativity: Detrimental effects of competition in a field setting. *Personality and Social Psychology Bulletin, 8,* 573–587.

Ames, C., & Ames, R. (1984). Systems of student and teacher motivation: Toward a qualitative definition. *Journal of Educational Psychology, 76,* 535–556.

Ames, C., & Archer, J. (1987a, April). *Achievement goals in the classroom: Student learning strategies and motivation processes.* Paper presented at the annual meeting of the American Educational Research Association, Washington, DC.

Ames, C., & Archer, J. (1987b). Mothers' beliefs about the role of ability and effort in school learning. *Journal of Educational Psychology, 79,* 409–414.

Anderman, E. M., & Maehr, M. L. (1994). Motivation and schooling in the middle grades. *Review of Educational Research, 64,* 287–309.

Anderson, R. C. (1995). The role of reader's schema in comprehension, learning, and memory. In R. B. Ruddel, M. R. Ruddel, & H. Singer (Eds.), *Theoretical models and processes of reading* (pp. 582–601). Newark, DE: International Reading Association.

Andrew, E., & Grubb, W. N. (1995). The power of curriculum integration: Its relationship to other reforms. In W. N. Grubb (Ed.), *Education through occupations: Integrating academic and vocational education in American high schools* (Vol. 1, pp. 39–56). New York: Teachers College Press.

Andrews, G. R., & Debus, R. L. (1978). Persistence and the causal perception of failure: Modifying cognitive attributions. *Journal of Educational Psychology, 70,* 154–166.

Arlin, P. K. (1975). Cognitive development in adulthood: A fifth stage? *Developmental Psychology, 11,* 602–606.

Aronoff, J., & Litwin, G. H. (1966). *Achievement motivation training and executive advancement.* Unpublished manuscript, Harvard University.

Aronson, E., Blaney, N., Stephan, C., Sikes, J., & Snapp, M. (1978). *The jigsaw classroom.* Beverly Hills, CA: Sage.

Aronson, E., & Mettee, D. R. (1968). Dishonest behavior as a function of differential levels of induced self-esteem. *Journal of Personality and Social Psychology, 9,* 121–127.

Astin, A. W. (1982). *Minorities in American higher education: Recent trends, current prospects, and recommendations.* San Francisco: Jossey-Bass.

Astin, A. W., Hemond, M. K., & Richardson, G. T. (1982). *The American freshman: National norms for fall 1982.* Los Angeles: University of California.

Atkinson, J. W. (1957). Motivational determinants of risk-taking behavior. *Psychological Review, 64,* 359–372.

Atkinson, J. W. (1964). *An introduction to motivation.* Princeton, NJ: Van Nostrand.

Atkinson, J. W. (1981). Studying personality in the context of an advanced motivational psychology. *American Psychologist, 36,* 117–128.

Atkinson, J. W. (1987). Michigan studies of fear of failure. In F. Halisch & J. Kuhl (Eds.), *Motivation, intention and volition* (pp. 47–60). Berlin: Springer.

Atkinson, J. W., & Raynor, J. O. (1974). *Motivation and achievement.* New York: Wiley.

Atwood, B., Williams, R. L., & Long, J. D. (1974). The effects of behavior contracts and behavior proclamations on social conduct and academic achievement in a ninth grade English class. *Adolescence, 9,* 425–436.

Axelrod, R. (Ed.) (1976). *Structure of decision: The cognitive maps of political elites.* Princeton, NJ: Princeton University Press.

Bailey, T. (1990). The changing world of work. *Educator,* Graduate School of Education, University of California, Berkeley, *4* (3), 10–11.

Bailey, T. (1993). Youth apprenticeship in the context of broad education reform. *Education Researcher, 22,* 16–17.

Bailin, S. (1987). Creativity and skill. In D. Perkins, J. Lockhead, & J. Bishop (Eds.), *Thinking: The second international conference* (pp. 323–332). Hillsdale, NJ: Erlbaum.

Bandura, A. (1971). *Social learning theory.* Morristown, NJ: General Learning Press.

Bandura, A., Grusec, J. E., & Menlove, F. L. (1967). Some determinants of self-monitoring reinforcement systems. *Journal of Personality and Social Psychology, 5,* 449–455.

Bandura, A., & Kupers, C. J. (1964). Transmission of patterns of self-reinforcement through modeling. *Journal of Abnormal and Social Psychology, 69,* 1–9.

Barker, R. G. (1942). Success and failure in the classroom. *Progressive Education, 19,* 221–224.

Barnes, M. S. (1894). *Studies in general history: Teacher's manual.* Boston: D. C. Heath.

Barron, F. (1965). The psychology of creativity. In F. Barron, W. C. Dement, W. Edwards, H. Lindman, L. D. Phillips, J. Olds, & M. Olds (Eds.),

278

New directions in psychology (Vol. 1). New York: Holt, Rinehart & Winston.

Battle, E. S. (1966). Motivational determinants of academic competence. *Journal of Personality and Social Psychology, 4,* 634–642.

Baumrind, D. (1991). Effective parenting during the early adolescent transition. In P. E. Cowan & E. M. Hetherington (Eds.), *Advances in family research* (Vol. 2, pp. 111–163). Hillsdale, NJ: Erlbaum.

Beck, I. L., & McKeown, M. G. (1988). Toward meaningful accounts in history texts for young learners. *Educational Researcher, 17* (6), 31–39.

Beery, R. G. (1975). Fear of failure in the student experience. *Personnel and Guidance Journal, 54,* 190–203.

Benjamin, M., McKeachie, W. J., Lin, Y. G., & Holinger, D. P. (1981). Test anxiety: Deficits in information processing. *Journal of Educational Psychology. 73,* 816–824.

Berg, I. (1970). *Education and jobs: The great training robbery.* New York: Praeger.

Berg, I., Bibb, R., Finegan, T. A., & Swafford, M. (1981). Toward model specification in the structural unemployment thesis: Issues and prospects. In I. Berg (Ed.), *Sociological perspectives on labor markets* (pp. 347–367). New York: Academic Press.

Berglas, S., & Jones, E. (1978). Drug choice as a self-handicapping strategy in response to noncontingent success. *Journal of Personality and Social Psychology, 36,* 405–417.

Biaggio, A. M. B. (1978). Achievement motivation of Brazilian students. *International Journal of Intercultural Relations, 2,* 186–195.

Binet, A. (1909). *Les idées modernes sur les enfants.* Paris: Flammarion.

Biological Sciences Curriculum Study (1968). *Biological science: An ecological approach.* Chicago: Rand McNally.

Birney, R. C., Burdick, H., & Teevan, R. C. (1969). *Fear of failure.* New York: Van Nostrand.

Bishop, John H. (1989, January–February). Why the apathy in American schools? *Perspective, 18,* 6–10, 42.

Boggiano, A. K., Barrett, M., Weiher, A. W., McClelland, G. H., & Lusk, C. M. (1987). Use of the maximal-operant principle to motivate children's intrinsic interest. *Journal of Personality and Social Psychology, 53,* 866–879.

Boggiano, A. K., Harackiewicz, J. M., Bessette, J. M., & Main, D. S. (1985). Increasing children's interest through performance-contingent reward. *Social Cognition, 3,* 400–411.

Boggiano, A. K., Main, D. S., & Katz, P. A. (1988). Children's preference for

279

challenge: The role of perceived competence and control. *Journal of Personality and Social Psychology, 54,* 134–141.

Boggiano, A. K., & Pittman, T. S. (1992). *Achievement and motivation: A social-developmental perspective.* Cambridge: Cambridge University Press.

Borkowski, J. G., Johnston, M. B., & Reid, M. K. (1987). Metacognition, motivation, and controlled performance. In S. Ceci (Ed.), *Handbook of cognitive, social, and neurological aspects of learning disabilities* (Vol. 2, pp. 147–174). Hillsdale, NJ: Erlbaum.

Botkin, M. J., & Weinstein, R. S. (1987). *Perceived social competence of friendship choice as a function of differential teacher treatment.* Unpublished manuscript.

Bransford, J. D., Nitsch, K. E., & Franks, J. J. (1977). The facilitation of knowing. In R. C. Anderson, R. J. Spiro, & W. E. Montague (Eds.), *Schooling and the acquisition of knowledge* (pp. 31–35). Hillsdale, NJ: Erlbaum.

Brattesani, K. A., Weinstein, R. S., & Marshall, H. H. (1984). Student perceptions of differential teacher treatment as moderators of teacher expectation effects. *Journal of Educational Psychology, 76,* 236–247.

Braverman, H. (1974). *Labor and monopoly capital: The degradation of work in the twentieth century.* New York: Monthly Review Press.

Bricklin, B., & Bricklin, P. M. (1967). *Bright child – poor grades.* New York: Dell.

Bringing children out of the shadows. (1988, Spring). *Carnegie Quarterly, 33* (2), 1–8.

Brophy, J., & Good, T. (1974). *Teacher–student relationships.* New York: Holt, Rinehart & Winston.

Brophy, J., & McCaslin, M. (1992). Teachers' reports of how they perceive and cope with problem students. *Elementary School Journal, 93,* 3–68.

Brown, A. L., & Campione, J. C. (1990). Communities of learning and thinking, or a context by any other name. *Contributions to Human Development,* special issue, D. Kuhn (Ed.), *21,* 108–126.

Brown, A. L., & Palincsar, A. S. (1989). Guided cooperative learning and individual knowledge acquisition. In L. B. Resnick (Ed.), *Knowing, learning, and instruction: Essays in honor of Robert Glaser* (pp. 393–451). Hillsdale, NJ: Erlbaum.

Brown, J., & Weiner, B. (1984). Affective consequences of ability versus effort ascriptions: Controversies, resolutions, and quandaries. *Journal of Educational Psychology, 76,* 146–158.

Brown, J. S., Collins, A., & Duguid, P. (1989). Situated cognition and the culture of learning. *Educational Researcher, 18* (1), 32–42.

280

Butler, R. (1988). Enhancing and undermining intrinsic motivation: The effects of task-involving and ego-involving evaluation on interest and performance. *British Journal of Educational Psychology, 58,* 1–14.

Butler, R., & Nisan, M. (1986). Effects of no feedback, task-related comments, and grade on intrinsic instruction and performance. *Journal of Educational Psychology, 78,* 210–216.

Campbell, D. N. (1974, October). On being number one: Competition in education. *Phi Delta Kappan, 56* (2), 143–146.

Campbell, D. T. (1986). Ethnocentrism of disciplines and the fish-scale model of omniscience. In D. E. Chubin, A. L. Porter, F. A. Rossini, & T. Connolly (Eds.), *Interdisciplinary analysis and research: Theory and practice of problem-focused research and development: Selected readings* (pp. 29–46). Mt. Airy, MD: Lomond.

Carse, J. P. (1986). *Finite and infinite games.* New York: Ballantine.

Carver, C. S., & Scheier, M. F. (1986). Functional and dysfunctional responses to anxiety: The interaction between expectancies and self-focused attention. In R. Schwarzer (Ed.), *Self-related cognitions in anxiety and motivation* (pp. 111–141). Hillsdale, NJ: Erlbaum.

Castenell, L. A. (1983). Achievement motivation: An investigation of adolescents' achievement patterns. *American Educational Research Journal, 20,* 503–510.

Cavana, G. R., & Leonard, W. H. (1985). Extending discretion in high school science curricula. *Science Education, 69,* 593–603.

Chapin, M., & Dyck, D. G. (1976). Persistence in children's reading behavior as a function of N length and attribution retraining. *Journal of Abnormal Psychology, 85,* 511–515.

Chapin, S. L., & Vito, R. (1988, April). *Patterns of family interaction style, self-system processes and engagement with schoolwork: An investigation of adolescents rated as at-risk, or not-at-risk for academic failure.* Paper presented at annual meetings of the American Educational Research Association, New Orleans.

Chase, W. C., & Simon, H. A. (1973). Perception in chess. *Cognitive Psychology, 4,* 55–81.

Clement, J. (1982). Analogical reasoning patterns in expert problem solving. *Proceedings of the Fourth Annual Conference of the Cognitive Science Society.* Ann Arbor: University of Michigan.

Cohen, E. J., & DeAvila, E. (1983). *Learning to think in math and science: Improving local education for minority children.* Final Report to the Walter S. Johnson Foundation. Stanford, CA: School of Education, Stanford University.

Cohen, H., & Filipczak, J. (1971). *A new learning environment.* San Francisco: Jossey-Bass.

Collins, M. D. (1975). *Survival kit for teachers (and parents).* Pacific Palisades, CA: Goodyear.

Collins, R. (1979). *The credential society: An historical sociology of education and stratification.* New York: Academic Press.

Combs, A. W. (1957). The myth of competition. *Childhood Education.* Washington, DC: Association for Childhood Education International.

Commanday, R. (1992). *Sources of self-esteem: Investigating factors underlying achievement motives of high ability Afro-American students from a low income community.* Unpublished doctoral dissertation, University of California at Berkeley.

COMPACT Dialogue: Connecticut Multi-state Performance Assessment Collaborative Team in Math and Science. (1989), 1(3). (A project sponsored by the National Science Foundation).

Condry, J. D., & Chambers, J. (1978). Intrinsic motivation and the process of learning. In M. R. Lepper & D. Greene (Eds.), *The hidden costs of reward: New perspectives on the psychology of human motivation* (pp. 61–84). Hillsdale, NJ: Erlbaum.

Connell, J. P. (1985). A new multidimensional measure of children's perceptions of control. *Child Development, 56,* 1018–1041.

Cooper, H., & Tom, D. (1984). Socioeconomic status and ethnic group differences in achievement motivation. In R. Ames & C. Ames (Eds.), *Research on motivation in education* (Vol. 1., pp. 209–242). New York: Academic Press.

Cooper, L., Johnson, D. W., Johnson, R., & Wilderson, R. (1980). The effects of cooperative, competitive and individualistic experiences on interpersonal attraction among heterogeneous peers. *Journal of Social Psychology, 111,* 243–253.

Coopersmith, S. (1967). *The antecedents of self-esteem.* San Francisco: Freeman.

Cordes, C. (1985, March). Venezuela tests 6-year emphasis on thinking skills. *APA Monitor, 16* (3), 26–28.

Covington, M. V. (1981). Strategies for smoking prevention and resistance among young adolescents. *Journal of Early Adolescence, 1,* 349–356.

Covington, M. V. (1985). Anatomy of failure-induced anxiety: The role of cognitive mediators. In R. Schwarzer (Ed.), *Self-related cognitions in anxiety and motivation* (pp. 247–263). Hillsdale, NJ: Erlbaum.

Covington, M. V. (1986). Instruction in problem solving and planning. In S. L. Friedman, E. K. Scholnick, & R. R. Cocking (Eds.), *Blueprints for thinking: The role of planning in cognitive development* (pp. 469–511). Cambridge: Cambridge University Press.

Covington, M. V. (1992). *Making the grade: A self-worth perspective on motivation and school reform.* Cambridge: Cambridge University Press.

Covington, M. V. (1996). The myth of intensification. *Educational Researcher, 25* (8), 22–27.

Covington, M. V., & Beery, R. G. (1976). *Self-worth and school learning.* New York: Holt, Rinehart & Winston.

Covington, M. V., Crutchfield, R. S., Davies, L. B., & Olton, R. M. (1974). *The Productive Thinking Program: A course in learning to think.* Address inquiries to: Professor Martin Covington, Psychology Department, 3210 Tolman Hall, University of California, Berkeley, CA 94720.

Covington, M. V., & Jacoby, K. E. (1973). *Productive thinking and course satisfaction as a function of an independence-conformity dimension.* Paper presented at the meeting of the American Psychological Association, Montreal.

Covington, M. V., & Omelich, C. L. (1978). *Sex differences in self-aggrandizing tendencies.* Unpublished manuscript, Department of Psychology, University of California, Berkeley.

Covington, M. V., & Omelich, C. L. (1979). Effort: The double-edged sword in school achievement. *Journal of Educational Psychology, 71,* 169–182.

Covington, M. V., & Omelich, C. L. (1981). As failures mount: Affective and cognitive consequences of ability demotion in the classroom. *Journal of Educational Psychology, 73,* 796–808.

Covington, M. V., & Omelich, C. L. (1984). Controversies or consistencies? A reply to Brown and Weiner. *Journal of Educational Psychology, 76,* 159–168.

Covington, M. V., & Omelich, C. L. (1985). Ability and effort valuation among failure-avoiding and failure-accepting students. *Journal of Educational Psychology, 77,* 446–459.

Covington, M. V., & Omelich, C. L. (1987). "I knew it cold before the exam": A test of the anxiety-blockage hypothesis. *Journal of Educational Psychology, 79,* 393–400.

Covington, M. V., & Omelich, C. L. (1988). I can resist anything but temptation: Adolescent expectations for smoking cigarettes. *Journal of Applied Social Psychology, 18,* 203–227.

Covington, M. V. & Roberts, B. W. (1994). Self-worth and college achievement: Motivational and personality correlates. In P. R. Pintrich, D. R. Brown, & C. L. Weinstein (Eds.), *Student motivation, cognition and learning* (pp. 157–187). Hillsdale, NJ: Erlbaum.

Covington, M. V., Spratt, M. F., & Omelich, C. L. (1980). Is effort enough, or does diligence count too? Student and teacher reactions to effort stability in failure. *Journal of Educational Psychology, 72*, 717–729.

Covington, M. V., & Tomiki, K. (1996). *Achievement motivation: Child-rearing antecedents, culture and ethnicity.* Unpublished manuscript, Institute of Social and Personality Psychology, University of California at Berkeley.

Covington, M. V., & Wiedenhaupt, S. (1997). Turning work into play: The nature and nurturing of intrinsic task engagement. In R. Perry & J. C. Smart (Eds.), *Effective teaching in higher education: Research and practice* (pp. 101–114). New York: Agathon Press.

Coyne, J. C., & Lazarus, R. S. (1980). Cognitive style, stress perception, and coping. In I. L. Kutash & L. B. Schlesinger (Eds.), *Handbook on stress and anxiety.* San Francisco: Jossey-Bass.

Cox, H., Swain, C., & Hartsough, C. S. (1982). *Student success at school.* Final Report: Elementary and Secondary Educational Act IV-C, Sonoma County Office of Education, Santa Rosa, California.

Crandall, V. C., Katkovsky, W., & Crandall, V. J. (1965). Children's beliefs in their own control of reinforcements in intellectual-academic achievement situations. *Child Development, 36*, 91–109.

Crandall, V. J., Preston, A., & Rabson, A. (1960). Maternal reactions and the development of independence and achievement behavior in young children. *Child Development, 31*, 243–251.

Csikszentmihalyi, M. (1975). *Beyond boredom and anxiety.* San Francisco: Jossey-Bass.

Cuban, L. (1990). Reforming again, again, and again. *Educational Researcher, 19*, 3–13.

D'Ambrosio, U. (1987). Ethnomathematics, what it might be. *International Study Group of Ethnomathematics Newsletter, 3*(1).

Darling-Hammond, L., & Wise, A. E. (1985). Beyond standardization: State standards and school improvement. *Elementary School Journal, 85*, 315–336.

Davids, A., & Hainsworth, P. K. (1967). Maternal attitudes about family life and child rearing as avowed by mothers and perceived by their underachieving and high-achieving sons. *Journal of Consulting Psychology, 31*, 29–37.

Davis, D. G. (1986, April). *A pilot study to assess equity in selected curricular offerings across three diverse schools in a large urban school district: A search for methodology.* Paper presented at the annual meeting of the American Educational Research Association, San Francisco.

de Charms, R. (1957). Affiliation motivation and productivity in small groups. *Journal of Abnormal and Social Psychology, 55,* 222–226.

de Charms, R. (1968). *Personal causation: The internal affective determinants of behavior.* New York: Academic Press.

de Charms, R. (1972). Personal causation training in the schools. *Journal of Applied Social Psychology, 2,* 95–113.

Deci, E. L. (1975). *Intrinsic motivation.* New York: Plenum.

Deci, E. L. (1992). The relation of interest to the motivation of behavior: A Self-Determination Theory perspective. In K. A. Renninger, S. Hidi, & A. Krapp (Eds.), *The role of interest in learning and development* (pp. 3–26). Hillsdale, NJ: Erlbaum.

Deci, E. L., & Ryan, R. M. (1987). The support of autonomy and the control of behavior. *Journal of Personality and Social Psychology, 53,* 1024–1037.

de Lange, J. (1987). *Mathematics, insight and meaning.* Vakgroep Onderzoek Wiskundeonderwijs en Onderwijscomputercentrum, Rijksuniversiteit Utrecht, the Netherlands.

Depreeuw, E. (1992). On the fear of failure construct: Active and passive test anxious students behave differently. In K. Hagtvet & T. Johnsen (Eds.), *Advances in test anxiety research* (Vol. 7, pp. 32–46). Amsterdam: Sets & Zeitlinger B.V.

Derry, S. H., & Murphy, D. A. (1986). Designing systems that train learning ability: From theory to practice. *Review of Educational Research, 56,* 1–39.

Deutsch, M. (1949). An experimental study of the effects of cooperation and competition upon group process. *Human Relations, 2,* 199–232.

Deutsch, M. (1979). Education and distributive justice. *American Psychologist, 34,* 391–401.

De Volder, M., & Lens, W. (1982). Academic achievement and future time perspective as a cognitive-motivational concept. *Journal of Personality and Social Psychology, 42,* 566–571.

Dewey, J. (1916). *Democracy and education.* New York: Macmillan.

Dewey, J. (1938/1963). *Experience and education.* New York: Collier.

Dickson, P. (1978). *The official rules: The definitive, annotated collection of laws, principles, and instructions for dealing with the real world.* New York: Delacorte.

Diener, C. T., & Dweck, C. S. (1978). An analysis of learned helplessness: Continuous changes in performance, strategy and achievement cognitions following failure. *Journal of Personality and Social Psychology, 36,* 451–462.

Diener, C. T., & Dweck, C. S. (1980). An analysis of learned helplessness: II.

The processing of success. *Journal of Personality and Social Psychology, 39,* 940–952.

Diggory, J. C. (1966). *Self-evaluation: Concepts and studies.* New York: Wiley.

Dillon, D., & Searle, D. (1981). The role of language in one first grade classroom. *Research in the Teaching of English, 15,* 311–328.

Doyle, A. C. (1967). *The annotated Sherlock Holmes* (Vol. 1). New York: Clarkson N. Potter.

Doyle, W. (1983). Academic work. *Review of Educational Research, 53,* 159–199.

Dryfoos, J. (1990). *Adolescents at risk: Prevalence and prevention.* New York: Oxford University Press.

Dweck, C. S. (1986). Motivational processes affecting learning. *American Psychologist, 41,* 1040–1048.

Dweck, C. S. (1990). Self-theories and goals: Their role in motivation, personality, and development. In R. Dienstbier (Ed.), *Nebraska symposium on motivation* (pp. 199–235). Lincoln: University of Nebraska Press.

Dweck, C. S., & Bempechat, J. (1983). Children's theories of intelligence: Consequences for learning. In S. G. Paris, G. M. Olson, & H. M. Stevenson (Eds.), *Learning and motivation in the classroom* (pp. 239–256). Hillsdale, NJ: Erlbaum.

Dweck, C. S., Chiu, C., & Hong, Y. (1995). Implicit theories: Elaboration and extension of the model. *Psychological Inquiry, 6* (4), 322–333.

Dweck, C. S., & Goetz, T. E. (1988). Attributions and learned helplessness. In J. H. Harvey, W. Ickes, & R. F. Kidd (Eds.), *New directions in attribution research* (Vol. 2, pp. 157–179). Hillsdale, NJ: Erlbaum.

Dweck, C. S., & Reppucci, N. D. (1973). Learned helplessness and reinforcement responsibility in children. *Journal of Personality and Social Psychology, 25,* 109–116.

Eccles, J. (1983). Expectancies, values and academic behaviors. In J. T. Spence (Ed.), *Achievement and achievement motives* (pp. 75–146). San Francisco: Freeman.

Edney, J. J. (1980). The commons problem: Alternative perspectives. *American Psychologist, 2,* 131–150.

Eggerman, R. W. (1982, July–August). Competition as a mixed good. *Humanist,* 48–51.

Eifferman, R. R. (1974). It's child's play. In L. M. Shears & E. M. Bower (Eds.), *Games in education and development* (pp. 75–102). Springfield, IL: Charles C. Thomas.

Eisenberger, R., & Cameron, J. (1996). Detrimental effects of reward: Reality or myth? *American Psychologist, 51* (11), 1153–1166.

Elleson, V. J. (1983, December). Competition: A cultural imperative. *Personnel and Guidance Journal, 62,* 195–198.

Engle, S. H., & Ochoa, A. S. (1988). *Education for democratic citizenship: Decision making in the social studies.* New York: Teachers College Press.

Epstein, K. K. (1989). *Early school leaving: What the leavers say.* Unpublished doctoral dissertation, University of California at Berkeley.

Erickson, F., & Mohatt, J. (1982). Cultural organization of participant structure in two classrooms of Indian students. In G. D. Spindler (Ed.), *Doing the ethnography of schooling: Educational anthropology in action* (pp. 132–175). New York: Holt.

Etaugh, C., & Brown, B. (1975). Perceiving the causes of success and failure of male and female performers. *Developmental Psychology, 11,* 103.

Felsenthal, H. M. (1970). Sex differences in teacher–pupil interactions and their relationship with teacher attitudes and pupil reading achievement. *Dissertation Abstracts, 30,* 3781–3782.

Fetterman, D. (1990, June). Wasted genius. *Stanford Magazine, 18* (2).

Fincham, F. D., & Cain, K. M. (1986). Learned helplessness in humans: A developmental analysis. *Developmental Review, 6,* 301–333.

Finn, J. D. (1989). Withdrawing from school. *Review of Educational Research, 59*(2), 117–142.

Fischer, C. (1982). *Ursachenerklärung im Unterricht.* Cologne: Böhlau Verlag.

Ford, G. R. (1974, July). In defense of the competitive urge. *Sports Illustrated,* 16–23.

Fordham, S., & Ogbu, J. U. (1986). Black students' school success: Coping with the "burden of 'acting white.'" *Urban Review, 18,* 176–206.

Foster, H. L. (1974). *Ribbin', jivin', and playin' the dozen: The unrecognized dilemma of inner-city schools.* Cambridge, MA: Ballinger.

Franco, J. N. (1983). A developmental analysis of self-concept in Mexican American and Anglo school children. *Hispanic Journal of Behavioral Sciences, 5,* 207–218.

Fredericksen, J., & J. R. Collins. (1989). A systems approach to educational testing. *Educational Researcher, 18* (9), 27–32.

Friedman, S. L., Scholnick, E. K., & Cocking, R. R. (Eds.) (1986). *Blueprints for thinking: The role of planning in cognitive development.* Cambridge: Cambridge University Press.

Friend, R. M., & Neale, J. M. (1972). Children's perceptions of success and failure: An attributional analysis of the effects of race and social class. *Developmental Psychology, 7,* 124–128.

Fyans, L. G., Maehr, M. L., Salili, F., & Desai, K. A. (1983). A cross-cultural

287

exploration into the meaning of achievement. *Journal of Personality and Social Psychology, 44,* 1000–1013.

Gardner, H. (1993). *Multiple intelligences: The theory and practice.* New York: Basic Books.

Gatchel, R. J., Paulus, P. B., & Maples, C. W. (1975). Learned helplessness and self-reported affect. *Journal of Abnormal Psychology, 84,* 732–734.

Getzels, J. W. (1975). Problem-finding and the inventiveness of solutions. *Journal of Creative Behavior, 9,* 12–18.

Gibbs, J. T. (1985). City girls: Psychosocial adjustment of urban black adolescent females. *Sage, 2,* 28–36.

Gick, M. L., & Holyoak, K. (1983). Schema induction and analogical transfer. *Cognitive Psychology, 15,* 1–38.

Gilbert, S. E., & Gay, G. (1985). Improving the success in school of poor black children. *Phi Delta Kappan, 66,* 133–137.

Goldberg, L. R. (1965). Grades as motivants. *Psychology in the Schools, 2,* 17–24.

Gottfredson, L. S. (1986). Societal consequences of the *g* factor in employment. *Journal of Vocational Behavior, 29,* 379–410.

Gottfredson, L. S., & Sharf, J. C. (1988). *Journal of Vocational Behavior,* special issue: *Fairness in employment testing, 33* (3), 225–230.

Graham, S. (1984a). Communicating sympathy and anger to black and white children: The cognitive (attributional) consequences of affective cues. *Journal of Personality and Social Psychology, 47,* 14–28.

Graham, S. (1984b). Teacher feelings and student thoughts: An attributional approach to affect in the classroom. *Elementary School Journal, 85,* 91–104.

Graham, S., & Barker, G. P. (1990). The down side of help: An attributional-developmental analysis of helping behavior as a low-ability cue. *Journal of Educational Psychology, 82,* 7–14.

Grant, W. V., & Eiden, L. J. (1982). *Digest of education statistics, 1982.* Washington, DC: National Center for Educational Statistics.

Greenberg, P. J. (1932). Competition in children: An experimental study. *American Journal of Psychology, 44,* 221–250.

Grenis, M. (1975, November). II. Individualization, grouping, competition, and excellence. *Delta Kappan, 57,* 199–200.

Grolnick, W. S., & Ryan, R. M. (1986). *Parent styles associated with children's school-related competence and adjustment.* Unpublished manuscript, University of Rochester.

Grubb, W. N. (1990). Reconstructing the high school. *Educator,* Graduate School of Education, University of California at Berkeley, *4* (3), 22–25.

Hall, P. (1980). *Great planning disasters*. Berkeley: University of California Press.

Hansen, D. A. (1989). Lesson evading and lesson dissembling: Ego strategies in the classroom. *American Journal of Education, 97*, 185–208.

Hanushek, E. A. (1989). The impact of differential expenditures on school performance. *Educational Researcher, 18*, 45–51, 62.

Harackiewicz, J. M., & Eliot, A. J. (1993). Achievement goals and intrinsic motivation. *Journal of Personality and Social Psychology, 65*, 904–915.

Harari, O., & Covington, M. V. (1981). Reactions to achievement behavior from a teacher and student perspective: A developmental analysis. *American Educational Research Journal, 18*, 15–28.

Hardin, G. J. (1968). The tragedy of the commons. *Science, 162*, 1243–1248.

Hare, B. (1985). Stability and change in self-perception and achievement among black adolescents: A longitudinal study. *Journal of Black Psychology, 11*, 29–42.

Harris, A. M., & Covington, M. V. (1989). *Cooperative team failure: A double threat for the low performer?* Unpublished manuscript, Department of Psychology, University of California at Berkeley.

Harter, S. (1974). Pleasure derived from cognitive challenge and mastery. *Child Development, 45*, 661–669.

Hayashi, T., Rim, Y., & Lynn, R. (1970). A test of McClelland's theory of achievement motivation in Britain, Japan, Ireland, and Israel. *International Journal of Psychology, 5*, 275–277.

Haycock, K., & Navarro, M. S. (1988, May). *Unfinished business: Fulfilling our children's promise*. Report from the Achievement Council, 1016 Castro Street, Oakland, CA 94607.

Healey, G. W. (1970). Self-concept: A comparison of Negro-, Anglo-, and Spanish-American students across ethnic, sex, and socioeconomic variables (Doctoral dissertation, New Mexico State University, 1969). *Dissertation Abstracts International, 30*, 2849.

Heider, F. (1958). *The psychology of interpersonal relations*. New York: Wiley.

Heilman, M. E., & Stopeck, M. H. (1985). Attractiveness and corporate success: Different causal attributions for males and females. *Journal of Applied Psychology, 70*, 379–388.

Helmke, A. (1988). The role of classroom context factors for the achievement-impairing effect of test anxiety. *Anxiety Research, 1*, 37–52.

Henry, J. (1957). Attitude organization in elementary school classrooms. *American Journal of Orthopsychiatry, 27*, 117–133.

Hermans, Hubert J. M., ter Laak, J. F., & Maes, C. J. M. (1972). Achievement

289

motivation and fear of failure in family and school. *Developmental Psychology, 6,* 520–528.

Hernstein, R. J., Nickerson, R. S., de Sanchez, M., & Swets, J. A. (1986). Teaching thinking skills. *American Psychologist, 41* (11), 1279–1289.

Hess, R. D., Chang, C. M., & McDevitt, T. M. (1987). Cultural variations in family beliefs about children's performance in mathematics: Comparisons among People's Republic of China, Chinese-American, and Caucasian-American families. *Journal of Educational Psychology, 79,* 179–188.

Heyman, G. D., & Dweck, C. S. (1992). Achievement goals and intrinsic motivation: Their relation and the role in adaptive motivation. *Motivation and Emotion, 16* (3), 231–247.

Hiebert, E., & Calfee, R. C. (1989). Advancing academic literacy through teachers' assessments. *Educational Leadership, 46* (7), 50–54.

Higgins, E. T. (1987). Self-discrepancy: A theory relating self and affect. *Psychological Review, 94,* 319–340.

Holt, J. (1964). *How children fail.* New York: Dell.

Hoppe, F. (1930). Untersuchungen zur Handlungs – und Affektpsychologie IV. Erfolg und Misserfolg. *Psychologische Forschung, 14,* 1–63.

Hull, F. M., Friedman, N. S., & Rodgers, T. F. (1982). The effect of technology on alienation from work. *Sociology of Work and Occupations, 9,* 31–57.

Hullfish, G., & Smith, P. (1961). *Reflective thinking: The method of education.* New York: Dodd, Mead.

Jamieson, I., Miller, A., & Watts, A. G. (1988). *Mirrors of work: Work simulations in schools.* New York: Falmer.

Janis, I. L. (1982). *Groupthink* (2nd ed.). Boston: Houghton-Mifflin.

Jervis, R. (1976). *Perception and misperception in international politics.* Princeton, NJ: Princeton University Press.

Jones, C. (1982, April). *High school and beyond: 1980 sophomore cohort first follow-up (1982) data file user's manual* (Report to the National Center for Educational Statistics, Contract OE 300-78-0208). Chicago: National Opinion Research Center.

Johnson, S. D. (1990). Teaching technical troubleshooting. *Educator,* Graduate School of Education, University of California at Berkeley, *4* (3), 18–21.

Juster, F. T. (1985). Preferences for work and leisure. In F. T. Juster & F. P. Stafford (Eds.), *Time, goods and well-being.* Ann Arbor: Institute for Social Research, University of Michigan.

Kagan, S., & Knight, G. P. (1981). Social motives among Anglo-American and Mexican-American children. *Journal of Research in Personality, 15,* 93–106.

Kagan, S., & Madsen, M. (1971). Cooperation and competition of Mexican, Mexican-American, and Anglo-American children of two ages under four instructional sets. *Developmental Psychology, 5,* 32–39.

Kaplan, R. M., & Swant, S. G. (1973). Reward characteristics in appraisal of achievement behavior. *Representative Research in Social Psychology, 4,* 11–17.

Karabenick, S. A., & Knapp, J. R. (1988). Help seeking and the need for academic assistance. *Journal of Educational Psychology, 80,* 406–408.

Keinan, G., & Zeidner, M. (1987). Effects of decisional control on state anxiety and achievement. *Personality and Individual Differences, 8,* 973–975.

Kelley, H. H. (1971a). *Attributions in social interactions.* Morristown, NJ: General Learning Press.

Kennedy, W. A., & Willcutt, H. C. (1964). Praise and blame as incentives. *Psychological Bulletin, 62,* 323–332.

Kirst, M. (1990, March). *Stanford Magazine,* p. 110.

Kleinfeld, J. (1972). Effective teachers of Eskimo and Indian students. *School Review, 83,* 301–344.

Knapp, R. H. (1960). Attitudes toward time and aesthetic choice. *Journal of Social Psychology, 56,* 79–87.

Knight, G. P., & Kagan, S. (1977). Development of prosocial and competitive behaviors in Anglo-American and Mexican-American children. *Child Development, 48,* 1385–1394.

Knight, J. J. (1974). Instructional dysfunction and the temporary contract. *Educational Technology, 14* (4), 43–44.

Kohl, H. (1967). *36 children.* New York: New American Library.

Kohlmann, C. W., Schumacher, A., & Streit, R. (1988). Trait anxiety and parental child-rearing behavior: Support as a moderator variable? *Anxiety Research, 1,* 53–64.

Kohn, A. (1986). *No contest: The case against competition.* Boston: Houghton-Mifflin.

Krohne, H. W. (1990). Developmental conditions of anxiety and coping: A two-process model of child-rearing effects. No. 33, *Mainzer Berichte zur Persönlichkeitsforschung.* Johannes Gutenberg-Universität Mainz, Psychologisches Institut, Abteilung Persönlichkeitspsychologie.

Krohne, H. W., Kohlmann, C. W., & Leidig, S. (1986). Erziehungsstildeterminanten kindlicher Angstlichkeit, Kompetenzerwartungen und Kompetenzen. *Zeitschrift für Entwicklungspsychologie und Pädagogische Psychologie, 18,* 70–88.

Krumboltz, J. (1990, January–February). Do schools teach kids to hate learning? *Stanford Observer*, p. 10.

Kruglanski, A. W. (1978). Endogenous attribution and intrinsic motivation. In M. Lepper & D. Greene (Eds.), *The hidden costs of reward: New perspectives on the psychology of human motivation* (pp. 85–107). Hillsdale, NJ: Erlbaum.

Kun, A. (1977). Development of the magnitude-covariation and compensation schemata in ability and effort attributions of performance. *Child Development, 48,* 862–873.

Kun, A., & Weiner, B. (1973). Necessary versus sufficient causal schemata for success and failure. *Journal of Research in Personality, 7,* 197–207.

Kunda, Z. (1990). The case for motivated reasoning. *Psychological Bulletin, 108,* 480–498.

Ladner, J. A. (1978). Growing up black. In J. H. Williams (Ed.), *Psychology of women: Selected writings* (pp. 212–224). New York: Norton.

Landrigan, P. J., & Carlson, J. E. (1995). Environmental policy and children's health. *Future of Children, 5,* 34–52.

Lave, J. (1988). *Cognition in practice.* Cambridge: Cambridge University Press.

Leonard, G. B. (1968). *Education and ecstasy.* New York: Delacorte.

Leonard, W. H., Cavana, G. R., & Lowery, L. F. (1981). An experimental test of an extended discretion approach for high school biology laboratory investigations. *Journal of Research in Science Teaching, 18,* 497–504.

Lepper, M. R. (1981). Intrinsic and extrinsic motivation in children: Detrimental effects of superfluous social controls. In W. A. Collins (Ed.), *Minnesota symposia on child psychology* (Vol. 14, pp. 145–214). Hillsdale, NJ: Erlbaum.

Lepper, M. R., Greene, D., & Nisbett, R. E. (1973). Undermining children's intrinsic interest with extrinsic rewards: A test of the "overjustification" hypothesis. *Journal of Personality and Social Psychology, 28,* 129–137.

Levin, B. B. (1990). *Portfolio assessment: Implications for the communication of effort and ability in alternative forms of assessment.* Unpublished paper, School of Education, University of California at Berkeley.

Levin, J. (1983, May). When winning takes all. *Ms., 11* (11), 92–94, 138–139.

Lewin, K. (Ed.) (1948). *Resolving social conflicts: Selected papers on group dynamics.* New York: Harper & Brothers.

Lindskold, S. (1978). Trust development, the GRIT proposal, and the effects of conciliatory acts on conflict and cooperation. *Psychological Bulletin, 85,* 772–793.

Lipman, M. (1985). Thinking skills fostered by the middle-school Philosophy for Children Program. In J. Segal, S. Chipman, & R. Glaser (Eds.), *Thinking and learning skills: Vol. 1. Relating instruction to basic research* (pp. 83–107). Hillsdale, NJ: Earlbaum.

Lipman, M., Sharp, A. M., & Oscanyan, F. S. (1977). *Ethical inquiry: Instructional manual to accompany Lisa.* Upper Montclair, NJ: Institute for the Advancement of Philosophy for Children.

Litwin, G. H., & Ciarlo, J. A. (1961). *Achievement motivation and risk-taking in a business setting.* Technical Report. New York: General Electric Company, Behavioral Research Service.

Locke, E. A., & Latham, G. P. (1984). *Goal setting: A motivational technique that works!* Englewood Cliffs, NJ: Prentice-Hall.

Lodico, M. G., Ghatala, E. S., Levin, J. R., Pressley, M., & Bell, J. A. (1983). Effects of meta-memory training on children's use of effective learning strategies. *Journal of Experimental Child Psychology, 35,* 263–277.

Lundgren, U. P. (1977). *Model analysis of pedagogical processes.* Stockholm, Sweden: Department of Educational Research, Stockholm Institute of Education.

Maehr, M. L. (1989). Thoughts about motivation. In C. Ames & R. Ames (Eds.), *Research on motivation in education* (Vol. 3). New York: Academic Press.

Maehr, M. L. (1991). The "psychological environment" of the school: A focus for school leadership. In P. Thurston & P. Zodhiates (Eds.), *Advances in educational administration* (pp. 51–81). Greenwich, CT: JAI Press.

Maehr, M. L., & Braskamp, L. A. (1986). *The motivation factor: A theory of personal investment.* Lexington, MA: D. C. Heath.

Maehr, M. L., & Midgley, C. (1991). Enhancing student motivation: A school-wide approach. *Educational Psychologist, 26,* 399–427.

Maehr, M. L., & Nicholls, C. (1980). Culture and achievement motivation: A second look. In N. Warren (Ed.), *Studies in cross-cultural psychology* (Vol. 2, pp. 221–267). New York: Academic Press.

Malone, T. W. (1981). Toward a theory of instrinsically motivating instruction. *Cognitive Science, 4,* 333–369.

Marecek, J., & Mettee, D. R. (1972). Avoidance of continued success as a function of self-esteem, level of esteem certainty, and responsibility for success. *Journal of Personality and Social Psychology, 22,* 98–107.

Marshall, H. H. (1988, December). Work or learning: Implications of classroom metaphors. *Educational Researcher, 9,* 9–16.

Martire, J. G. (1956). Relationships between the self-concept and differences in the strength and generality of achievement motivation. *Journal of Personality, 24,* 364–375.

Maugh, T. (1987, March 4). Gifted reported dropping out. *San Francisco Chronicle*, p. F7.

Mayer, R. E. (1989). Models for understanding. *Review of Educational Research, 59*, 43–64.

McClellan, J. (1978). What is a futurist? *Futures Information Exchange, 2*, 1–2.

McClelland, D. C. (1955). Some social consequences of achievement motivation. In M. R. Jones (Ed.), *Nebraska symposium on motivation* (Vol. 3, pp. 41–65). Lincoln: University of Nebraska Press.

McClelland, D. C. (1958). Methods of measurement of human motivation. In J. W. Atkinson (Ed.), *Motives in fantasy, action, and society* (pp. 7–42). Princeton, NJ: Van Nostrand.

McClelland, D. C. (1961). *The achieving society.* Princeton, NJ: Van Nostrand.

McClelland, D. C. (1965). Toward a theory of motive acquisition. *American Psychologist, 20*, 321–333.

McClelland, D. C. (1972). What is the effect of achievement motivation training in the schools? *Teachers College Record, 74*, 129–145.

McClelland, D. C. (1985). *Human motivation.* Cambridge: Cambridge University Press.

McClelland, D. C., & Winter, D. G. (1969). *Motivating economic achievement.* New York: Free Press.

McInerney, D. M. (1988). *Cross-cultural studies of achievement motivation: Educational implications and research directions for the future.* Macarthur Institute of Higher Education, Sydney, Australia.

McKeachie, W. J., Pintrich, P. R., & Lin, Y. G. (1985). Teaching learning strategies. *Educational Psychologist, 20*, 153–160.

McNabb, T. (1987). *The effects of strategy and effort attribution training on the motivation of subjects differing in perceived math competence and attitude toward strategy and effort.* Unpublished manuscript, American College Testing Program, Iowa City, IA.

Merton, R. K. (1949). *Social theory and social structure.* Glencoe, IL: Free Press.

Mettee, D. R. (1971). Rejection of unexpected success as a function of the negative consequences of accepting success. *Journal of Personality and Social Psychology, 17*, 332–341.

Meyer, W. U., Bachmann, M., Biermann, U., Hempelmann, M., Plöger, F. O., & Spiller, H. (1979). The informational value of evaluative behavior: Influences of praise and blame on perceptions of ability. *Journal of Educational Psychology, 71*, 259–268.

Miller, L. K., & Hamblin, R. L. (1963). Interdependence, differential rewarding, and productivity. *American Sociological Review, 28,* 768–778.

Millroy, W. L. (1991). An ethnographic study of the mathematical ideas of a group of carpenters. *Learning and Individual Differences, 3,* 1–25.

Mincer, J. (1989, May). Human capital and the labor market: A review of current research. *Educational Researcher, 18,* 27–34.

Mineka, S., & Henderson, R. W. (1985). Controllability and predictability in acquired motivation. *Annual Review of Psychology, 36,* 495–529.

Mineka, S., & Kihlstrom, J. F. (1978). Unpredictable and uncontrollable events: A new perspective on experimental neurosis. *Journal of Abnormal Psychology, 87,* 256–271.

Mischel, W., & Liebert, R. M. (1966). Effects of discrepancies between observed and imposed reward criteria on their acquisition and transmission. *Journal of Personality and Social Psychology, 3,* 45–53.

Mizokawa, D. T., & Ryckman, D. B. (1988, April). *Attributions of academic success and failure to effort or ability: A comparison of six Asian American ethnic groups.* Paper presented at the annual meeting of the American Educational Research Association, New Orleans.

Monte, C. F., & Fish, J. M. (1989). The fear-of-failure personality and academic cheating. In R. Schwarzer, H. M. van der Ploeg, & C. D. Spielberger (Eds.), *Advances in test anxiety research* (Vol. 6, pp. 87–103). Lisse, Netherlands: Swets & Zeitlinger.

Morris, R. (1977). *Increasing participation through the use of normative interventions.* Unpublished doctoral dissertation, Stanford University.

Mushak, P. (1992). Lead: A critical issue in child health. *Environmental Research, 59,* 281–309.

National Academy of Sciences, Panel on Secondary School Education for the Changing Workplace (1984). *High school and the changing workplace, the employer's view.* Washington, DC: National Academy Press.

Nelson, L. L., & Kagan, S. (1972). Competition: The star-spangled scramble. *Psychology Today, 6* (4), 53–56, 90–91.

Nelson-Le Gall, S. (1985). Help-seeking behavior in learning. In E. W. Gordon (Ed.), *Review of research in education* (Vol. 12, pp. 55–90). Washington, DC: American Educational Research Association.

Newell, A., & Simon, H. A. (1972). *Human problem solving.* Englewood Cliffs, NJ: Prentice-Hall.

Newman, R. S. (1990). Children's help-seeking in the classroom: The role of motivational factors and attitudes. *Journal of Educational Psychology, 82,* 71–80.

Newman, R. S., & Goldin, L. (1990). Children's reluctance to seek help with schoolwork. *Journal of Educational Psychology, 82,* 92–100.

Nicholls, J. G. (1975). Causal attributions and other achievement-related cognitions: Effects of task outcome, attainment values, and sex. *Journal of Personality and Social Psychology, 31,* 379–389.

Nicholls, J. G. (1978). The development of the conceptions of effort and ability, perception of academic attainment, and the understanding that difficult tasks require more ability. *Child Development, 49,* 800–814.

Nicholls, J. G. (1984). Achievement motivation: Concepts of ability, subjective experience, task choice, and performance. *Psychological Review, 91,* 328–346.

Nicholls, J. G. (1989). *The competitive ethos and democratic education.* Cambridge, MA: Harvard University Press.

Nicholls, J. G., Patashnick, M., & Nolen, S. B. (1985). Adolescents' theories of education. *Journal of Educational Psychology, 77,* 683–692.

Nickerson, R., Perkins, D. N., & Smith, E. C. (1985). *The teaching of thinking.* Hillsdale, NJ: Erlbaum.

Nixon, R. M. (1962). *Six crises.* Garden City, NY: Doubleday.

Nolen, S. B. (1987, April). *The hows and whys of studying: The relationship of goals to strategies.* Paper presented at the annual meeting of the American Educational Research Association, Washington, DC.

Nolen, S. B. (1988). Reasons for studying: Motivational orientations and study strategies. *Cognition and Instruction, 5* (4), 269–287.

Nuttin, J. (1984). *Motivation, planning and action: A relational theory of behavior dynamics.* Hillsdale, NJ: Erlbaum.

Nuttin, J., & Lens, W. (1985). *Future time perspective and motivation: Theory and research method.* Hillsdale, NJ: Erlbaum.

Oakes, J. (1985). *Keeping track: How schools structure inequality.* New Haven, CT: Yale University Press.

Oakes, J. (1987, October). *Improving inner-city schools: Current directions in urban district reform.* State University of New Jersey, Rutgers and the Rand Corporation.

Oakes, J. (1992). Can tracking research inform practice? *Educational Researcher, 20,* 12–21.

Ogbu, J. U. (1978). *Minority education and caste: The American system in cross-cultural perspective.* New York: Academic Press.

Oka, E. R., & Paris, S. G. (1987). Patterns of motivation and reading skills in underachieving children. In S. J. Ceci (Ed.), *Handbook of cognitive, social, and neuropsychological aspects of learning disabilities* (Vol. 2, pp. 115–145). Hillsdale, NJ: Erlbaum.

Olsen, C. (1991). *Achievement orientation and context effects on intensive motivation for learning a task*. Unpublished doctoral dissertation, University of California at Berkeley.

Olton, R. M., & Crutchfield, R. S. (1969). Developing the skills of productive thinking. In P. Mussen, J. Langer, & M. V. Covington (Eds.), *Trends and issues in developmental psychology* (pp. 68–91). New York: Holt, Rinehart & Winston.

Olton, R. M., Wardrop, J. L., Covington, M. V., Goodwin, W. L., Crutchfield, R. S., Klausmeier, H. J., & Ronda, T. (1967). *The development of productive thinking skills in fifth-grade children*. Technical Report, Research and Development Center for Cognitive Learning. Madison: University of Wisconsin.

Omelich, C. L. (1974). *Attribution and achievement in the classroom: The self-fulfilling prophecy*. Paper presented at the meeting of the California Personnel and Guidance Association, San Francisco.

Orlick, T. (1982). *The second cooperative sports and games book*. New York: Pantheon.

Ornstein, R., & Ehrlich, P. (1989). *New world, new mind*. New York: Doubleday.

Osterman, P. (1989). The job market for adolescents. In D. Stern & D. Eichorn (Eds.), *Adolescence and work: Influences of social structure, labor markets, and culture* (pp. 235–256). Hillsdale, NJ: Erlbaum.

Paris, S. G., Lipson, M. Y., & Wixson, K. K. (1995). Becoming a strategic reader. In R. B. Ruddel, M. R. Ruddel, & H. Singer (Eds.), *Theoretical models and processes of reading* (pp. 582–601). Newark, DE: International Reading Association.

Parsons, J. E., Meece, J. L., Adler, T. F., & Kaczala, C. M. (1982). Sex differences in attributions and learned helplessness. *Sex Roles, 8*, 421–432.

Paterson, D. (1956). *The conservation of human talent*. Walter Van Dyke Bingham Lecture, Ohio State University.

Patterson, J. (1987). *1987 and beyond: Choices for the future*. Center for Educational Planning, Santa Clara County Office of Education, 100 Skyport Drive, San Jose, CA 95115.

Perkins, D. N. (1982). General cognitive skills: Why not? In S. Chipman, J. Segal, & R. Glaser (Eds.), *Thinking and learning skills: Current research and open questions* (Vol. 2). Hillsdale, NJ: Erlbaum.

Perkins, D. N., Jay, E., & Tishman, S. (1993). Beyond abilities: A dispositional theory of thinking. *Merill-Palmer Quarterly, 39*, 1–21.

Perkins, D. N., & Salomon, G. (1987). Transfer and teaching thinking. In

D. N. Perkins, J. Lockhead, & J. Bishop (Eds.), *Thinking: The Second International Conference* (pp. 285–303). Hillsdale, NJ: Erlbaum.

Perkins, D. N., & Salomon, G. (1988). Teaching for transfer. *Educational Leadership, 46* (1), 22–32.

Perry, R. P., & Struthers, C. W. (1994, April). *Attributional retraining in the college classroom: Some causes for optimism.* Presented at "Sustainable Educational Effects: A Motivational Analysis" at the American Educational Research Association annual meeting, New Orleans.

Phye, G. D., & Andre, T. (Eds.) (1986). *Educational Psychology: Vol. 3. Cognitive classroom learning: Understanding, thinking, and problem solving.* New York: Academic Press.

Pintrich, P. R. (1988). A process-oriented view of student motivation and cognition. In J. S. Stark & L. Mets (Eds.), *Improving teaching and learning through research: New directions for institutional research* (Vol. 57, pp. 55–70). San Francisco: Jossey-Bass.

Pintrich, P. R. (1989). The dynamic interplay of student motivation and cognition in the college classroom. In C. Ames & M. Maehr (Eds.), *Advances in motivation and achievement: Vol. 6. Motivation enhancing environments* (pp. 117–160). Greenwich, CT: JAI Press.

Pintrich, P. R., & De Groot, E. V. (1990). Motivational and self-regulated learning components of classroom academic performance. *Journal of Educational Psychology, 82,* 33–40.

Pittman, T. S., & Boggiano, A. (1992). Psychological perspectives on motivation and achievement. In A. K. Boggiano & T. S. Pittman (Eds.), *Achievement and motivation: A social-developmental perspective* (pp. 1–8). Cambridge: Cambridge University Press.

Pittman, T. S., Boggiano, A. K., & Ruble, D. N. (1983). Intrinsic and extrinsic motivational orientations: Interactive effect of reward, competence feedback, and task complexity. In J. Levine & M. Wang (Eds.), *Teacher and student perceptions: Implications for learning* (pp. 319–340). Hillsdale, NJ: Erlbaum.

Porter, A. (1989). A curriculum out of balance: The case of elementary school mathematics. *Educational Researcher, 18,* 9–15.

Powell, B., Ames, C., & Maehr, M. L. (1990). *Achievement goals and student motivation in learning disabled and at-risk children.* Paper presented at the annual meeting of the American Educational Research Association, Boston.

Pratte, R. (1988). *The civic imperative: Examining the need for civic education.* New York: Teachers College Press.

Pressley, M. (1995). More about the development of self-regulation: Com-

298

plex, long-term, and thoroughly social. *Educational Psychologist, 30,* 173–188.

Ramirez, M., & Castaneda, A. (1974). *Cultural democracy, biocognitive development, and education.* New York: Academic Press.

Ramirez, M., & Price-Williams, D. R. (1976). Achievement motivation in children of three ethnic groups in the United States. *Journal of Cross-Cultural Psychology, 7,* 49–61.

Raven, B. H., & Eachus, T. M. (1963). Cooperation and competition in means-independent triads. *Journal of Abnormal and Social Psychology, 28,* 768–778.

Raynor, J. O. (1969). Future orientation and motivation of immediate activity: An elaboration of the theory of achievement motivation. *Psychological Review, 76,* 606–610.

Raynor, J. O. (1982). Motivational determinants of music-related behavior: Psychological careers of student, teacher, performer, and listener. In J. O. Raynor & E. E. Entin (Eds.), *Motivation, career striving, and aging* (pp. 309–329). Washington, DC: Hemisphere.

Raynor, J. O., & Entin, E. E. (1982). *Motivation, career striving, and aging.* Washington, DC: Hemisphere.

Reasoner, R. W. (1973). A matter of priority. *California School Boards, 32,* 24–28.

Reasoner, R. W. (1986). *Building self-esteem.* Consulting Psychologists Press, 557 College Ave., Palo Alto, CA 94306.

Reich, R. B. (1989, January). Must new economic vigor mean making do with less? *NEA Today,* special issue: *Issues '89,* 13–19.

Resnick, L. (1987). *Education and learning to think.* Washington, DC: National Research Council, National Academy Press.

Reuman, D. A. (1988). *How social comparison mediates effects of ability grouping in mathematics on achievement expectancies.* Paper presented at the Annual Meeting of the American Education Research Association, New Orleans, LA.

Reusser, K. (1987, March). *Problem solving beyond the logic of things.* Cited in A. H. Schoenfeld, *On Mathematics as sense making: An informal attack on the unfortunate divorce of formal and informal mathematics.* Paper presented at OERI/LRCD Conference on Informal Reasoning and Education, Pittsburgh.

Richmond, B. O., & Weiner, G. P. (1973). Cooperation and competition among young children as a function of ethnic grouping, grade, sex, and reward condition. *Journal of Educational Psychology, 64,* 329–334.

REFERENCES

Riessman, F. (1988, Summer). Transforming the schools: A new paradigm. *Social Policy, 19* (1), 2–4.

Rist, R. C. (1970). Student social class and teacher expectations: The self-fulfilling prophecy in ghetto education. *Harvard Educational Review, 40,* 411–450.

Rocklin, T., & O'Donnell, A. M. (1986, August). *Self-adapted testing: A performance-improving variant of computerized adaptive testing.* Paper presented as a poster at the annual meeting of the American Psychological Association, Washington, DC.

Rosen, B. C., & D'Andrade, R. (1959). The psychosocial origins of achievement motivation. *Sociometry, 22,* 185–218.

Rosen, R. (1959). Race, ethnicity, and the achievement syndrome. *American Sociological Review, 24,* 47–60.

Rosenbaum, M. E. (1980). Cooperation and competition. In P. B. Paulus (Ed.), *Psychology of group influence* (pp. 291–326). Hillsdale, NJ: Erlbaum.

Rosenberg, J. (1965). *Society and the adolescent self-image.* Princeton, NJ: Princeton University Press.

Rosenberg, M., & Simmons, R. G. (1973). *Black and white self-esteem: The urban school child.* Washington, DC: American Sociological Association.

Rosenholtz, R. S., & Rosenholtz, S. J. (1981). Classroom organization and the perception of ability. *Sociology of Education, 54,* 132–140.

Rosenholtz, S. J. & Simpson, C. (1984). Classroom organization and student stratification. *Elementary School Journal, 85,* 1–17.

Rosenholtz, S. J., & Wilson, B. (1980). The effect of classroom structure on shared perceptions of ability. *American Educational Research Journal, 17,* 75–82.

Rosenthal, R., & Jacobson, L. (1968). *Pygmalion in the classroom: Teacher expectation and pupils' intellectual development.* New York: Holt, Rinehart & Winston.

Rothblum, E. D., Solomon, L. J., & Murakami, J. (1986). Affective, cognitive and behavioral differences between high and low procrastinators. *Journal of Counseling Psychology, 33,* 387–394.

Rowe, M. (1972). *Wait-time and rewards as instructional variables: Their influence on language, logic, and fate-control.* Paper presented at the meeting of the National Association for Research in Science Teaching.

Rubin, H. L. (1980). *Competing: Understanding and winning the strategic games we all play.* New York: Lippincott & Crowell.

Rumbaut, R. G. (1995). A legacy of war: Refugees from Vietnam, Laos and Cambodia. In S. Pedraza and R. G. Rumbaut (Eds.), *Origins and destinies: Immigration, race, and ethnicity in America.* Belmont, CA: Wadsworth.

300

Russell, W. J. (1988, March). Editorial: Presidential campaigns and educational policy. *Educational Researcher, 17* (2), 4, 12.

Rustemeyer, R. (1984). Selbsteinschätzung eigener Fähigkeit – vermittelt durch die Emotionen anderer Personen. *Zeitschrift für Entwicklungspsychologie und Pädagogische Psychologie, 16,* 149–161.

Ryals, K. R. (1969). *An experimental study of achievement motivation training as a function of the moral maturity of trainees.* Unpublished doctoral dissertation, Washington University, St. Louis, MO.

Sadoski, M., & Paivio, A. (1995). A Dual Coding view of imagery and verbal processes in reading comprehension. In R. B. Ruddell, M. R. Ruddell, & H. Singer (Eds.), *Theoretical models and processes of reading* (pp. 582–601). Newark, DE: International Reading Association.

Sanders, M., Scholz, J. P., & Kagan, S. (1976). Three social motives and field independence-dependence in Anglo American and Mexican American children. *Journal of Cross-Cultural Psychology, 7,* 451–461.

Saxe, G. B. (1988). Candy selling and math learning. *Educational Researcher, 17,* 14–21.

Schaffer, M. (1994). Children and toxic substances: Confronting a major public health challenge. *Environmental Health Perspectives, 102,* suppl. 2, 155–156.

Schneider, S. H. (1989). *Global warming.* San Francisco: Sierra Club Books.

Schoenfeld, A. H. (1985). *Mathematical problem solving.* New York: Academic Press.

Schoenfeld, A. H. (1989). *Reflections on doing and teaching mathematics.* Paper presented at a conference, Mathematical Thinking and Problem Solving, Berkeley, CA.

Schorr, L. B. (1988). *Within our reach: Breaking the cycle of disadvantage.* New York: Anchor/Doubleday.

Schwarzer, R., Jerusalem, M., & Schwarzer, C. (1983). Self-related and situation-related cognitions in test anxiety and helplessness: A longitudinal analysis with structural equations. In R. Schwarzer, H. M. van der Ploeg, & C. D. Spielberger (Eds.), *Advances in anxiety research* (Vol. 2, pp. 35–43). Hillsdale, NJ: Erlbaum.

Schwarzer, R., Jerusalem, M., & Stiksrud, A. (1984). The developmental relationship between test anxiety and helplessness. In H. M. van der Ploeg, R. Schwarzer, & C. D. Spielberger (Eds.), *Advances in test anxiety research* (Vol. 3, pp. 73–79). Hillsdale, NJ: Erlbaum.

Scribner, S. (1984). Studying working intelligence. In B. Rogoff & J. Lave (Eds.), *Everyday cognition: Its development in social context* (pp. 9–40). Cambridge, MA: Harvard University Press.

Sears, P. S. (1940). Levels of aspiration in academically successful and unsuccessful children. *Journal of Abnormal and Social Psychology, 35,* 498–536.

Seligman, M. E. P. (1975). *Helplessness: On depression, development, and death.* San Francisco: Freeman.

Seligman, M. E. P., Maier, S. F., & Geer, J. (1968). The alleviation of learned helplessness in the dog. *Journal of Abnormal Psychology, 73,* 256–262.

Seligman, M. E. P., Maier, S. F., & Solomon, R. L. (1971). Unpredictable and uncontrollable aversive events. In F. R. Brush (Ed.), *Aversive conditioning and learning.* New York: Academic Press.

Shade, B. (1987). Ecological correlates of the educative style of Afro-American children. *Journal of Negro Education, 56,* 88–99.

Shanker, A. (1988, July). *State of our union.* Speech to American Federation of Teachers Convention, San Francisco, CA.

Shapiro, G. (1986). *A skeleton in the darkroom: Stories of serendipity in science.* New York: Harper & Row.

Shaw, M. E. (1958). Some motivational factors in cooperation and competition. *Journal of Personality, 26,* 155–169.

Shepard, L. A. (1989). Why we need better assessment. *Educational Leadership, 46* (7), 4–9.

Shirts, R. G. (1969). *Star power: Director's instructions.* Western Behavioral Science Institute, 1150 Silverado, La Jolla, CA 92037.

Silberman, C. E. (1970). *Crisis in the classroom: The remaking of American education.* New York: Vintage.

Silverstein, B., & Krate, R. (1975). *Children of the dark ghetto: A developmental psychology.* New York: Praeger.

Singh, S. (1977). Achievement motivation and economic growth. *Indian Psychological Review, 14,* 52–56.

Skaalvik, E. M., & Hagtvet, K. A. (1990). Academic achievement and self-concept: An analysis of causal predominance in a developmental perspective. *Journal of Personality and Social Psychology, 58,* 292–307.

Skinner, E. A., Wellborn, J. G., & Connell, J. P. (1990). What it takes to do well in school and whether I've got it: A process model of perceived control and children's engagement and achievement in school. *Journal of Educational Psychology, 82,* 22–32.

Slavin, R. E. (1983). When does cooperative learning increase student achievement? *Psychological Bulletin, 94,* 429–445.

Slavin, R. E. (1984). Students motivating students to excel: Cooperative incentives, cooperative tasks, and student achievement. *Elementary School Journal, 85,* 53–64.

Slavin, R. E. (1987). Ability grouping and student achievement in elementary schools: A best-evidence synthesis. *Review of Educational Research, 57*, 293–336.

Slavin, R., & Oickle, E. (1981). Effects of cooperative learning teams on student achievement and race relations: Treatment by race interactions. *Sociology of Education, 54*, 174–180.

Smiley, P. A., & Dweck, C. S. (1994). Individual differences in achievement goals among young children. *Child Development, 65*, 1723–1743.

Smith, E. (1982). The black female adolescent: A review of the educational career and psychological literature. *Psychology of Women Quarterly, 6*, 261–288.

Smith, T. W., Snyder, C. R., & Handelsman, M. M. (1982). On the self-serving function of an academic wooden leg: Test anxiety as a self-handicapping strategy. *Journal of Personality and Social Psychology, 42*, 314–321.

Smits, B., & Meyer, W. U. (1985). *Lehrerreaktionen auf Erfolg und Misserfolg bei für begabt und unbegabt gehaltenen Schülern.* Katholieke Universiteit, Nijmegen, the Netherlands.

Snyder, C. R. (1984, September). Excuses, excuses: They sometimes actually work – to relieve the burden of blame. *Psychology Today, 18*, 50–55.

Snyder, C. R., & Higgins, R. L. (1988). Excuses: Their effective role in the negotiation of reality. *Psychological Bulletin, 104*, 23–35.

Snyder, M. L., Stephan, W. G., & Rosenfeld, C. (1976). Egotism and attribution. *Journal of Personality and Social Psychology, 33*, 435–441.

Sofia, J. P. (1978). *The influence of specific goal setting conferences on achievement, attributional patterns and goal setting behavior of elementary school boys.* Unpublished doctoral dissertation, School of Education, University of California at Berkeley.

Solomon, L. J., & Rothblum, E. D. (1984). Academic procrastination: Frequency and cognitive-behavioral correlates. *Journal of Counseling Psychology, 31*, 503–509.

Sowder, L. (1987, June). *Searching for affect in the solution of story problems in mathematics.* Paper presented at the annual meeting of the American Educational Research Association, San Diego.

Spence, J. T., & Helmreich, R. L. (1983). Achievement-related motives and behaviors. In J. T. Spence (Ed.), *Achievement and achievement motives* (pp. 7–74). San Francisco: Freeman.

Spenner, K. I. (1985). The upgrading and downgrading of occupations: Issues, evidence, and implications for education. *Review of Educational Research, 55*, 125–154.

Stack, C. B. (1974). *All our kin: Strategies for survival in a black community.* New York: Harper & Row.

Stake, R., & Easley, J. (1978). *Case studies in science education* (Vols. 1 & 2). Urbana: Center for Instructional Research and Curriculum Evaluation and Committee on Culture and Cognition, University of Illinois at Urbana-Champaign.

Steele, C. M. (1988). The psychology of self-affirmation: Sustaining the integrity of the self. In L. Berkowitz (Ed.), *Advances in experimental social psychology* (Vol. 21, pp. 261–302). New York: Academic Press.

Steele, S. (1989a). Being black and feeling blue. *American Scholar, 58,* 497–508.

Steele, S. (1989b, February). The recoloring of campus life. *Harper's Magazine,* pp. 47–55.

Steinberg, L., Dornbusch, S. M., & Brown, B. B. (1992). Ethnic differences in adolescent achievement: An ecological perspective. *American Psychologist, 47,* 723–729

Stephan, W. G., Rosenfield, D., & Stephen, C. (1976). Egotism in males and females. *Journal of Personality and Social Psychology, 34,* 1161–1167.

Stern, D. (1984). School-based enterprise and the quality of work experience: A study of high school students. *Youth and Society, 15,* 401–427.

Stern, D., Hoachlander, E. G., Choy, S., & Benson, C. (1986, March). *One million hours a day: Vocational education in California public secondary schools.* Policy Paper #PP86-3-2. PACE, School of Education, University of California, Berkeley, CA 94720.

Stern, D., Raby, M., and Dayton, C. (1992). *Career academies: Partnerships for reconstructing American high schools.* San Francisco: Jossey-Bass.

Sternberg, R. J. (1985). Instrumental and componential approaches to the nature and training of intelligence. In S. Chipman, J. Segal, & R. Glaser (Eds.), *Thinking and learning skills: Current research and open questions* (Vol. 2). Hillsdale, NJ: Erlbaum.

Sternberg, R. J. (1986). *Critical thinking: Nature, measurement, and improvement.* Washington, DC: National Institute of Education.

Stevenson, J. A. (1921). *The project method of teaching.* New York: Macmillan.

Strober, M. (1987, Spring). The scope of microeconomics: Implications for economic education. *Journal of Economic Education, 18,* 135–149.

Strober, M. (1990, January–February). Kindling students' passion for economics. *Stanford Observer.*

Stulac, J. (1975). *The self-fulfilling prophecy: Modifying the effects of a unidimensional perception of academic competence in task-oriented groups.* Unpublished doctoral dissertation, Stanford University.

Suarez-Orozco, M. M. (1989). *Central American refugees and U.S. high schools: A psychosocial study of motivation and achievement*. Stanford, CA: Stanford University Press.

Teevan, R. C., & Fischer, R. (1967). *Hostile press and childhood reinforcement patterns: A replication*. Unpublished manuscript. Lewisburg, PA: Bucknell University.

Tetlock, P. E. (1985). Toward an intuitive politician model of attribution process. In B. R. Schlenker (Ed.), *The self in social life*. Hillsdale, NJ: Erlbaum.

Thurow, L. C. (1975). *Generating inequality: Mechanisms of distribution in the U.S. economy*. New York: Basic Books.

Tishman, S., Jay, E., & Perkins, D. N. (1993). Teaching thinking dispositions: From transmission to enculturation. *Theory into practice, 32* (3), 147–153.

Tishman, S., Perkins, D. N., & Jay, E. (1995). *The thinking classroom: Learning and teaching in a culture of thinking*. Boston: Allyn Bacon.

Tobias, S. (1989, September). Tracked to fail. *Psychology Today, 23,* 54–58, 60.

Toffler, A. (1970). *Future shock*. New York: Random House.

Tomiki, K. (1997). *Influences of cultural values and perceived family environments on achievement motivation among college students*. Unpublished master's thesis, University of California at Berkeley.

Tracey, C. B., Ames, C., & Maehr, M. L. (1990). *Attitudes and perceptions of competence across regular, at-risk, and learning disabled students*. Paper presented at the annual meeting of the American Educational Research Association, Boston.

Trimble, K., & Sinclair, R. L. (1986, April). *Ability grouping and differing conditions for learning: An analysis of content and instruction in ability-grouped classes*. Paper presented at the annual meeting of the American Educational Research Association, San Francisco.

Wakefield, J. (1988). Problem finding in the arts and sciences. *Questioning Exchange, 2,* 133–140.

Weiner, B. (1972). *Theories of motivation: From mechanism to cognition*. Chicago: Markham.

Weiner, B. (1974). *Achievement motivation and attribution theory*. Morristown, NJ: General Learning Press.

Weiner, B., Frieze, L., Kukla, A., Reed, L., Rest, S., & Rosenbaum, R. (1971). Perceiving the causes of success and failure. In E. E. Jones, D. E. Kanouse, H. H. Kelley, R. E. Nisbett, S. Valins, & B. Weiner (Eds.), *Attribution: Perceiving the causes of behavior* (pp. 95–121). Morristown, NJ: General Learning Press.

305

Weiner, B., Heckhausen, H., Meyer, W., & Cook, R. (1972). Causal ascriptions and achievement behavior: A conceptual analysis of effect and re-analysis of locus of control. *Journal of Personality and Social Psychology, 21*, 239–248.

Weiner B., & Kukla, A. (1970). An attributional analysis of achievement motivation. *Journal of Personality and Social Psychology, 15*, 1–20.

Weinstein, R. S. (1976). Reading group membership in first grade: Teacher behaviors and pupil experience over time. *Journal of Educational Psychology, 68*, 103–116.

Weinstein, R. S. (1981, April). Student perspectives on achievement in varied classroom environments. In P. Blumenfeld (Chair), *Student perspectives and the study of the classroom*. Symposium conducted at the meeting of the American Educational Research Association, Los Angeles.

Weinstein, R. S. (1985). Student mediation of classroom expectancy effects. In J. B. Dusek, V. C. Hall, & W. J. Meyer (Eds.), *Teacher expectancies* (pp. 329–349). Hillsdale, NJ: Erlbaum.

Weinstein, R. S. (1993). Children's knowledge of differential treatment in school: Implications for motivation. In T. M. Tomlinson (Ed.), *Hard work and high expectations: Motivating students to learn*. National Society for the Study of Education Series. Berkeley, CA: McCutchan.

Wertheimer, M. (1959). *Productive thinking*. New York: Harper & Row.

Whitehead, A. N. (1929). *The aims of education*. New York: New American Library.

Wieland-Eckelmann, R., Bösel, R., & Badorrek, W. (1987). *Coping styles, temporal patterns of states, and performance*. Paper presented at the Eighth International Conference of the Society for Test Anxiety Research, Bergen, Norway.

Wiggins, G. (1989, May). A true test: Toward more authentic and equitable assessment. *Phi Delta Kappan, 70* (9), 703–713

Wiggins, G. (1991). Standards, not standardization: Evoking quality student work. *Educational Leadership, 48*, 18–25.

Wilson, T. D., & Linville, P. W. (1985). Improving the performance of college freshmen with attributional techniques. *Journal of Personality and Social Psychology, 49*, 287–293.

Winter, D. G. (1987). Leader appeal, leader performance, and the motive profiles of leaders and followers: A study of American presidents and elections. *Journal of Personality and Social Psychology, 52*, 196–202.

Winter, D. G., & Carlson, L. A. (1988). Using motive scores in the psychobiographical study of an individual: The case of Richard Nixon. *Journal of Personality, 56*, 75–103.

Winterbottom, M. R. (1953). The relation of need for achievement to learning experiences in independence and mastery. In J. Atkinson (Ed.), *Motives in fantasy, action and society* (pp. 453–478). New York: Van Nostrand.

Woodson, C. E. (1975). *Motivational effects of two-stage testing*. Unpublished manuscript, Institute of Human Learning, University of California, Berkeley.

Wurman, R. S. (1989). *Information anxiety*. New York: Doubleday.

Zoeller, C., Mahoney, G., & Weiner, B. (1983). Effects of attribution training on the assembly task performance of mentally retarded adults. *American Journal of Mental Deficiency, 88,* 109–112.

Zuckerman, M. (1979). Attribution of success and failure revisited, or: The motivational bias is alive and well in attribution theory. *Journal of Personality, 47,* 245–287.

AUTHOR INDEX

SUBJECT INDEX

ability
  attributional interpretations, 58–61, 81–3
  learnable aspects, 21
  promotion of positive beliefs in, 147–9
  self-worth dynamics, 78–83, 137–8, 146–8
  static versus plastic view of, 147–9
  strategic planning view of, 148
ability attributions
  developmental changes, 81–3
  ethnic group differences, 63
  in failure-prone students, 58–61, 99
  learned helplessness effects, 67–70
  retraining, 70–1
  self-worth dynamics, 78–83, 137–8, 146–8
  in success-oriented students, 58–60
ability game, 110–17
  "equity game" contrast, 19
  failure interpretations in, 110–1
  and negative reasons for learning, 17–18
  scarcity of rewards in, 109–25
  school as, 110–17
  self-worth negative effects, 137–8
ability grouping/tracking
  castelike minority groups, 126
  irrational goal-setting effects of, 120
  negative effects, 112–14, 120, 130
  refugee placement in, 113–14
  self-esteem effects, 113
  self-fulfilling prophecy relationship,
    114–17
absolute standards
  advantages, 143–4
  motivational effects, 30–2, 143
  relative standards comparison, 30–1
achievement expectations, 118–21
achievement tests, see test scores
"acting white," 96–8
African Americans, see blacks
aggressiveness, 242
analogies, in problem-solving, 172–3
anxiety-prone students
  absolute standards advantage, 31
  child-rearing influences, 49
  mastery learning benefits, 162
apprenticeship, 141
Asian American children
  authoritarian parenting, 50

effort attributions, 63
  peer-group dynamics, 50–1
aspiration levels, 28–9
  and absolute standards, 30–2
  Hoppe's experiments, 28–9
attitudes toward achievement, 48
attributional retraining, 70–1
  age factors, 71
  failure-oriented students, 70–1
attributions, 14–15, 56–76
  and achievement motivation theory,
    14–15
  cooperative behavior obstacle, 186–7
  developmental changes, 81–3
  educational implications, 63–74
  and emotions, 57–8
  ethnic differences, 62–3
  in failure-accepting students, 99
  in failure-avoiding students, 58–61, 64, 71
  learned helplessness effects, 67–70
  need achievement theory relationship,
    58–9
  sex differences, 61–2
  in success-oriented students, 58–60
  theory of, 14–15
authentic tasks
  and Career Placement game, 209
  motivational guidelines, 140–1
  and testing, 228–9
authoritarian homes
  achievement motivation influence, 50
  peer-group interaction, 50–1
authoritative homes
  achievement motivation influence, 50
  peer-group interaction, 50–1
automation, 246

BioAlert game, 207–8, 259
blacks
  achievement motivation differences, 44–7
  "acting white" burden, 96–8
  attributional patterns, 62–3
  community college enrollment, 250
  competition effects on, 125–8
  disidentification dynamics, 95–6
  drop-out rates, 5
  dropping-out reasons, 127–8

315

underachievement (*cont.*)
   and ideal-self/actual self discrepancy,
      88–9
   parental influences, 49–50
   as self-handicapping strategy, 88–9
   and teacher rewards/punishments, 67
unemployment, 238–41
unidimensional classrooms, 111–2
   moderation of, 130–1
   self-esteem effects, 111–2, 130–1
   and social relationships, 112

verbal ability, 111–2
vocabulary tests, 229–30
vocational education
   academic education integration, 225
   serious games role in, 223–4

"warehousing of children," 125
wishful thinking, 117
"witch-hunt syndrome," 107–8
women, attributional differences, 61–2
word-recognition vocabulary tests, 229–30
work ethic
   developmental changes, 82–3
   educational policy emphasis, 74, 227
   and need achievement theory, 34
   teacher reinforcement of, 65–7
work life, 220–30
   competition myths, 237–49
   educational reform application, 220–1
   "enterprise training" for, 221
   and human nature myth, 236
   serious games relationship, 222–30
writing skills, 5